Pierre Lambert de la Motte
The Unknown Father of Modern Missions

Françoise Fauconnet-Buzelin

Translated by Jefferies Foale CP

Pierre Lambert de la Motte
The Unknown Father of Modern Missions

First Vicar Apostolic of Cochinchina, 1624–1679

Françoise Fauconnet-Buzelin

Translated by Jefferies Foale CP

Adelaide
2024

Françoise Fauconnet-Buzelin
The origins of the Paris Foreign Mission Society
Pierre Lambert de la Motte (1624–1679)
Perrin
www. editions-perrin. fr
© Perrin, 2006 ISBN 2. 262. 02528. 2
English Translation: Jefferies Foale CP
Editor: Bill McCarthy FMS

All rights reserved. Except for any fair dealing permitted under the Copyright Act, no part of the publication may be reproduced by any means without prior permission. Inquiries should be made in the first instance with the publisher.

ISBN
978-1-923006-46-1   Soft
978-1-923006-47-8   Hard
978-1-923006-48-5   Epub
978-1-923006-49-2   PDF

Published by:

Making a lasting impact
An imprint of the ATF Press Publishing Group
owned by ATF (Australia) Ltd.
PO Box 234
Brompton, SA 5007
Australia
ABN 90 116 359 963
www.atfpress.com

Table of Contents

Foreword ix
Introduction xi
Introduction to the Vietnamese edition 2015 xv
English Translator's Introduction xix

Chapter 1 Heir to the Great Century 1
    A man of his time 1
    The rise of an ambitious family in troubled times 3
    A precocious child in search of his vocation 5
    The misfortunes of war 7
    A devout councillor in search of a role model 9
    The rebel 12
    '*Vanitas vanitatum*' 14
    Conversion and reconversion 16
    The hermitage 18
    The pilgrim 21
    An ordination under the sign of mission 23
    The beginning of the call to the foreign missions 24
    Director of the Office of the Poor 25
    An influential precursor 28

Chapter 2 French Bishops for Asia 31
    Reasons for a reform and new measures to be adopted 31
    First attempts 33
    Alexandre de Rhodes 34
    Proposals with varying degrees of acceptance 35
    Beneath the surface 37
    The *Instructions* 40

	Between Roman strategy and French interests	41
	Pierre Lambert leads the way	45
	The end of an era	47
Chapter 3	**The Discovery of Asia**	**51**
	The desert experience	51
	A lie with serious consequences	53
	On the outskirts of the forbidden zone	54
	Examples and counter-examples from religious in Asia	56
	First impressions of Siam	59
	The outbreak of hostilities	62
	The Jesuit Question	64
	Abusive denunciations or justified accusations?	67
	The key to the problem	69
Chapter 4	**Dialogue–the way forward**	**73**
	The first false start	73
	Time for reflection	75
	Pallu, a calming influence	76
	Differences of opinion	78
	Provisional reconciliation	81
	The Bourges mission	84
	The thorny issue of trade and other material necessities	87
	Pallu returns to Europe	89
Chapter 5	**Consolidations and Fractures**	**93**
	News from Cochinchina	93
	First exchanges with Phra Narai	95
	Comings and goings in the port of Ayutthaya	97
	The forces at work	101
	The Fragoso affair	104
	All is grace	106
	Royal favours and great projects	109
	An unfortunate initiative	111
	The pastoral letter against the trade of the clerics	113
	False hopes involving the court	116
	The return of Jacques de Bourges	120

Chapter 6	**Pastoral visits to Vietnam**	**125**
	François Deydier in Tonkin	125
	The arrival of Pierre Lambert	129
	Ordinations and synod	132
	The Lovers of the Cross	134
	Tensions in Ayutthaya	140
	Four very suspicious deaths	142
	News from Rome	144
	A perilous expedition to help the Church of Cochinchina	146
	The governor's feast	148
	Clandestine administration	152
Chapter 7	**Diplomatic exercises**	**155**
	Pallu, Rome and the directors	155
	New confrontations	160
	The reunion: Pallu rebels.	162
	A contested election: Louis Laneau as Vicar Apostolic	166
	Suspicions, rumours and whispers	169
	The receptions of Phra Narai	173
	An ambiguous position	175
	The official appeal from Cochinchina	176
Chapter 8	**Last battles, last victories**	**183**
	A suspicion laden pause	183
	An emergency situation in Cochinchina	185
	A triumphant visit	188
	Resolute opponents	192
	The last stand	195
	The state of affairs	199
	Under the sign of the cross	203
	Posthumous tributes	208
Chapter 9	**A Missiology in Search of Balance**	**211**
	A consistent record	211
	The right use of human resources	214
	The subtleties and contradictions of adaptation to local customs	218
	The father of the Vietnamese clergy	221
	The auxiliary personnel	225

Chapter 10 A spiritual heritage to be rediscovered   **229**
    An initial conflict   230
    The Pauline model   232
    The obedience of faith   235
    Inner abandonment   237
    A harmonious and fruitful synthesis   241
    The missionary, a contemplative in action   243

Epilogue   **245**
    The ruin of the mission of Siam   245

Bibliography   **249**

Index of Names   **253**

Foreword

The history of the missions aroused great interest amongst French Catholics in the nineteenth and early twentieth centuries, but that interest has now faded. In the current context of secularisation and religious indifference, the objectives and methods of the Missions are criticised and the missionary identity itself is unclear. The missionary, often likened to the coloniser and formerly exalted as a paradigm of zeal, heroism and devotion, no longer attracts such admiration. In such a climate, the idea of publishing the biography of a missionary bishop of the seventeenth century, a man unknown to the general public, and one frequently criticized by mission authorities, seems to be rather pointless or a remarkable act of self-denial.

Seven years ago, I came close to sharing these sentiments with the officials of the Foreign Mission Society of Paris who entrusted me with the task of writing the life of Pierre Lambert de la Motte, Titular Bishop of Beirut and first Vicar Apostolic of Cochinchina. Considered a secondary founder and of far less importance than his colleague François Pallu, la Motte had within the Society a reputation for austerity, rigidity and intransigence that initially discouraged me. Moreover the research was difficult and wearisome due to the massive amount of documentation available and its contradictory nature. But then came a surprise from on high! In the course of my research I discovered not only a remarkable man but also a slice of Church history that had been concealed and it was a revelation. This historic 'Apocalypse' (in the etymological sense of the word—taken from the book of Revelation) at first overwhelmed me before absorbing all my attention and 'sympathy' (still in the etymological sense). Without claiming to have uncovered the whole truth about this important episode which deserves the attention of many researchers, I simply wish that the reader, without necessarily sharing my enthusiasm and attachment to a character who has become very dear to me, may find in these pages the opportunity to enrich and renew his understanding of the history of the Missions.

F. F. B.

Forty years after the publication of the Conciliar Decree Ad Gentes by Paul VI and fifteen years after the celebrated encyclical of John Paul II Redemptoris Missio, the Church of France was faced with ageing, the difficulty of taking responsibility for its missionary past and the projection of itself into a global future. It is at this time that Pierre Lambert de la Motte emerges as a figure currently relevant and therefore avant-garde for his time, a man who spreads a great breath of fresh air over missionary historiography and will most likely overturn many accepted ideas.

Because of the questions and challenges this research raised, it required an argumentation that was both rigorous and solidly based, but which the general reader might find somewhat tedious. This book, therefore, offers an abridged and slightly modified form of the full text published by the Paris Foreign Mission Society.

Introduction

The life of Pierre Lambert de la Motte took place in a context of conflict rather than peace and harmony: battles, mutual misunderstandings, a dialogue of the deaf who opposed one another in Asia, against the backdrop of colonial rivalries and religious competition, the Jesuits under Portuguese patronage with Spanish religious, then with the first French lay missionaries. Even if nowadays this conflict, in broad outline and therefore improperly described by the simplistic expression 'the Rites Dispute,' no longer affects in a personal way those involved in the Missions, it remains alive nevertheless in the collective consciousness of the congregations concerned. Whether it is acknowledged or not, in fact the wound opened within the missionary milieu through the control of the Missions by Rome effected from 1622 (the year of the creation of the Congregation of Propaganda Fide as well as the canonisation of Ignatius of Loyola and Francis Xavier) to 1773, the date of the suppression of the Jesuits by Clement XIV, this wound, not having been properly cleaned has never been completely healed. If this conflict had repercussions so passionate, and so long-lasting, it is because it goes beyond the scope of doctrinal differences and power rivalries within the Church.

It feeds on the great changes that affected the consciousness of Christian Europe between the sixteenth and eighteenth centuries. It was born, in fact, on terrain freshly ploughed by the conquest of the New World (and therefore the institution of missionary 'sponsorship'), by the Wars of Religion (and therefore the reform codified by the Council of Trent), and finally by the advent of humanism which the Jesuits, the spearhead and elite corps of the Catholic counter-reformation, made the focus of their pedagogy. This conflict ended, due to a lack of combatants, with the end in France of the rule by divine right of the monarchy, the material ruin of the Church, freedom of conscience and in the minds of a significant part of the population a solid anticlericalism based on the rights of reason as opposed to religious obscurantism. Thus the French Revolution signalled the collapse of the Constantinian style system on which the Society of Jesus had based its Asian missiology for a hundred and fifty years.

It was a missiology that aimed at conversion by argument based on reason. It targeted the elite and the ruling bodies of the most civilized countries in order to lead their people to the obedience of faith. In other words, at the end of the century of the Enlightenment, this same revolution sounded the death knell of the great missionary illusion of the Jesuits, meaning the creation in every human society throughout the world of a universal type of Christian man. He would be educated and formed, depending on his culture of origin on the Jesuit model and under the almost exclusive authority of the fathers, this model itself being conceived as the ideal humanist. Nothing could be more logical: when the humanist creed, supported by the Cartesian credo, takes precedence over Christian revelation, it is not the Gospel but the Declaration of the Rights of Man that becomes the charter for humanity.

If this matter had, and continues to have, such an impact in France, it is because it has been publicised, amplified and therefore automatically distorted by the media of the time, in this instance the writers, in the seventeenth and especially in the eighteenth centuries, It unfolded against the backdrop of the Jansenist crisis, it became a matter of opinion which distorted inextricably the true facts of the matter. In the list of people involved in this great politico-religious drama, alongside ecclesiastical actors are the greatest names in the literature of the period: Corneille and Pascal, Molière and Racine, to mention only the leading characters. It is through them that the debate has moved from the realm of the experts to the public at large, that is to say, the educated elite of the seventeenth century and the Age of Enlightenment. As these authors have never ceased to be read and studied in France, it is partly because of them that the debate retains its sharpness even today.

In this vast arena that was as much ideological as strictly religious, Pierre Lambert de la Motte is an unknown figure and a target. He is unknown, not only to the public, but to certain qualified people also. For example, it is surprising that some serious works, that focus on the Norman spiritual environment from which he came, scarcely mention his name, or omit it completely, whereas his confrere and friend, François de Montmorency-Laval, who inhabited the same world, always occupies a prominent place in these writings.

As far as the history of the Missions is concerned, it is clearly impossible to ignore the first French Vicar Apostolic, since this mystic who was passionate about solitude and prayer was a pitiless prosecutor who fiercely denounced what he considered to be missionary excesses or deviations. It was this vehemence that made him a target, to whom are directed the deep-seated resentment and anger engendered by the polemic. There was the resentment of the Jesuits, clearly enough: he was their bête noire, and they were the bane of his life. There was a sense of disquiet amongst the directors of the Paris Foreign Missions Society, who were closely linked to the French Jesuits. They expected a more favourable treatment from a prelate. Also there was concern felt by some of his confreres who, in spite of their attachment or admiration for him, could not agree wholeheartedly with what they regarded as his extremism. Finally there was a lack of enthusiasm, or at least hesitant acceptance of him throughout history among the priests of the Paris Foreign Missions Society who never succeeded in consciously integrating his legacy and have generally preferred the more attractive Bishop François Pallu whose extraordinary journeys boosted the image of the missionary adventurer.

And yet, for anyone who looks more closely into the history of the spirituality of the Paris Foreign Missions Society, this heritage is clear and undeniable, if not always obvious. It is there, at least in the secrecy of its charism and in its founding objective, that is, to plant indigenous churches and enable them to grow, regardless of the cost entailed, until they are autonomous, then to fade away or even disappear in order to let them live. Because of this principle, which is a complete contradiction of the concept of tutelage promoted by the patronage system, Pierre Lambert de la Motte is really the spiritual father of the institute he founded conjointly with François Pallu and their first companions. These men, Louis Laneau, François Deydier, Jacques de Bourges, also deserve to be better known and recognized. These men had no ambition to plant the cross in infidel lands, as the common practice was at that time, nor to dazzle the Asian leaders with the prestige of science and civilization and therefore European and Christian Truth.

Rome had entrusted them with a more obscure, but nevertheless essential mandate: that of forming a native clergy which would enable young Asian Christian communities to escape from dependence on the West, hoping thereby to limit persecution. However, long before being appointed Vicar Apostolic of Cochinchina, Pierre Lambert de la Motte had planted the cross, more deeply no doubt than any other in the centre of his soul, the centre of his heart and the centre of his life. And from this centre issued a strange radiation that was fascinating, disturbing and overpowering in its intensity. And yet it was essential, as it nourished his first companions, and carried the Society of Foreign Missions through the dangerous convulsions of its birth and beyond, into the painful mystical depth of its history.

The first Vicar Apostolic of Cochinchina was an eminent participant in a spiritual movement which renewed the French church in the seventeenth century. He resolutely chose to free the Mission from colonial stagnation, for example the methodological debates generated by humanism, in order to immerse it in the radical mystery of the Redemption. Also his fight bypassed in its deepest dimension, the framework of a simple conflict of jurisdiction or exotic episode, which is an anachronism today, the old quarrel about nature and grace. The mystical missiology of Pierre Lambert de la Motte, which makes the contemplation of the Cross the source of all authentic apostolic fruitfulness, takes on today a new resonance in a debate that appears to be just as crucial and equally passionate, a debate in which a Catholic orthodoxy proclaiming Christ as the only saviour is opposed to theologians advocating an approach that is less exclusive of mediation.

Lambert de la Motte was criticized during his lifetime for weakness in theology, even a certain illuminism. However, it would be interesting to study closely what his experience and spiritual insights can bring to contemporary missiological reflection. Is it altogether extravagant to wonder whether, well before the negative effects of the colonialism of the nineteenth century, an excessive confidence in human means and the power of reason extolled by the Jesuits did not result in certain deviations and render fruitless an approach based on spiritual experience at the very beginning of the Mission in Asia? Is this perhaps a possible prelude to a form of dialogue that appears as a priority today and that only authentic Christian mystics of the calibre of Lambert de la Motte could try? The answer cannot be given with certainty, but the question should be asked, because ultimately it underpins the history that follows.

Introduction to the Vietnamese edition 2015

Historian Francoise Fauconnet-Buzelin, PhD in history of art, curator of heritage preservation, and director of research in the Society of Foreign Missions of Paris, is the author of biographies of many missionaries, especially of two books about Bishop Pierre Lambert de la Motte:

The first book: *Le père inconnu de la Mission modern, Pierre Lambert de la Motte, premier vicaire apostolique de Cochinchine, 1624-1679: The Forgotten Father of Modern Mission, Pierre Lambert de la Motte, The First Apostolic Vicar of Cochinchina, 1624-1679,* Archives des Missions Étrangères, Paris 2006. This book is written for professionals in history.

The second book: *Aux sources des Missions Étrangères, Pierre Lambert de la Motte (1624-1679): Finding the Origin of the Society of Foreign Missions, Pierre Lambert de la Motte (1624-1679),* Perrin, Paris 2006. In this book, the author restates the contents of the first book, but more concisely and simply, for the general audience. In the words of the author, 'this book is a compendium and a slight "adjustmentversion" (légèrementremaniée) of the full book published by the Society of Foreign Missions of Paris'.

Readers can see 'slight adjustment' most clearly in the title and in the last two chapters (IX and X) of the compendium book.

The title of the first book attracts readers' attention to Bishop Lambert as 'The Forgotten Father of Modern Mission'. It is a broad vision. Meanwhile, the title of the second book also focuses on that 'Forgotten Father', but this time she sees him specifically in relationship with 'the Society of Foreign Missions'. The author writes in the Introduction: 'Bishop Pierre Lambert de la Motte is the true spiritual father of the Society which he founded with Bishop Francois Pallu and his early companions such as missionary priests Louis Laneau, Francois Deydier, Jacques de Bourges . . .'. This sentence explains the meaning of the title: when 'finding the origin of the Society of Foreign Missions', we perceive Bishop 'Pierre Lambert de la Motte' as the main origin, and even more deeply, as 'the true spiritual father' but 'forgotten' of the Society.

The most interesting part of this book, in our opinion, lies in the last two chapters. Chapter IX: 'Finding a Balanced Way for Missionary' and Chapter X: 'Rediscovering a Spiritual Heritage', although it has regained the contents which were scattered throughout many chapters of the first book, now, however, the author reorganised more succinctly on the basis of subtle and profound theological and spiritual reflections. It can be said that these two chapters help readers directly grasp the charism and spirituality of Bishop Lambert and indirectly the charism and spirituality of his spiritual children, the most prominent of which are sisters of the Congregation of the Lovers of the Holy Cross and lay men and women belonging to the Association of the Male and Female Lovers of the Holy Cross of Our Lord Jesus Christ (now known as the Association of the Secular Lovers of the Holy Cross), that the author did not know have been re-founded in Vietnam since 1987.

Among the specific contents of the introduction written for the first book, we would like to repeat here only two things: first, 'the unique feature of the historian Francoise Fauconnet-Buzelin is not only presenting the external events related to Bishop Pierre Lambert's activities, especially his tense confrontation with Jesuit missionaries under the Portuguese Padroado regime, but also looking into the inner depths of the Bishop, whom she often called a great "mystic", whose core is love for Jesus Christ Crucified, the foundation of spirituality of the Lovers of the Holy Cross.' Second, 'the historian has demonstrated her loyalty to the critical point of view to maintain objectivity, that is, she did not hesitate to point out some of the weaknesses that she considered to be mistakes of Bishop Pierre Lambert in his diplomatic activities with political organizations'.

We hope that the translation of these two books will be beneficial for the Family of the Lovers of the Holy Cross and for those who want to learn about Bishop Pierre Lambert de la Motte.

Fr Phi Khanh Vuong Dinh Khoi, OFM
Counselor of Study Group of Spirituality of Lovers of the Holy Cross

Sai Gon, Ash Wednesday 2015, 345th Anniversary of the Profession Mass of two first sisters of the Lovers of the Holy Cross, Ane and Paula, in Pho Hien on Ash Wednesday 1670, in the presence of their Founder, that marked the birth of the Congregation of the Lovers of the Holy Cross.

English Translator's Introduction

This book was originally published in French under the title, *Aux sources des Missions Étrangères, Pierre Lambert de la Motte (1624-1679)*, (Finding the Origin of the Society of Foreign Missions, Pierre Lambert de la Motte (1624-1679), Perrin, Paris 2006. It was written to make the contents of the author's original scholarly research project, *The Forgotten Father of Modern Mission, Pierre Lambert de la Motte, The First Apostolic Vicar of Cochinchina, 1624-1679*, Perrin, Paris 2005, on La Motte accessible to a wider readership, and it includes perhaps the author's most valuable contribution, a deep reflection contained in the final two chapters.

Simply translating the French title is problematic. French readers may read 'Foreign Missions' as intended to refer to the Paris Foreign Mission Society, readers of English do not. More importantly, the scope of the book goes far beyond the origins of the Paris Foreign Mission Society, dealing as it does with La Motte's role, sent from Rome, at the cutting edge of the Roman challenge to the Portuguese Government monopoly on colonial Church control, and the dramatic tale of his life and death struggle with the endemic violations in Asia of a corrupt and broken system. He endured misunderstanding and disbelief in France, even among his own backers who were swayed by the reputation, power and influence of his opponents. No one could believe him, though no one was ever more careful of his facts. This led to him being practically written out of history until our day. Further, La Motte pioneered the formation and ordination of Vietnamese clergy and founded the "Lovers of the Holy Cross" Vietnamese religious sisters, destined in times of persecution to become the backbone of the Church in Vietnam, and who now number over nine thousand.

La Motte stands as a towering figure in the history of missions, a saintly mystic of unparalleled vision, courage, faith and integrity, who surely merits a place among the saints.

In view of all this, the English translation is offered under the title, 'The Unknown Father of the Modern Mission, Pierre Lambert de la Motte, first Vicar Apostolic of Cochinchina, 1624–1679'.

I can never pay worthy tribute to my editor, in fact, co-translator, Marist Brother Bill McCarthy FMS for his tireless work in assuring accuracy, readability and appropriate style throughout. Thanks also to Fr Tom McDonough, CP, Passionist Provincial Superior, who encouraged me in this 'hobby', this labour of love, and guaranteed the cost of publication. Thanks also to Sister Anna Le Van Nga MTG for her encouragement and patience.

Jefferies Foale CP
Saigon September 2023

Chapter 1
Heir to the Great Century

A man of his time

Although he is almost unnoticed in the eyes of French religious history, Pierre Lambert de la Motte belongs, with every fibre of his being, to that 'great century of souls', the seventeenth century. It has been referred to as a 'Century of Saints', during which the heights of mysticism merged with an outpouring of charity. It was an innovative age when clergy and laity, men and women, scholars and humble united their passion and zeal in an extraordinary religious effervescence. It was a century illuminated by great men and women: François de Sales, Cardinal de Bérulle, Madame Acarie, Vincent de Paul, John Eudes, Jean-Jacques Olier, Gaston de Renty, Bossuet, Fénelon, and so many others. They were carried along, inspired, imitated and served by a multitude of simpler but no less ardent souls, favoured at times by remarkable mystical graces: humble religious women, shepherds and cowherds, entertainers, servants, seamstresses.

The Spirit blows where it will, sometimes disconcertingly, as in the years of religious euphoria which followed the bloody trauma of the Wars of Religion in France. After decades of ruthless fratricidal struggles, the leaders of the Catholic reconstruction were men and women animated by the most sublime aspirations just as others had been driven by the most murderous impulses in the preceding century. Because they strove to transform the violence of their predecessors into service of others and sacrifice of themselves, everything about them was extreme: heroism, mortification, conflict, renunciation and generosity. Mothers abandoned their children for the love of God (like Jeanne de Chantal and Marie of the Incarnation), young spouses separated after a few years of marriage to embrace religious life (like the Duke and Duchess of Ventadour), ten-year-old children and uneducated women had spiritual experiences that totally changed their lives.

Pierre Lambert de la Motte was a member of this world; he was one of those 'extremists' whose attitudes might surprise, shock or even disgust us today. Let us beware, however, of stopping at the superficial reactions of our 'modern' sensitivity—which is perhaps, only a sign of spiritual desensitization—if we want even the slightest understanding of this story.' Something has been lost that will not return. Historiography is a contemporary way of practising mourning,' wrote Michel de Certeau in *La Fable mystique*.[1] Spiritually, many of the people we are about to meet will be for us beings from 'another world.' Like Mary Magdalene in the garden of the tomb, we will have to accept our inability, given this inevitable separation, to comprehend them, Our task will be all the more challenging, since we have only a few specific sources with which to trace the French career of Pierre Lambert de la Motte: a genealogy constructed in the 1950s by a descendant of the family, Henry de Frondeville, and the biography written in 1685 by Jean-Charles de Brisacier, the superior of the seminary of the Paris Foreign Missions Society. This biography written with the help of live testimonies and a diary of the future Bishop of Beirut, which has disappeared unfortunately, is of great value, but it must be used with some caution because it is not free of the hagiographic or at least apologetic style of this literary genre. Indeed, because the biography focuses on the religious aspect, and hence La Motte's edifying characteristics, Brisacier leaves in the shadows not only his human and psychological traits, but especially the political and social context in which he lived.

However, with the passing of time, after three and a half centuries, it is possible to see how influential this context was in the development of a personality gifted from childhood with an exceptional character, but also how influential were particularly significant historical circumstances. Only a deep, unprejudiced immersion in the troubled political climate and the heightened religious atmosphere of seventeenth century France can facilitate the rediscovery of the personal and social coherence of a man too often presented as excessive or even abnormal, whereas he merely shared the spiritual

---

1. Michel de Certeau, *La Fable mystique, xvie-xviie siècles* (Paris: Gallimard, 1982), 21.

radicalism of the most zealous of his contemporaries. The detailed portrait of Brisacier is almost too remarkable because it isolates La Motte from his historical background. To better define this character, it will be necessary to place him in a broader context while trying to determine from the small amount of evidence available, the place of Pierre Lambert de la Motte in the different milieux through which he passed in succession. We will be able to make a better judgment then, about the way this mystic, prayerful man, faithful to his Ignatian formation, was an outstanding man of action who worked tirelessly for 'the greater glory of God', first of all in his own country, then 'as far away as the ends of the earth'.

The rise of an ambitious family in troubled times

Pierre Lambert was born in January 1624 into a family of the judicial nobility that had been established in Normandy since the fifteenth century. In 1461, his ancestor, William Lambert, formerly the wine steward in the court of Charlotte of Savoy,[2] was made Viscount d'Auge by King Louis XI who gave him a house in Lisieux. In five generations, his descendants climbed all the rungs that allowed Pierre entry to the highest rank of officials, namely magistrates of the sovereign courts. At the same time, they considerably increased their heritage by well-planned marriages with wealthy daughters of the bourgeoisie of Lisieux. At the beginning of the sixteenth century great-grandfather, William II, took the title of Sieur de La Motte[3] from the name of a property he acquired in the vicinity of Lisieux.

This was the first step toward ennoblement, which occurred two generations later. His grandson Pierre, born in 1575, exercised judicial functions as lieutenant of the short dress,[4] a distinctive sign of nobility.

The Lambert family, however, experienced a difficult time when, between 1589 and 1593, Normandy became the stronghold of the pretender to the throne of France, Henry of Navarre, who had not yet renounced Protestantism. Committed Catholics, they took part in a conspiracy designed to deliver Lisieux to the supporters of King Philip

---

2. On 22 July 1461, Charlotte became Queen of France.
3. The title of Seigneur or Sieur is the French equivalent of a Lord. This was also one of the oldest titles within mediaeval nobility.
4. A deputy officer to the Provost of Paris responsible for capturing criminals.

II of Spain. During the unrest, one of them, John, was arrested and their most beautiful house, Mauduit, was burned down. Meanwhile, in Rouen, Nicolas Heudey of Pommainville, adviser to the Parlement[5] and maternal grandfather of Pierre Lambert, voted in 1591 in favour of the bull of excommunication of the future King Henry IV. The political choices of the future Bishop of Beirut were marked out in advance, well before his birth. From his father, Pierre Lambert, vice-bailiff of Evreux, and from his mother, Catherine de Heudey of Pommainville, daughter of a Rouen councillor, he inherited an ultra-Catholic, pro-Spanish and anti-Protestant conviction. He was thus predestined to find himself later in the ranks of the last militants of the devout party that gathered around Marie de Medicis[6] and Cardinal de Bérulle[7] upon the death of Henry IV, and that tasted defeat from the repeated attacks of Richelieu[8] and Mazarin.[9] From the outset he found himself on the side of the adversaries, who were also the losers.

Yet when, on the morning of 16 January 1624, the infant, a few days old, was carried to the baptismal font of the church of Saint-Jacques in Lisieux, a bright future seemed to open before him. His ancestry destined him for a brilliant administrative career, favoured by a whole network of family relationships that opened the door to the most influential milieu of Normandy, that of the parliamentarians. He could also count on the support of one of his cousins, the famous Capuchin preacher Zacharie de Lisieux, who was at one time chaplain to Queen Henriette of England.

Pierre was only a few months old when his father abandoned his duties as vice-bailiff of Evreux and moved to Lisieux to the house

---

5. Originally there was only one Parlement, which was in Paris, but the number grew to thirteen. They were the highest judicial courts in the kingdom, second in authority only to the king himself. They were not the same as a legislative body such as the English Parliament.
6. Marie de' Medicis, 26 April 1575–3 July 1642, was Queen of France and Navarre as the second wife of King Henry IV of France.
7. Cardinal Pierre de Bérulle, 4 February 1575–October 2, 1629, cardinal and statesman who founded the French Congregation of the Oratory, reformed clerical education in France.
8. Cardinal Richelieu, 9 September 1585–4 December 1642, was a French clergyman and statesman.
9. Cardinal Mazarin, 4 July 1602–9 March 1661, an Italian by birth, was a diplomat and politician who served as the chief minister to the Kings of France Louis XIII and Louis XIV from 1642 to his death in 1661.

of his mother Marie Mauduit, a widow for thirty years. With him were his wife, his eldest daughter Marie, born in 1623, and the newborn child. Five more children were born there of whom only two survived: Marie, the fourth born in 1627, and Nicolas, the last in 1631. But after a few years, Pierre's father quarrelled with his mother and left the Mauduit house for the Lambert house, the cradle of the family, located at the other end of the town. Periodically, parents and children would enjoy the fresh air in their country houses, la Motte and la Boissière, beautiful timber-framed houses, that can be seen even today at the western exit of Lisieux. The early education of little Pierre was ensured, as in all noble families, by an ecclesiastical tutor. The child was serious, reserved and showed a surprising maturity from a young age. 'Those who had the advantage of being responsible for his education attest that there was almost nothing childish in his childhood', said his biographer Jean-Charles de Brisacier. 'From the age of eight, he showed the seriousness of a mature man. He handled his advantages over other children without haughtiness or ostentation. A liveliness of spirit was joined to a soundness of judgment, a love of study to a retentive memory, and the strength of genius to the beauty of a naturalness that was as gentle as it was firm.'[10]

A precocious child in search of his vocation

A calm and disciplined boy, Pierre took little part in the games of his peers, preferring to meditate alone. At the time of his first communion, attracted by religious life and no doubt affected by his reading of the *Imitation of Jesus Christ*, he had a moving spiritual experience that he recalled thirty years later, at the beginning of his missionary life.

> I remembered an idea that had preoccupied me for a long time when I was about nine years old in the town of my birth. I asked myself this question: would I like to become a member of a religious congregation? I realized that I definitely had no desire to enter any of the local religious congregations, since their members did not seem to lead a life of great perfection. But then I thought of a different kind of religious group of

---

10. Jean-Charles de Brisacier. *Vie de Mgr Lambert de la Motte* (Life of Bishop Lambert de la Motte). Polycopié inédit, Archives des Missions Étrangères de Paris (AMEP, Archives of the Foreign Missions of Paris), volume 000102, Ch. I.

> people very much to my liking, to whom I felt strongly attracted. They were called the Lovers of the Cross. Their life seemed so admirable to me that if I had known where I might find such people, I would have made every effort, at whatever cost, to belong to their Company. But not having found any such group in the world, I have never since been attracted to enter any religious house, even though I have always held in high esteem those houses which are faithful to the aims of their Institute, and which I have regarded as nurseries of heaven.[11]

From then on, he redoubled his piety and charity. He distributed all his pocket money to the poor and, as his biographer tells us, became 'so charitable towards the poor that, through repeatedly asking the household manager for bread for them, he sometimes put her in a bad mood, and in order to obtain from her what he desired, he tried to soften her up and win her over by all sorts of means.'[12] Thus, the missionary zeal that would later carry him to the ends of the earth was already manifested in a naive and childlike form. 'He often formulated questions or answers of a pious nature that surprised everyone, and when he was in the country, instead of attaching himself to companions nearby, he chose to walk alone, so as to be able to approach the little peasant children he met without being seen; for then, he would ask them about their catechism, and by his willingness to listen he would encourage them to understand and to remember what he was saying to them.'[13]

At the age of nine, this extraordinarily precocious child showed a radical religious commitment but did not find, in the effervescence that was then sweeping the Church of France, a place that corresponded to his aspirations. Everywhere, however, new or reformed orders were flourishing. The Jesuits educated the finest French youth, soon to be rivalled by the Oratorians. Among the contemplatives, Jean de Saint-Samson gave the Carmelites of Brittany a new mystical impetus. Even the most austere orders were able to offer the most brilliant of their members excellent careers in the world: Father Joseph de Paris, a Capuchin, wove the fabric of French diplomacy throughout Europe,

---

11. Compte rendu d'oraison du 3 novembre 1663. AMEP, volume 116, 559.
12. Compte rendu. 559. Az.
13. Compte rendu. 559.

and Father Mersenne's scientific knowledge attracted the most eminent members of Parisian God-fearing society to the convent of the Minims[14] in the Place Royale. There was no lack of choice for an intelligent boy, brought up in material ease and awareness of his social superiority.

But Pierre, always haunted by his desire for the absolute, dreamed of a model that did not exist. So he submitted to the family tradition and entered the Jesuit college in Caen, a very reputable establishment that gave the best human, intellectual and religious training to the young elite of Lower Normandy. Caen was then a rapidly growing city with a population of nearly 20,000 inhabitants. Renowned for the quality of its intellectual and cultural life, it was nicknamed the Athens of Normandy.[15] It was the university capital of Normandy, attracting students from all over western France, also from England and Holland. The college taught arts, civil law, canon law, medicine and theology. Pierre Lambert would be formed in a cosmopolitan and refined environment, although provincial, which was characterized by the excellence of its humanist teaching. His rhetoric teacher at the Jesuit school was Father Jacques le Faure, who later became provincial of the Chinese mission. Pierre was an excellent student who distinguished himself by the brilliance of his intellect and the depth of his piety. His membership in the Marian society of the college, which brought together the elite of the students for a more demanding formation, nourished his devotion to the Blessed Virgin while developing his sense of spiritual rigour and commitment to the world.

The misfortunes of war

Pierre Lambert's college years were marked by a series of family and social crises that profoundly affected his sensibility. In 1635, after several years of latent conflict, France solemnly declared war on Spain. Serious unrest broke out in Lorraine. Louis XIII decided

---

14. The Minims, officially known as the Order of Minims, are a Roman Catholic congregation of friars founded by Saint Francis of Paola in fifteenth-century Italy. The congregation soon spread to France, Germany and Spain, and continues to exist today.
15. Normandy is one of the provinces of France, occupying the region west of Paris. Rouen is the capital.

to restore order himself and called the vassals and the free men of Normandy to his side. Despite his advanced age and pro-Spanish convictions, Pierre Lambert, the father, had to go and fight for the king. The military campaign, however, turned out to be short-lived for the former vice-bailiff of Evreux who, at the age of sixty, returned to service after more than ten years of retirement. He died of illness after a few months, and was buried in the church of Saint-Etienne in Nancy. He left in Lisieux a widow with four children aged from four to twelve years, a substantial patrimony and several lawsuits pending against his mother and brothers. His succession was not simple.

In Caen, Pierre, his eldest son, although affected by the loss of his father, continued his studies brilliantly. He did not know that his misfortunes were only beginning. In 1635, the capture of Corbie by the Spaniards made Normandy a frontier province. Refugees flocked there. It was a rich region that the State tended to consider as the breadbasket of France, so it was heavily taxed for men, food and money. The Normans alone paid one-fifth of the total tax and new taxes were created to support the war effort. The population, pressured and frustrated, weakened by endemic famines, decimated by the plague which affected the country for fifteen years, reacted with violence. The revolt of the va-nu-pieds (bare-footed ones), one of the most serious popular uprisings of the century, broke out in May 1639 in Rouen. In July, it reached Caen. On August 26, a crowd of 2,000 people, many of them women, led by a leader named Bras-nu (Bare-arm), looted the house of a tax collector, and then, in the following days, those of a tax clerk, a middle class citizen and two wealthy merchants. Riots, ransackings and assassinations of officers followed one another in Avranches, Bayeux, Coutances, Mortain and Carentan. At Lisieux, on his properties of La Motte and La Boissière, the young Pierre Lambert had acquired the habit of relieving the misery of the peasants as far as he could. He was now the witness to suffering which he was unable to alleviate, and to the revolt of the poor against the members of his own social class whom they held responsible for their misfortunes. Perhaps he did not see the riots that took place in the summer, during the vacation period, but he was in Caen when the terrible repression of the revolts began.

Richelieu, indeed, was not satisfied with the actions of the lieutenant general of Normandy, the Duke of Matignon, who arrested Bras-nu and other rioters. He sent from Paris a young colonel renowned for his bravery in battle, Jean de Gassion, nicknamed 'War', at the head of a troop of 5,000 foreign mercenaries. On November 29, Gassion entered Caen and, after a successful tour of the southern part of the province, returned on December 22. His methods were traditional and effective: rape, pillage, defenestration, public executions. Neither women nor children were spared. The population was terrorized, and everything was done to keep it that way. Bras-nu, arrested, was 'broken alive,' and what remained of his body was exposed at the gates of the city.

The military action was soon followed by judicial action. It was the chancellor, Séguier, who was in charge. His justice was as swift as Gassion's military methods. In Caen, on 16 January 1640, he suspended all the officers and replaced them with commissioners. The prisons were overcrowded, mostly with people who were unable to pay their taxes, their only crime. In the midst of the general distress, the religious of the Jesuit college were quick to come to the aid of the most disadvantaged.

These dramatic events must have been particularly painful for Pierre Lambert because he had just suffered two successive bereavements with the death of his paternal grandmother, Marie Mauduit in 1638, then that of his mother, Catherine Heudey in 1640. The orphans were placed under the guardianship of Pierre Fermanel, a wealthy shipowner from Rouen who disappeared four years later. Pierre, the eldest son, suddenly the breadwinner of the family, had to give up his plans, still latent, of religious commitment. He continued his studies in law at the University of Caen and, at the age of 22, briefly held a position as a lawyer in the Parlement of Paris before buying a position as a councillor at the Court of Aids in Rouen where he took up his duties in 1646. In addition to his official activities, he also had to settle the complex business of inheritance left to him by his parents. In spite of the procedural customs of the time, his clarity of judgment, his fundamental honesty and his benevolence allowed him to reconcile all parties and to restore peace in his family.

A devout councillor in search of a role model

Rouen, the second largest city in the kingdom, did not escape the general crisis that had affected French society since the death of Louis XIII. Behind the prosperous facade of its business community, a restlessness of the people transformed the Norman capital into a veritable social powder keg. For years, the city had to deal with the influx of a horde of miserable peasants who were ruined by the burden of taxes or who were fleeing the famine and epidemics that ravaged the surrounding countryside. The plague, which in 1637 killed more than one and a half thousand patients of the hospital, did not stop this galloping over-population. Between 1600 and 1640, the number of inhabitants of the city increased from 60,000 to 89,000. The streets, squares and forecourts were invaded by idle and destitute crowds, aggravating the problems of supply, the risks of contagion, the dangers of riots and the feeling of insecurity. The municipal authorities and the sovereign courts tried to manage this explosive situation as best they could, but their task was a delicate one, for their stance in favour of the people during the revolts of 1639 had earned them the distrust of the central government.

From 1640, as commissioner 'for income tax and the levying of the land tax', Etienne Pascal, a former adviser to the Court of Aids[16] of Clermont-Ferrand, oversaw the collection of the many taxes imposed on the province. A widower, he settled in rue des Murs-Saint-Ouen with his three children: Gilberte, the eldest, aged 20, Blaise aged 16, already a mathematician of note, and Jacqueline aged 14, who was successful in the world of theatre and literature. It was the young girl's precocious talent that earned the Pascal family, upon their arrival in Rouen, the friendship of Pierre Corneille, the king's adviser to the administration of Waters and Forests and the Table of Marble,[17] and also a successful playwright whose last play, *Le Cid*, performed two years earlier, was a triumph that revolutionized the Parisian theatre scene.

It was thus in a very sensitive political and social context, and in the most delicate professional sector, that of taxation and finance, that Pierre Lambert, at the age of twenty-two, took his first steps as king's adviser. He was too devout to seek the friendship of a man

---

16. The Courts of Aids were sovereign courts in *Ancien Régime* France, primarily concerned with customs, but also other matters of public finance. The Ancien Regime refers to the political and social system in France before the Revolution of 1789.
17. In Paris, the Table of Marble took its name from the large marble table in the Salle du Palais in Paris where the Constable, the Admiral and the Grand Master of the Waters and Forests exercised their jurisdiction.

of the theatre like Corneille, and too well trained by the Jesuits to compromise himself with the Jansenist sympathies of an Étienne Pascal. The former member of the college of Caen adhered, as he should, to the Congregation of the Assumption, also called Congregation of the Gentlemen, which brought together more than a thousand members who, like him, came from the seven hundred most famous and wealthy families of Rouen: bourgeois, merchants and members of the sovereign courts. From this group was also recruited the main body of the recently formed Company of the Blessed Sacrament created in 1645. All of them were active in the service of the city's many charitable endeavours: visits to the sick of the Hôtel-Dieu, to the galley slaves and to the prisoners; the Foundlings' Work; the Assistance of Lorraine created in 1640 to help the victims of war; the project to create a general hospice for the able-bodied poor, which took shape in 1651.

In his private life, this handsome, rich young man of just over twenty years of age, with a noble bearing, who 'naturally liked to be well-dressed' and was an excellent catch, imposed on himself an almost monastic chastity. He did so in a society where gallant conquests were not regarded as forbidden to married men, nor even to certain worldly members of the clergy. 'Having lodged in private, he did not want any women in his household; he did not even allow any to enter his house under the pretext of rendering some service, and he had his valets available to serve him in everything as a rule. Thus his house, whether in the city or in the country, was more like a seminary than the home of a man of the world, and when his friends came to see him, he spoke to them about salvation with such fervour that they always departed better men than when they had come.'[18]

Faithful to the teachings of his Jesuit masters, he received spiritual direction from Father Julien Hayneuve, instructor of the third year at the novitiate in Rouen and disciple of the greatest formator of missionaries in Canada, Louis Lallemant. Through this contact, the young magistrate became familiar with a new form of missionary spirituality marked by the example of the first martyrs of New France[19] who became his models: Isaac Jogues, Jean de Brébeuf,

---

18. Brisacier. *Vie.* Ch. II.
19. New France refers to much of the territory in eastern Canada and USA. It was held by France as a colony from 1534 to 1763, after which Britain took possession of it and included it in the British Empire.

Gabriel Lallemant[20] and their companions, all of whom were imbued with the same demand for asceticism, abnegation, sacrifice and love of the Cross. To profit the more from the instruction of his teachers, he moved to a house near the Jesuit chapel, the usual setting for his devotions.

The rebel

But soon the outbreak of the wars of the Fronde[21] upset the functioning of Rouen's institutions and dragged Pierre Lambert into a political battle he had not foreseen. Indeed, the social situation, worrying for several years, suddenly worsened in 1648. The exceptional rains of spring and summer spoiled the harvests, and famine threatened again. Moreover, while in Paris the first confrontations between the Parlement and the Court had just occurred, a prelude to the Fronde, and the plague reappeared in the vicinity of Rouen. In addition to these natural disasters, there were calamities caused by men: the troops of the Duke of Orléans came to establish their winter quarters in the suburbs of the city at the expense of the inhabitants, who had to ensure their accommodation and subsistence. This burden proved to be unbearable for the people who rose up again. In November and December the crowd, galvanized by the women, invaded the town hall and the courthouse. Councillors, and even the first president of the Parlement, were insulted. As ten years before in Caen, on the side of the privileged, Pierre Lambert witnessed this misery, this revolt, and the class egoism of his peers who sought only to safeguard their privileges.

At the same time, while the peace of Westphalia finally put an end to the conflict with the Habsburgs on the northern front, the political situation deteriorated in Paris where the Parlement, supported by the people and the archbishop's coadjutor, Jean-François de Gondi, the future Cardinal de Retz, hardened its opposition to Mazarin's government. Factions were formed, plots were hatched, which for five years, as alliances changed, maintained the civil war and destruction

---

20. Isaac Jogues (d 1646), Jean de Brébeuf (d 1649) and Gabriel Lallemant (d 1649) were martyred in Canada by Indians amongst whom they carried out their missionary work.
21. The Fronde was the name for a series of civil wars in France between 1648 and 1653.

throughout the country. On one side were the queen, the prime minister and the court, supported by the Great Condé, a prince of royal blood. On the other side were several great men of the kingdom led by Condé's brother, Armand de Bourbon, Prince of Conti, and his sister Anne-Geneviève, Duchess of Longueville, wife of the governor of Normandy. Events came to a head on the night of 5–6 January 1649 when, after celebrating the Epiphany, the queen, her sons and her followers fled to Saint-Germain while Condé organized the siege of Paris. On January 10, the Duke of Longueville followed his wife in the rebellion, broke with Mazarin and dragged the Parlement of Rouen in his wake. On the 18th the city refused to accept the new governor appointed by the king, the Count of Harcourt, and warmly welcomed its insurgent leader who, arriving clandestinely on a boat, took possession of the old palace. Deputies of the different sovereign courts then formed a council destined to assist the duke who, in his fight against the central power, was declared a rebel and guilty of treason. On January 30, the council, composed of heterogeneous elements who acted outside the law, decided to seize the money of the State and appointed three delegates to divert the revenue of taxes on behalf of Longueville: Duval de Bonneval, a councillor of requests; Carré, a master of the accounts; and Lambert de la Motte, a councillor at the court of grants. It is clear, therefore, that the young magistrate took the side of the rebellion and, at twenty-five years of age, already enjoyed sufficient esteem to be given this mission of trust.

The delegates were sent to Alençon and Caen to organize the movement of funds in co-operation with the treasurers of France. On this occasion, Pierre Lambert had to deal, for strictly professional reasons, with one of his future spiritual directors, Jean de Bernières, the treasurer of France in Caen. This was the only political mission of the Fronde councillor, because the Parlement of Paris, facing the threat of Spanish interference engineered by Conti, wasted no time in negotiating with Mazarin. On March 11, the peace of Rueil put an end to this first episode of the Fronde. In Rouen too, the parties were reconciled and on April 9, patricians and people gathered in the cathedral to sing a *Te Deum* and celebrate peace.

The arrest of the Duke of Longueville, a few months later, did not rekindle the revolt because the patricians of Rouen, exasperated by their governor's appetite for power, played the loyalty card this time, and above all, that of their self-interest. On February 1, the city gave an enthusiastic welcome to the king, the queen and the prime minister who came to assure themselves of the province's loyalty. In the ranks of the patricians, Pierre Lambert attended the sumptuous receptions given in honour of the royal visitors. On February 6, he was presented, like all his colleagues of the sovereign courts, to the king and queen and the next day to the prime minister. From then on, Normandy did not change and was one of the few provinces spared the civil war that lasted until 1653.

'Vanitas vanitatum'

By this date, Pierre Lambert, too, had learned a lesson from the events and from the role he had played in them. At twenty-nine years of age he was able to take advantage of the return to favour of the Duke of Longueville and have his services appreciated and thereby gain new favours. But, disillusioned by the opportunism of the dignitaries who were mainly concerned with preserving their privileges, he no longer believed in political action as a means of putting into practice true Christian values and of improving the situation of the underprivileged. For some time now, he had been experiencing a disgust for the world, which turned him away from creatures, and an attraction for God alone. While continuing to fulfil his civil and charitable duties, he felt more and more attracted to people devoted to the Church and he often left Rouen to devote himself to the works of piety of his connections in Lower Normandy. In 1649, while vacationing at La Boissière, he met the new parish priest of Pré d'Auge, Dominique Georges, a friend of Bourdoise and former formator at the seminary of Saint-Nicolas du Chardonnet. Together they founded an ecclesiastical conference, the Cambremer Conference, for the training of priests according to the model initiated in Paris by Vincent de Paul. Shortly after, he made important donations to John Eudes for the construction of the seminary in Coutances, and in October 1653, he financed a Eudist mission in Lisieux. Moreover, as the marriage of his second sister to Jacques de Grieu, Sieur of Estimauville and of Paperottes in January of the same year put an end to the heaviest of his family obligations, he felt free to devote himself fully to the spiritual attraction he had always felt.

A simple incident was sufficient to precipitate his decision.' He naturally liked to be well dressed,' narrates Brisacier, 'but it pleased God to detach him from this vanity through an unexpected accident from which, fortunately, he benefited by the victory he gained over himself. One day, being invited to a gathering for the signing of the marriage articles of one of his relatives who was settling in Rouen, he went there on horseback, very attractively attired; suddenly his horse took fright—I don't know why—and all of a sudden it threw him into a stream which left him in a real mess. At that moment, he remembered the fall of St. Paul, and so he said to himself: 'There you are! Such vanity gets its just reward!' So saying, he had the courage to present himself in this state to the company. After being humbled in this way, he had little difficulty with most external practices of virtue. 'Moved with gratitude to God for the grace he had just received, he resolved anew to give himself to God with an undivided heart and without reserve.'[22]

This fall, which he interpreted as a sign from heaven, provoked a true inner conversion in the young magistrate who was disappointed by the vanities of this world but still attached to it by the bonds of social proprieties and civil responsibilities.' Engaged in the world and in public affairs at the urging of my relatives, and having lived for some years in this state of ingratitude to God,' he wrote later, 'when I was experiencing my greatest prosperity, it pleased God in His boundless mercy to give me a disgust for creatures and to call me to Himself. I was so deeply involved in the world and in business matters that, however diligent I was, it took me five years to free myself from it'. Knowing that he still had to travel a long way to achieve the absolute detachment to which he aspired, Pierre Lambert decided to change his life radically and, ignoring the objections of his colleagues, he took leave of his responsibilities. At the end of the year 1654—when in Paris, on the night of November 23, Blaise Pascal had an indelible experience, the 'certainty of God'[23]—he left for the Hermitage in Caen.

---

22. Brisacier. *Vie.* Ch. II.
23. Blaise Pascal, a brilliant scientist and philosopher, at age thirty-one had an intense religious vision that changed his life. Henceforth he devoted himself to religious writing, opposing the Enlightenment worldview of complete rule by reason. He was a member of the Jansenist religious group.

Conversion and reconversion

In the middle of the seventeenth century, Caen was undoubtedly one of the most religious cities in France, the centre of influence of a spiritual movement that historians call the 'Norman mystical milieu.' In 1643 Jean Eudes founded the Congregation of Jesus and Mary there. With the help of his two lay friends, Baron Gaston de Renty and the treasurer of France, Jean de Bernières, Pierre Lambert multiplied his charitable initiatives and the reorganization of rural missions. The centre of all these initiatives was the Hermitage, a sort of spiritual cenacle 'neither convent nor desert,' which 'welcomed for a temporary stay those who wished to prepare for the integration of the Christian into social life by assiduous personal prayer'.[24] It was in this environment where religious people sought to combine the demands of worldly commitment with those of mystical experience that the young magistrate tried to find a way to transition between his old and his new life. Through its particular purpose, the Hermitage kept him in contact with the former while enabling him to be initiated gradually into the latter.

To all outward appearances the Hermitage of Caen was the headquarters of the local branch of the Company of the Blessed Sacrament and, according to Chantal Quillet, probably constituted the Norman sodality originating from the Marian congregation of the college of Caen. Pierre Lambert found there both confreres and former colleagues, clerics and lay people, all animated by the same ideal. He continued to engage with them in charitable works and shared their missionary concerns which were mainly focused on Canada. However, unknown to the general public, the Hermitage was also a cenacle for about ten people who, under the direction of Jean de Bernières, sought 'a pathway to an inner experience of the divine'.[25]

Now, to be precise, the crisis that Pierre Lambert experienced also had a twofold aspect, the one exterior and the other interior. Externally, it was comparable to the general disillusionment which struck the last militants of the party involved in the Tissue of the Fronde. After Mazarin's victory, which was also a victory for reason

---

24. Chantai Quillet. *Le Rôle des laïcs, des « dévots », dans le renouveau spirifuel du XVIIe siècle*. Unpublished.
25. Quillet. *Le Rôle des laïcs*.

of State,[26] no one in France could still entertain the hope of restoring a society based entirely on Catholic values. An emblematic figure of the devout ideal, Gaston de Renty, one of the pillars of the Hermitage, died of exhaustion on 24 April 1649, as he spent the last of his strength helping the victims of the siege of Paris. With him disappeared the most authentic and accomplished model of the 'Christian gentleman'. Henceforth, the figure of the devout man, increasingly less evident in society, tended to be characterised by formal behaviour that Molière caricatured with success in the character of Tartuffe.[27]

Pierre Lambert was aware of the risk of spiralling downward; he had already perceived it in the egocentric and self-interested behaviour of his peers during the disturbances in Rouen and this is precisely what caused the second phase, the inner phase of his crisis. From this time on, he travelled along a double lane in the course of his spiritual journey, comparable to the one described by Saint Paul in his Second Letter to the Corinthians: 'Even though our outer nature is wasting away, our inner nature is being renewed day by day' (2 Cor 4:16). The first way, that of the outer nature wasting away, was the automatic consequence of his act of social renunciation. It was accompanied by suffering and psychological questioning that was only natural. 'Those who had seen him in Rouen, a few months earlier, carrying out his duties and earning the esteem of everybody in his department, which had appointed him to attend to important matters several times, in the fulfilment of which he had acquired a great reputation, at first regarded his retirement to Caen as a ridiculous indiscretion,' Brisacier reported. 'Even spiritually enlightened people told him that they could not approve of his action. Moreover, his servants, bored by not seeing him return home, came to ask him for their leave. He knew the way they had behaved since his departure and this made him consider himself from then on to be like those dead or dying ecclesiastics whose furniture was easily stolen. This he recorded in his own words in a small diary written in his own hand.'[28]

---

26. Reason of State refers to a particular way of thinking about government. It refers to the choice of rulers to act in ways that go against the dictates of both natural and positive law with the aim of acquiring, preserving, and augmenting the rule of the State.
27. *Tartuffe* was the name of a play written by the famous playwright, Moliere in the seventeenth century. The character, Tartuffe, is a hypocrite who pretends to be virtuous.
28. Brisacier. *Vie*. Ch. I.

Loneliness, incomprehension, abandonment, even betrayal were the first legitimate feelings which generated another more serious one: doubt.

> All of this, together with the experience that he soon had of being stripped of his judicial office, which he had resolved to sell, was a serious temptation for him. The devil represented to him that he was about to commit an act of absolute madness, that he would remain without authority, without credit and without esteem. Moreover, in a few days time, if he wished to continue to follow the attraction he felt, he might be without friends and without assets, reduced to a poverty, which was indeed voluntary, but real. He would be universally condemned by everyone for having left a job where he was of service to the public in order to follow a little-used road whose end he himself did not know.[29]

In the desert of the Hermitage, the brilliant councillor Lambert was tempted by honours and riches in its most subtle and pernicious form, that of justification by works. The awareness of his competence, reinforced by his care for efficiency in matters of this world inherited from his Ignatian formation, rebelled at the prospect of renouncing all his human skills. The law and the logic of the world shook the determination that had driven him from it. For long months, under the direction of Jean de Bernières, he worked meticulously at the mortification of his self-love and achieved not only a detachment from material goods but also an abandonment of his own desires in order to follow the will of God. He undertook the reconstruction of the interior man on the ruins of the exterior man.

The hermitage

Formed like Pierre Lambert by the Jesuits of Caen, Jean de Bernières, himself a Franciscan tertiary, was greatly influenced by the spirituality of his spiritual director, Chrysostom of Saint-Lô, a religious of the Third Order of Saint Francis. Chrysostom taught him his doctrine of 'detachment from created things' according to which perfection consisted in stripping oneself of interest in all created things in order to devote himself to God alone. As a layman with interests in the

---

29. Brisacier. *Vie.* Ch. I.

world, Bernières tried to reconcile this doctrine with the occupations and concerns of social life, much as the Carmelites strove to reconcile the active with the contemplative life. He achieved this by centring his spiritual life on union with Christ, who, through his divine and human natures enabled people to achieve union with God. But this union was obtained only at the price of a permanent contradiction that humans must accept with reference to the interior and exterior sufferings of Christ, whose humanity is the model.

The teaching of Jean de Bernières was very close to that of the French School of spirituality in its Christocentrism, and more especially in the concept of detachment dear to Father de Condren, the spiritual father of two staunch supporters of the Hermitage, Gaston de Renty and Jean Eudes. His teaching was strongly influenced by the Franciscan ideal of poverty, humility and love of the Cross. But it also bore the mark of Ignatian voluntarism, and of the method of introspection and psychological analysis of the Exercises: 'As with a statue, the saints are made by the blows of hammer and chisel',[30] said Bernières. The disciple of the Hermitage thus lived in a state of perpetual tension, torn between his quest for the divine presence and the resistance of nature, between the movements of the spirit and those of the flesh. Standing in an unstable balance between the lower and the upper part of his soul, he was continually crucified in the world, for he could only find peace, rest and beatitude in God, the only centre. 'His soul experiences the happiness of annihilation, and tastes life in death, which means that God has taken possession of it in its present state, so that as soon as the soul awakens, it finds itself in a passive union with Our Lord in its very depths.' The soul, then, experiences great calm, tranquillity and sweetness; God bestows on it a 'great certainty of his presence, and an experiential knowledge of who he is.'[31]

At the Hermitage, this path, so painful and mortifying for human nature, was nevertheless mitigated by the practice of true companionship; each person could express his or her own experience and benefit from that of others. 'During all that time I never heard any topic of conversation other than prayer', reported Henri-Marie Boudon, who stayed there for three months.

---

30. *Dictionnaire de spiritualité*. Volume 1, col. 1524–1525. (Paris: Beauchesne, 1937–1996).
31. *Dictionnaire*.

> Nothing else was talked about during the time of recreation or at any other time, and in truth, it was the most enjoyable recreation in this holy place. Remarkably, it was never boring. Days, months and years were spent talking about the same topic, which seemed to be ever new, and it was this that provided direction in a unique way to God alone, the only place of our true rest. Idle talk and worldly news had no place in the Hermitage. There were no set exercises of piety, because the whole day was given over to prayer. Early morning rising was followed by a continual application to God throughout the day.[32]

Spiritual direction, written accounts of prayer experiences, conversations about spirituality and communication through letter writing made the Hermitage a kind of experimental laboratory of the mystical life. It was a crucible where the most private movements and experiences of souls mingled and interacted. Those involved included noble souls such as Gaston de Renty and Jean Eudes already mentioned, also Henri-Marie Boudon, François de Montmorency-Laval, Jean Baptiste Saint Jure and, through correspondence or proximity, bishops Jean-Pierre Camus and Philippe Cospéan, also religious women: Marie de l'Incarnation, Mechtilde du Saint-Sacrement, Ursule de la Conception, Jourdaine de Bernières, and lay people like the humble Marie des Vallées.

Thus was established an extremely varied and extensive network, whose members were linked by a profound moral and spiritual unity, in spite of the distance and the differences of state of life. Jean de Bernières also attached great importance to the union of prayer which made it possible to maintain bonds beyond physical separation. Like all the great spiritual masters from the Hermitage, Pierre Lambert acquired from this model, in addition to the priority given to the life of prayer, a great respect for individual initiative, a flexible attitude to rules and regulations based on community welfare rather than on unquestioning obedience, practical and personal participation in works of charity, complementarity without competition between clergy and laity, in short, a community spirit founded on an ideal of 'liberty, equality, fraternity'. Such a perspective was quite revolutionary

---

32. Maurice Souriau, *Deux Mystiques normands au xviie siècle, Gaston de Renty et Jean de Bernières* (Paris: Librairie Académique Perrin et Cie, 1913), 201–202.

at a time when Rome was reinforcing the hierarchical control of clerics as far as possible and the absolutism of Louis XIV was taking hold in France.

This liberal spirit was undoubtedly one of the points on which the habitués of the Hermitage deviated most from their Jesuit masters, of whom they were, otherwise, steadfast allies in the struggle against Jansenism and in their fidelity to Rome. In place of the much more methodical way of functioning practised in the Marian congregations, Jean de Bernières substituted an individualized approach to spiritual growth which, although extremely demanding, was based more on the interior abandonment of the directee than on the voluntary application of a method. The profound respect for individual freedom to which it testified thus tempered the impression of excessive rigour and disregard for human nature that the Hermitage teaching gave at first sight, and explained the attachment of its members to their experiences in this place. For these elite souls, ready for every type of spiritual heroism, this outlook on life was a substitute for the obedience *perinde ac cadaver* ('even as a corpse')[33] of the Jesuit discipline, an invitation to consent to self-sacrifice and mystical death, in order to reach the heights of union with God through all the pitfalls of life in the world.

The pilgrim

After having spent some painful months of solitude and doubt in this harsh school of interior self-denial, Pierre Lambert decided in April 1655 to definitively resign his magistrate's office in order to receive holy orders. Already, he saw the possibility of a missionary career, for Jean de Bernières, one of the main leaders of the missions in Canada, had approached him to become the first Vicar Apostolic of the French colony that had been established since the beginning of the century in North America. He accompanied him to Paris to present him to the Assembly of the Missions, a committee of the Company of the Blessed Sacrament responsible for presenting candidates to Rome. But the move was not successful, due to political intrigues and the

---

33. This phrase refers to a promise made by a Jesuit to have no opinion or will of his own or any mental reservation whatever, even as a corpse (perinde ac cadaver). He would unhesitatingly obey each and every command that he received from his superiors and the Pope.

opposition of the Archbishop of Rouen who did not want to give up his right of jurisdiction over New France. Pierre Lambert thus returned to Caen free of all ties and with no other intention than to persevere in his path of self-denial and radical renunciation.

To rid himself of his worldly outlook, he decided to undertake a 'pilgrimage of abjection' to Rennes in order to make a novena at the tomb of John of St Samson, a great Carmelite mystic considered to be the French John of the Cross.[34] A unique practice of the Hermitage was the pilgrimage of abjection which required a penitent to make a journey on foot, dressed as a poor man without money, in order to experience as concretely as possible the situation of the most destitute members of society, that is the beggars and other vagabonds who constituted one of the most serious social problems of the time. The pilgrimage enabled people who were well respected, who were rich and familiar with good works, to purify their practice of charity by stepping through the looking glass,[35] that is to say, by putting themselves on the same footing as the least of the reprobates. It was in the same spirit that Vincent de Paul was chained to the bench of a galley in the place of a convict.

On 25 July 1655, dressed in coarse linen, his hair cut short like that of a peasant, Pierre Lambert left Caen on foot, with a sack on his shoulder, without money or food, obliged to beg for food and lodging. But an even more painful ordeal awaited him in Rennes. Aware of the popular excitement caused in the city by this strange pilgrim, the Carmelites refused him hospitality and therefore also the benefit of the spiritual conversation he had hoped to have with them. There he was condemned to spend his nights in a disreputable inn, exposed to the taunts and provocations of the populace, and to spend his days 'waiting in silence, near the tomb of John of St Samson, for whatever communication it might please God to have with him'. Passivity, dereliction, abandonment. The pilgrim spent his novena in an atmosphere that was completely in keeping with that of his mediator,

---

34. The distance from Caen to Rennes by road is about 154 km.
35. A novel entitled *Alice Through the Looking-Glass* was published in 1871 by Lewis Carroll. It was the sequel to *Alice's Adventures in Wonderland* (1865). Alice entered a fantastical world by climbing through a mirror into the world that she can see beyond it. There she found that, just like a reflection, everything was reversed, including logic, e. g. running helped one remain stationary. For Pierre Lambert, his situation as a rich man was reversed.

whose grace finally appeared. Brisacier tells us that 'after experiencing several hours of extreme dryness of soul and depression, suddenly he received such penetrating and vivid enlightenment concerning the imitation of the poverty and the renunciation of the Son of God that, at the end of the time he spent in Rennes, he was a changed man. The interior transformation into the humble man Jesus surpassed the exterior change that he had effected when he put on the clothes of a poor man.'[36]

This pilgrimage marked an important turning point in Pierre Lambert's spiritual evolution. As far as it is possible to judge from appearances, it constituted his entrance exam into the mystical life. It was to be followed by many other graces and many trials. On his return to Caen, finally rid of the 'old man,' the former councillor knew that he would never again put on his magistrate's robes. He was now ready to embrace the priestly state of life that, for some years, his friend John Eudes had been endeavouring to restore in all its rigour and dignity. It was to his school that Pierre Lambert went to prepare himself.

An ordination under the sign of mission

At the end of October 1655, Pierre Lambert went to the seminary of Coutances of which he was a benefactor. Perhaps he was thinking of exercising his ministry within the Congregation of Jesus and Mary, this seminary being its house of formation. A few weeks later, after his retreat, he went to Bayeux to receive holy orders from the hands of his bishop, Mgr Servien. On December 21, his ordination as a deacon was the occasion of a new mystical experience.' It was said to him in the depths of his soul, after Holy Communion,' writes Brisacier, 'that the Son of God and the Holy Spirit dwelling within him, would make him, in time, a martyr of love, a promise that filled him with consolation and whose effect he looked forward to with complete confidence.'[37]

On December 27, Pierre Lambert was ordained a priest and immediately he left for Coutances to prepare for his first Mass by means of another retreat. It was celebrated on February 8, the feast of

---

36. Brisacier. *Vie*. Ch. V.
37. Brisacier. *Vie*. Ch. V.

the Heart of Mary. On that day, the new priest received two further revelations during his meditation. 'On the morning of that important day', Brisacier again relates, 'the indwelling Spirit assured him that he was destined to be dedicated to a death that would last throughout his life; when offering and drinking the Blood of the Lamb sacrificed for all people, he himself must expect to be immolated and to suffer greatly till his last breath, in order to contribute to the conversion and the sanctification of souls.'[38]

The beginning of the call to the foreign missions

That same evening, he noted in his diary:

> It seems to me that the burning love of God that I experienced today during Mass and after Mass, has been focused with greater intensity on the peoples who have never known him rather than on those who already have some knowledge of him. It seems to me that I must go and seek out these poor blind people beyond the seas whom God wants to draw out of darkness, through the merit of his blood poured out for all.' His biographer commented pertinently that this was 'a premonition all the less suspect, as it was written in his own hand on the very day it was revealed to him, that is to say, at a time when he had been told not to think of Canada and when he was not yet thinking of the Indies, to which, nevertheless, he was destined to go by God, unknown to him or to anyone else.[39]

Two specific intuitions about the future emerged from these experiences: firstly, a victimhood spirituality which bore the mark of John Eudes' conception of the priesthood and through him the understanding of the French school of spirituality, and secondly, a persistent missionary call in spite of circumstances that seemed to oppose it. Uncertain, therefore, of his future, torn between a mysterious attraction in his consciousness for the foreign missions and a much more concrete invitation from his friend John Eudes to work in the parish missions of France, Pierre Lambert, in order to allow himself time for discernment, planned to return to Paris

---

38. Brisacier. *Vie.* Ch. V.
39. Brisacier. *Vie.* Ch. V.

to study theology at the Sorbonne[40] while leading a contemplative and solitary life. But another call unexpectedly brought him back to Rouen to assume new social responsibilities.

Director of the Office of the Poor

In spite of his mystical experiences, which shocked many of his former acquaintances, Pierre Lambert did not lose his reputation for integrity, competence and dedication that he had acquired during his civilian career. Moreover, in this century of great religious effervescence, he was not the only one in his milieu to have indulged in behaviour which, even if it deviated from social conventions and could be misunderstood, nevertheless appeared less excessive, and certainly less foolish then, than it does today. No doubt his accession to the priesthood reassured those around him and allowed him to confirm his conversion while restoring him to a socially acceptable position. The new Pierre Lambert was no longer a fringe member of society experiencing a spiritual crisis but a worthy ecclesiastic who could once again be entrusted with responsibilities commensurate with his abilities.

Now, in the spring of 1656, an important position for which Pierre Lambert seemed to be ideally qualified was freed up in Rouen by the death of its incumbent, that of Director of the Bureau of the Poor. It was one of the most important administrative functions of the city, which consisted in organizing all the aid to be given to those who were then called the 'able-bodied poor', that is to say, to all those in need, except the sick and infirm, who were in the care of the General Hospital. And in the middle of this century, there was no shortage of needy people in the capital of Normandy.

The plague, crop failures, wars and looting ruined the countryside and caused a massive rural exodus. Stripped of their property, driven by hunger, widows, orphans, unemployed peasants and demobilized soldiers swelled the already substantial crowd of beggars in the city. The wealthy feared that this influx of idle and destitute people would lead to new revolts and epidemics. Fear, as much as charity, impelled the city's leaders to take care of them and to supervise them in order

---

40. The Sorbonne is a prestigious university in Paris, founded in the thirteenth century by Robert de Sorbon.

to neutralize the danger they posed to the whole population. This was the time when, in Rouen as in many other large French cities, 'the great enclosure of the poor' was organized, the time when charitable action became a public institution.

After hesitating for a long time, because he no longer wished to appear in the world, Pierre Lambert, urged on by his friends, finally accepted this new position. As soon as he took office in 1656, he began to tackle the problem of poverty in a personal and innovative way that made him, along with Vincent de Paul, one of the great promoters of public welfare in France. His guiding idea was that it was not enough to feed and house the poor, that is, to ensure their simple material subsistence while preventing them from harming society, but that it was just as important to take care of their human empowerment: to educate them, to give them a trade and to help them discover their dignity as human beings, that is, as children of God.

The task was immense, because not only did hundreds of 'enclosed' (abandoned children, teenagers and able-bodied old people who were taken of their own free will or by force from the streets and housed at the General Hospital) depend on the Bureau of the Poor, but also a house for newly converted Protestants and a refuge for repentant girls depended on the Bureau. Another task of the Bureau was the distribution of alms to the poor of the thirty-three parishes of the city and its suburbs.

Anxious to help everyone with the greatest possible humanity, respectful of the individual dignity of the poor, whose clothing he had worn during his pilgrimage to Rennes, Pierre Lambert alternated official measures with personal approaches. So as not to offend their pride, he visited poor people at night, those ashamed of their situation. He was called upon for general confessions, abjurations, reconciliations, or even, according to the expression of the time, to 'stop public scandals.' He was often requested by prominent people such as Archbishop François II Harlay de Champvallon and the Duke and Duchess of Longueville to solve difficult problems. He nevertheless maintained a fraternal familiarity with the most humble, occasionally sharing children's meals at the Hospital; also, he spent hours in prayer and discussion to persuade a dangerous preacher to recant or to convince a prostitute to change her life.

In order to carry out his favourite work, the education of abandoned children, Pierre Lambert relied on existing structures that he developed and perfected. As early as the middle of the 16th century, in order to combat begging and idleness, the Bureau of the Poor had already created four schools for destitute boys and two for girls. They were taught good conduct, catechism, reading, writing and the rudiments of the most common trades. It was the beginning of vocational education, placed under the direction of the clergy and financed by benefactors. But the system, for lack of suitable teachers, soon collapsed.

After 1645, the deterioration of the social situation in the city reignited the problems. The influx of vagrants required new police regulations and the local craft industry lacked skilled labour. Catholic activists from the Company of the Blessed Sacrament and Marian congregations wanted to counter the influence of Protestant schools. In the new buildings of the General Hospital, two priests assisted by a master writer instructed boys 'in the Christian religion.' These boys were locked up from the age of eight. After six years of apprenticeship in manual work, they could obtain a master's degree that enabled them to get a qualified job. The girls were entrusted to lay mistresses, the 'black ladies,' so-called because of their costume; they were especially noted for their austerity.

As soon as he took office, Pierre Lambert took control. He was assisted by two benefactors of the Bureau, brothers François and Laurent Le Cornu de Bimorel. Pierre Lambert persuaded them to devote their fortune to the poor and to come and reside with him at the General Hospital. Next, he employed a lay teacher, Adrien Nyel, as general bursar in charge of teaching reading, writing and catechism, and also the person responsible for the supervision of the male staff, the teenage apprentices and the children. The new bursar also had to recruit teachers in order to found schools in different parts of the city. For ten years, Adrien Nyel carried out his duties with admirable dedication before being called to Rheims. He returned to end his days at the General Hospital of Rouen to which he had promised perpetual fidelity. The role he performed as general bursar was the first example of the declericalization of charitable education.

With the employment of Adrien Nyel it was possible to reorganize the education of boys. But neither was the education of girls neglected. Pierre Lambert appealed to a recently created congregation, founded by Madame de Villeneuve in the Paris region in 1640, the Daughters of the Cross, a society of widowed or unmarried women in secular dress, dedicated to the instruction of little girls. At the time when he had travelled to Paris in 1657, Pierre Lambert contacted these new teachers and arranged for two of them to assist him at the General Hospital. Two years later, at the request of their patron Madame d'Aiguillon, he sent them to Le Havre to found a new teaching establishment which they entrusted to a competent woman whom they trained, before returning to Rouen.

An influential precursor

The capital of Normandy thus became a model for the organization of popular education which was to serve as a point of reference for many establishments. Those in charge of the Caen and Lisieux offices took advice from Pierre Lambert and when, in 1659, Nicolas Barré arrived in Rouen, he had no difficulty in finding dedicated and motivated women among the Third Order of Minims from whom he recruited his first teachers for non-fee-paying schools. A few years later, Nicolas Roland from Rheims came to Rouen to find a model for his Sisters of the Holy Child Jesus, who were also dedicated to the teaching of poor girls. Meanwhile in Rheims, Adrien Nyel laid the foundations of the Institute of the Brothers of the Christian Schools before handing the baton to John Baptist de La Salle. Thus, when Pierre Lambert de la Motte arrived in Rouen in May 1656, it took him only a few months to lay the foundations of an ambitious and innovative social program that developed far beyond Normandy.

Yves Poutet wrote:

> His activity went far beyond the sphere of the Company of the Blessed Sacrament and the General Hospital of Rouen. It was both multifaceted and original, inspirational of initiatives rather than reliant on the suggestions of others. Gifted with a subtle intelligence, a clever dialectician, a psychologist by temperament, Pierre Lambert knew how to put forward convincing arguments that disconcerted his adversaries. His exceptional gifts and his rare dynamism created, if not enemies, at least fierce opponents. His charity had no bounds. It extended to all the distressed and to all forms of Catholic spiritual life. In relation to God, it sacrificed neither the Trinity, nor the Incarnation, nor the child Jesus, nor the Virgin Mary, nor Saint Joseph. As regards others, it supported every worthy

cause; it extended a helping hand to the most underprivileged, to the rejects of society, to the ignorant. Without any fanfare, it encouraged, suggested, provided funds, and prepared relief.[41]

This excessive activity did not disrupt Pierre Lambert's spiritual life in the least even though, as his biographer tells us, 'so many different occupations almost overwhelmed him, but far from diminishing his union with God, they only served to increase it. He was usually more united to God in the midst of his troubles than he was at the time of his retreat and during the hours he devoted to contemplation in his oratory'.[42] A man of prayer by nature and a man of action from necessity, Pierre Lambert succeeded, at the cost of exceptional self-discipline, in reconciling the two forms of life. Being an ascetic, he placed himself under the direction of a confessor, Father Simon Hallé of the Order of Minims who initiated him into the penitential discipline of his Order. From that time on, he really had only one meal a day and was satisfied with a light repast in the evening. Being a contemplative, he devoted four or five hours a day to prayer, very early in the morning before Mass and in the evening before retiring to bed. Being an intellectual, he devoted his evenings to the study of theology with an Irish teacher from the Sorbonne.

A truly Catholic spirit, he associated himself with many forms of devotion: he was a member of the Confraternity of the Rosary, the Third Order of Minims and the Congregation of Gentlemen founded by the Jesuits. Always concerned about the formation of the clergy, he was the main architect of the creation of the new Eudist seminary in Rouen, a very delicate undertaking which met with fierce opposition from the Jansenists. However, in the course of such a full and fruitful life, the secret call of the mission did not go away and soon, without his awareness of it, circumstances led him in a new direction.

In the spring of 1657, Pierre Lambert had to make a trip to Paris on behalf of the General Hospital of Rouen. He took the opportunity to visit his young brother Nicolas who was a seminarian in Paris living with some of his fellow seminarians in a hostel in the rue Saint-Dominique. These young men all belonged to the group of Good Friends, formed and directed by a Jesuit, Father Bagot; they were among the elite of Clermont College. They led a very strict and pious

---

41. Yves Poutet. *Le xviie siècle et les origins lassaliennes*. t. 1. (Rennes: 1970.), 490–494.
42. Brisacier. *Vie*. Ch. XII.

life and since the arrival of Alexander de Rhodes in Paris four years earlier, they had been campaigning for apostolic vicars to be sent to Asia. In their company, the missionary desire of the director of the Bureau of the Poor was awakened with increased intensity. After a short stay in Rouen, during which he obtained the approval of his spiritual director, Pierre Lambert returned to Paris and submitted his application, as well as the rest of his fortune, for what was then called the China missions. This initiative was make him a key player in missionary history.

Chapter 2
French Bishops for Asia

Reasons for a reform and new measures to be adopted

When Pierre Lambert volunteered to go to Asia as a simple missionary, he became part of a long-standing project that had its origins two years before his birth, in the creation of the Congregation De Propaganda Fide (more commonly called 'Propaganda') in Rome in 1622. This new congregation, responsible for the conquest of Protestantism in Europe, but also for the evangelization of all known lands on the surface of the globe, came into being ten years after one of the greatest disasters in missionary history: the banning of Christianity in Japan and the beginning of the first great persecution of the Church in Asia. These dramatic events put an end to the great illusion, maintained for more than half a century by the first successes of Francis Xavier, of a rapid and peaceful conversion of Asia. They also provoked in the upper echelons of the Catholic Church, already shaken by the European schism of the Reformation, a critical awareness of its responsibilities and failures.

As early as 1624, investigations commissioned by Cardinal Francis Ingoli, the first Secretary of Propaganda, drew up a damning assessment of the state of the distant missions entrusted by Rome to the care of the kings of Spain and Portugal through a system of patronage since 1494. The conclusions of these investigations, presented to the cardinals in three successive memoranda dated 1625, 1628 and 1644, were quite distressing: the missions were undermined by quarrels and rivalries between seculars and regulars; religious and Jesuits, Portuguese and Castilians. Political leaders interfered improperly in ecclesiastical affairs, and vice versa. Many missionaries were more concerned with enrichment or entertainment than with the fulfilment of their spiritual functions. Many neglected to learn the local languages, despised or mistreated indigenous people and denied them access to instruction and holy orders. Everywhere the authority of the Holy See was controlled or scorned in the name of secular interests. In Asia especially, in the sphere of the Portuguese Padroado (Patronage),[1] religious engaged in trade in an abusive and scandalous manner.

In this climate of decadence and corruption, redeemed here and there by exemplary lives, a few priority objectives were urgently needed: selecting more carefully those leaving for the missions (because the religious orders tended to get rid of elements that posed problems for them in Europe); limiting the privileges generously granted to religious during the previous century; fighting against abuses and scandals, especially by forbidding clerics to engage in commerce; sending missionaries who were independent of civil authorities who could, if not reform, at least initially inform the Holy See objectively about the measures to be taken; taking the necessary steps to form a native clergy in order to diminish the occasions of persecution; limiting the European presence in the new Christian communities, thereby allowing the overseas churches to become autonomous in time.

It was precisely this last measure that was lacking in Japan. In spite of repeated requests from Rome, the various Portuguese Jesuit bishops appointed for this country from 1588 onwards ordained very few local priests and, above all, favoured the expansion of their own order to the detriment of the formation of a secular clergy capable of assuming pastoral responsibilities in the absence of foreign missionaries.

---

1. The Portuguese 'Padroado' refers to an arrangement between the Portuguese government and the Holy See from the mid-fifteenth century by which the Portuguese government was granted a certain jurisdiction over Catholic church administration in lands acquired by Portuguese maritime expeditions to Africa and Asia. The privileges extended to the designation of candidates for bishoprics and church benefices. The Portuguese government was expected to provide adequate support to the dioceses and religious establishments in its territory. [In the course of time the Padroado became a source of annoyance to the Holy See as it interfered with the progress of the missions. It was dismantled in the twentieth century.

First attempts

In 1637, faced with the magnitude of the Japanese tragedy, Propaganda decided to try a new emergency strategy: the confidential dispatch of independent apostolic vicars from Portugal in order to ordain Japanese priests who were so sorely lacking in times of persecution. For years, Propaganda had been urging the last bishop of Japan, the Jesuit Diego Valente, who had taken refuge in Macau,[2] to give his Church some native priests, but he died in 1633 without having set foot on the archipelago, from which the last missionaries were taken one after another without being replaced.

Faced with this stumbling block, Francis Ingoli changed his methods and had the Indian Mathieu de Castro, titular bishop of Chrysopolis, and the Italian Franciscan Anthony of Santo-Felice, titular archbishop of Myra, consecrated in the greatest secrecy in order to send them to Japan as Vicars Apostolic with episcopal powers under the sole control of Propaganda.

Leaving by land to avoid the control of Lisbon,[3] the two men were nevertheless identified and intercepted, by order of the archbishop, as soon as they arrived in Goa.[4] After many adventures, they were sent back to Rome without ever having been able to approach their mission territory. At the same time, the French Capuchin Ephrem de Nevers, a missionary of Propaganda appointed to the English trading post of Madras, was kidnapped by the Portuguese; he then spent the years from 1649 to 1652 in the jails of the Goa Inquisition.[5] He owed his release, not to the intervention of the Holy Office, which threatened in vain to excommunicate all the clergy of Goa, but to the much more decisive initiative of his friend, the Muslim king of Golconda,[6] who sent his troops to surround the Portuguese city of St. Thomas of Meliapur with orders to burn it down if the Capuchin was not released.

---

2. Macau is a peninsula at the mouth of the Pearl River, China. It was a Portuguese colony from 1557 until 1999 when it was transferred to China.
3. Lisbon is the capital city of Portugal where the government was established.
4. In 1510 the Portuguese defeated the ruling sultan in Goa, a city on the west coast of India, and ruled there until 1947 when it was annexed by India.
5. In order to combat heresy, the Catholic Church established a group of institutions in Europe and other countries. In Goa an Inquisition was set up in 1560 and eventually abolished in 1812.
6. Golconda was a sultanate in southern India which at one time consisted of 21 provinces. It existed from 1518 until 1687.

Such was the atmosphere that prevailed in the missions of Asia at the beginning of the 17th century. The Portuguese, whose colonial power was declining, did not want to give up an inch of their religious power and openly opposed Propaganda. They were more or less openly assisted in this by the Jesuits who had always been very close to the Lisbon court and who sought to maintain the overwhelming numerical superiority they held in Asia. Moreover, over the years, the missionaries of the Society of Jesus had acquired many exemptions and privileges which assured them of virtually unlimited freedom of action. They were not keen to have bishops interfere in the government of missions which they had founded with their own methods and which they generally considered to be their reserved territories.

Alexandre de Rhodes

However, it was a Jesuit, Alexandre de Rhodes, who took the initiative to make the decision that, after many struggles and difficulties, permitted the installation of an ordinary indigenous hierarchy in the new Asian churches. Born in 1591 into a family of Spanish Jewish origin which had been living in Avignon since the fifteenth century, Alexandre de Rhodes entered the Society of Jesus in Rome at the age of 18. Appointed to the mission of Japan, which he could not reach because of persecution, he was sent in 1624 to Cochinchina where his confreres François Buzomi and Diego Carvalho had founded the first Christian communities in the country around a group of Japanese refugees. Called to Tonkin in 1627 because of his good knowledge of the Vietnamese language, Alexandre de Rhodes worked there successfully for three years, but he was expelled in 1630 after the promulgation of an edict banning Christianity. During the fifteen years that followed, he made several trips back and forth between Macau and Cochinchina from where he was definitively banished in 1645 after his catechist, André Phu Yen, was executed before his eyes. It was then that he was chosen by his superiors to go to Rome to defend the interests of the Jesuit missions in Asia.

Considered one of the greatest, if not the greatest missionary in Vietnam, Alexandre de Rhodes was strongly attached to the new churches of Cochinchina and Tonkin, but he feared for their future, for he had seen the same disturbing scenario repeated in these two countries as in Japan: missionaries, closely linked to the interests of

Portuguese merchants, had benefited from a favourable reception of the Annamite leaders,[7] but their fate, like that of the Christians, depended very much on the fluctuations of political and economic relations between Macau and the local governments.

The people welcomed the preaching of Christianity, but the mandarins and bonzes, jealous of their prerogatives, tried by all possible means to harm the converts. The catechists, dedicated and well trained by the Fathers, did a remarkable job but were not able to replace the European priests when they were expelled, as happened to de Rhodes personally on five occasions. If the persecution continued and if the missionaries were definitively banished or exterminated as in Japan, then the flourishing communities of Tonkin and Cochinchina, acquired at such a high cost, would experience the same inexorable extinction. The remedy was still the same, the one that was lacking in Japan: a native clergy and, to train its members, the urgent dispatch of several bishops.

One of the great advantages of Alexandre de Rhodes, which possibly contributed to his soundness of judgment, was his relative political neutrality for the time. He was neither Portuguese, although he worked as a missionary of Portuguese Padroado (Patronage), nor French, as later French historians would have us believe, but a subject of the Pope. He therefore put the interests of the Church before any form of national interest. He arrived in Rome in June 1647 full of confidence, determined to defend his ideas for the development of a Vietnamese clergy.

Proposals with varying degrees of acceptance

Naturally, the cardinals of the Propaganda gave him a warm welcome and even suggested that he should return to his mission with the title of bishop. But he refused, believing that his Jesuit confreres, attached to other ways of operating and generally hostile to the episcopate, would never agree to work under his authority. As for the pope, he was not convinced by the arguments of the Jesuit from Avignon and did not reply to the multiple petitions that Rhodes addressed to him. Nor he did approve of the ambitious project of Propaganda which

---

7. Annam, a largely mountainous area, is the central region of Vietnam, between Tonkin in the north and Cocinchina in the south.

proposed the sending to Asia of a body made up of a patriarch, two or three archbishops and a dozen bishops. Perhaps they thought that if the Portuguese authorities succeeded in neutralizing isolated individuals, they would not dare to attack head-on such a significant contingent.

But Innocent X was hardly in a position to engage in such a provocation, for he found himself in an awkward political situation, caught between the two Catholic powers that benefited from Patronage, Spain and Portugal. Indeed, they were competing with each other. Favouring the Spaniards, he was under pressure from the Portuguese sovereign who, in retaliation, refused to appoint bishops to the vacant posts. In 1649, there was no longer a bishop in Brazil or in Africa; there was only one in Portugal and two in Asia—in Goa and Cranagor—which aggravated the situation of neglect of most of the missions.

Disappointed by the attitude of Rome, Alexandre de Rhodes went to Paris where he hoped to find a more favourable response to his project. He arrived in the French capital on the 27th January 1653, and was warmly welcomed at the court and amongst zealous groups associated with the Company of the Blessed Sacrament. His passionate descriptions of the Christianity of Cochinchina and Tonkin aroused the enthusiasm of the young Jesuits, many of whom volunteered for these new missions. The Good Friends of the College of Clermont, directed by his confrere Jean Bagot, responded in similar fashion. Three of them, François Pallu, François de Montmorency-Laval and Bernard Piques, caught his attention and, on March 7, Alexandre de Rhodes proposed their candidature to Propaganda.

In Rome, however, there was still hesitation, because the Italians did not like the French and were suspicious of their temperament, which they considered too enthusiastic and not sufficiently resolute. Moreover, Propaganda wanted to be able to count on men absolutely committed to its orders and it considered that the Parisian volunteers were too closely linked to the Jesuits whose influence it feared. For his part, the King of Portugal, worried about his patronal power, announced that, on the fleet of March 1655 he would send twenty-five new Jesuits to Asia, among them eleven Frenchmen who had volunteered for the missions in China. Alexandre de Rhodes, on the other hand, was not part of the team. He lost the game and was to pay dearly for his commitment to the Christians of Vietnam whom he would never see again. Considered undesirable by the Portuguese, who did not forgive him for an initiative against their power, he was sent to a mission independent of the Padroado, in Persia. He died eight years later in Ispahan on 5 November 1660, without knowing that the first French Vicar Apostolic, Pierre Lambert de la Motte, whom he had never met, had just set out for his mission in Cochinchina. It was not until the death of Innocent X in January 1655 and the election of his successor, Alexander VII, who was more attentive to the fate of the distant missions, that the situation changed again. Taking advantage of this change of reign, a small delegation of French activists set out for Rome in the spring of 1656 to sound out the intentions of the new Pope. Supported by the assembly of the clergy of France and the highest authorities of the country, it counted among its members François Pallu, the first candidate retained by Alexandre de Rhodes.

But in spite of a favourable and benevolent welcome from the Pontiff, negotiations dragged on without apparent results. In Paris, worried about this delay, the leaders of the Assembly of Foreign Missions decided to send to the rescue Pierre Lambert de la Motte, who had just declared his desire to serve in the missions. They hoped that his great legal skills and his expertise as a negotiator would help to break the deadlock. They had so much confidence in him that they put his name second, just after that of François Pallu, on the new list of candidates they were proposing to the Pope for the position of Vicar Apostolic.

On 18 November 1657, Pierre Lambert de la Motte arrived in Rome. In the absence of precise information, historians have made many assumptions about his exact role in the negotiations with the Vatican authorities, a role that is still difficult today to define precisely. It seems certain, however, that it was he who, during a long meeting with Cardinal Alberici, Secretary of Propaganda, succeeded in gaining acceptance of the principle concerning the nomination of French Vicars Apostolic for Asia. Officially, it is believed that he removed the major obstacle, which was financial, by guaranteeing the income of the Vicars Apostolic from his personal fortune.

Beneath the surface

This was certainly a determining factor, but the sequence of events suggests that the pope and the cardinals of Propaganda may have had less material reasons for placing their complete trust in him and thereby risking a venture which, humanly speaking, had very little chance of success because of the considerable opposition it aroused. For in Rome it was well known that the Jesuits, as well as the Portuguese authorities, were hostile to the presence of Vicars Apostolic in Asia and would ally themselves with the authorities of Padroado to hinder them.

All the letters of warning addressed to François Pallu by William Lesley, the editor of the *Instruction* of Propaganda, throughout the year 1659 testify to this double distrust. 'You people are good, zealous, well-intentioned, sincere and frank, but the other nations and especially the Portuguese are not like that; they are shrewd, cunning and deceitful. The religious formed among them put the interests of their country above that of the Church; that is why I am very much afraid that they will snare you in their nets to prevent your journey.'[8] 'His Holiness will do nothing and will certainly not be willing to send Jesuits with you. Certainly it is not the intention of Rome that they accompany you. However, it is necessary to keep in touch with them. By all means avoid breaking off relations, but take it for granted that they will be able to prevent you from doing much, and will want to do so if you are not their friends from the start. If they bother you because of what you are doing or saying, cooperate with them as far as you can, in good conscience, to satisfy them, but keep Rome well informed of all that is happening, and ask for the necessary orders.'[9] 'As for you, all these gentlemen have always had, and still have a very high opinion of your goodness, zeal and sincerity, virtues that would have motivated you from the beginning and caused you to undertake your journeys. But there are too many inconsistencies in this affair from the Jesuit Fathers, the Spaniards and especially the Portuguese; and even now we suspect that these same adversaries will not let you travel, that you will have more difficulties from them than from the infidels to whom you are going to preach the Gospel.'[10]

---

8. LetterofWilliam Lesley to François Pallu, 8 September 1659. *Documents historiques de la Société des Missions étrangères*. Annotated by Adrien Launay. (Paris: 1904), 258.
9. Letter of William Lesley to François Pallu, 29 September 1659. *Documents historiques*, 260.
10. Letter of William Lesley to François Pallu, 23 November 1659, *Documents historiques*, 261.

In receiving Pallu and his friends, the Roman authorities probably feared that they were much too closely tied to the Jesuits, much too dependent on them to be able to defend themselves in the conflict that would inevitably be waged in Asia, and this is doubtless the reason why they still hesitated. Perhaps, also, and this is only an hypothesis, they also recognized in Pierre Lambert, despite his very close ties with the Fathers of the Society of Jesus, the right man for the job, a man sufficiently experienced and competent on the administrative level to fulfill the function of Vicar Apostolic, and sufficiently practised in self-denial on the spiritual level to resist the attacks and trials inherent in this mission of sabotage which did not dare to say its name. For to attack the Portuguese Padroado was also to attack the Jesuits, since the interests of both had been linked for a century. For one of their former disciples to do so was to expose himself to misunderstanding, to general reprobation, to exclusion and, for a Frenchman of that time, to the accusation of treason and, even worse, to that of Jansenism which was enough to ruin his reputation.

By his voluntary humiliations, by his long practice of interior mortification, Pierre Lambert had unknowingly been preparing himself for a long time for a task that was thankless, heart-breaking and bereft of all solace. He was also well able to keep secrets, to bear the weight of darkness and dereliction that would inevitably fall on him as a result of the double-dealing of a pontifical authority mired in its contradictions. 'He left France with his mind set against the Jesuits which made him act against them in all that he undertook',[11] a disoriented Pallu wrote one day. Given all that we know of Pierre Lambert's past, his relationships and his position in French religious affairs, these dispositions can only date from his stay in Rome. It must therefore be assumed that he received unofficial instructions there, which he later followed. In behaving towards the Jesuits with a strictness that was sometimes misunderstood by his confreres and that earned him the resentment of the directors in Paris, he did not receive even the slightest reprimand from the Vatican authorities.

Whatever the secret content of these negotiations, about which we can only speculate, Pierre Lambert's short stay in Rome was decisive.

---

11. Letter of François Pallu to MM. Brisacier, Gazil, Fermanel et Bésard, Siam, 3 September 1673. AMEP, volume 27, 322. Cited in Henri Chappoulie. *Une controverse entre missionnaires à Siam au XVIIe siècle. Le religiosus négociator du jésuite français J. Tisannier.* (Université de Paris, 1943).

Back in Rouen, the director of the Bureau of the Poor, who had returned to France after Easter, was soon fighting an underground battle against the Jansenists for the creation of a Eudist seminary. Then on 13 May 1658, Propaganda nominated him, as well as François Pallu, as Vicars Apostolic for Asia.

The pope gave his approval on June 8 and, on July 29, published a brief naming the two Frenchmen Bishops of Heliopolis and Beirut.[12] On August 17, Propaganda assigned the Apostolic Vicariate of Tonkin to the former and that of Cochinchina to the latter.[13] On November 17, having received the rochet[14] from the pope, François Pallu was consecrated Bishop in the crypt of the Vatican Basilica by Cardinal Antoine Barberini, prefect of Propaganda. At the end of January 1659, he was back in Paris to prepare for his departure and to await the instructions that would guide the actions of the Vicars Apostolic.

The *Instructions*

Propaganda had, in fact, only decided to send Vicars Apostolic to Asia in order to regain control of the missions, and it expected these new agents to conform faithfully to its views. With this in mind, it carefully prepared a text that would become a landmark in missionary history, the Roman *Instruction* of 1659.[15] The editor was an Irish clergyman, William Lesley, an ardent defender of the French against the claims of the Portuguese and the Jesuits, whom he did not spare. Before submitting his copy to the cardinals, he had to consult all the registers

---

12. The two Frenchmen were titular bishops which means that they did not have a diocese. According to the custom in the Catholic Church, they were given the title of a bishopric that had ceased to exist, in this case, the former dioceses of Heliopolis and Beirut.
13. In Vietnam, Cochinchina was the southern region and Tonkin the northern region of the country.
14. The rochet is a white garment, descending to about knee level, often trimmed with lace, that is worn by bishops.
15. The *Instruction* of 1659, also known as the *Magna Charta* of the Congregation, (that is of Propaganda), was addressed to all of the Vicariates Apostolic in China and Indochina, and contained directives for all missionaries. Two of these are particularly noteworthy: the invitation for the promotion of indigenous clergy and an explicit commitment to inculturation, which included a prohibition against combating local customs and traditions of a given country, except when they stood in opposition to faith or morals. Internet. https://www. vatican. va/roman_curia/congregations. (Accessed 14/12/2022)

of Propaganda for many months and draw up an exhaustive report on the state of the missions. It was not until November 1659, one year after the consecration of François Pallu, that the official directives governing the conduct of the Vicars Apostolic arrived in Paris.

These directives were inspired by some great principles such as the refusal of secularization and politicization, respect for indigenous cultures, the attainment of autonomy by the local churches and the consolidation of their relationship with the Holy See. But they also give specific instructions which show that in Rome there were no illusions about the difficulties of all kinds that awaited the Vicars Apostolic. They recommended, therefore, that they go by land to avoid contact with the Portuguese, that they travel under a false identity and use a false pretext, without revealing their nationality or their status as missionaries, and inform Rome of everything that was happening in the missions.

The official text of these directives constitutes the Roman charter for modern missions. The intentions of Propaganda were clearly stated and showed a careful examination of the various missionary methods, including the most innovative. In particular, there was a clear approval of the Jesuits' 'inculturation methods', but also a categorical, if implicit, condemnation of their political involvement and secular activities.

One can also guess, with certain restrictions, that Propaganda was perfectly conscious that it did not have the means to implement its policy. Very modern in its intentions, the *Instruction* therefore remained utopian in the politico-religious context of the time. The Vicars Apostolic would have to interpret and apply the directives as best they could, each according to his own cultural perceptions and personal temperament. But whatever their good will and sincerity, they would pay the price for this discrepancy between principles and reality and would ultimately become the victims of their obedience to Rome.

Between Roman strategy and French interests

During the two years between his return from Rome and his departure on mission (from Easter 1658 to June 1660), Pierre Lambert's activity, which went unnoticed, seems to have been confined to the affairs of Rouen. He hardly appeared on the official Parisian scene where

François Pallu seemed on the other hand to have been omnipresent. Born in Tours in August 1626, François Pallu was the tenth of eighteen children of an honourable family from Tours which gave three of its seven daughters and four of its eleven sons to the Church, two of whom attached themselves to the Society of Jesus. His maternal grandfather, Gautier, was the last elected mayor of Tours. His paternal grandfather, then his father, both named Etienne, successively held the positions of alderman and then mayor-designate of the city, a position which was tantamount to ennoblement for them and their lineage. François Pallu, like Pierre Lambert, belonged to the nobility of the robe, but at a more recent and slightly lower level, his father having been a simple councillor and then a lawyer at the bailiwick of Tours.

On the other hand, the little information we have suggests that the Pallu family was less overtly ambitious, but more conformist than the Lambert family. Through Anne Pallu, aunt of François, married to Jacques Bonneau, one of Mazarin's main agricultural tenants they were allied with Colbert[16] and the two bishops Gault of Marseille (Eustache and Jean-Baptiste). During the Fronde, they were on the side of Mazarin, which was another notable difference from the Lambert family. This political contrast will be found in the respective attitudes of the two Vicars Apostolic towards power.

Back in Paris a few months after his colleague, François Pallu, although matured by his long association with the circles of pontifical power, did not seem to have fully understood the intentions of Propaganda and consequently made a certain number of false moves which earned him serious reprimands. However, the Roman instructions were clear: if the traps of the Padroado were to be avoided, it was necessary to leave without the knowledge of the Portuguese authorities, therefore as discreetly and as quickly as possible; above all, the land route should be taken. But for more than two years, François Pallu persisted in seeking a route by sea. Was he afraid of the dangers and hardships of travelling through the deserts of the Middle East? Was he sincerely persuaded that the maritime route was the most economical and rapid? Or was he influenced by those close to him: on the one hand, the Jesuits and their friends, who

---

16. Jean-Baptiste Colbert was the First Minister of State from 1661 until 1683, a man who had a great influence on the politics and finance of France.

could not bear the idea of a separation between the Vicars Apostolic and the missionaries of the Society and therefore recommended an agreement with Portugal? On the other hand, was he influenced by the business community—financiers, ship owners and merchants who were to some extent associated with the Company of the Blessed Sacrament—who saw in the appointment of French Vicars Apostolic a good means of developing commercial relations overseas, merchants and missionaries relying on each other for the greater prosperity of the Church and of France? All these factors must have added to the very real difficulties of organization for the first Vicar Apostolic to have been delayed in France for more than three years.

His first error of judgment consisted in requesting from Lisbon the authorization to borrow Portuguese ships, an authorization which was apparently granted by mistake at first and was then refused. Although this initiative provoked a strong rebuke from Rome, the Bishop of Heliopolis continued to seek a maritime solution and proposed a contract of association with the Company of Madagascar that was ultimately unsuccessful. Then in August 1659, François Pallu supported the creation of a trading company for China, designed by the Company of the Blessed Sacrament and modelled on the Dutch East Indies Company. Its 'principal aim would be to facilitate, by its establishment, the passage of bishops appointed by His Holiness to go abroad and work for the glory of God and the conversion of souls'.[17]

The Company of the Blessed Sacrament, which had used all of its influence in the appointment of the Vicars Apostolic, felt totally involved in the organization of their mission. However, its conceptions being of lay and French inspiration did not coincide exactly with the clerical and Roman views of Propaganda, which led to a certain number of misunderstandings. The cardinals, familiar with diplomatic intrigues, had recommended absolute discretion. But, notwithstanding their instructions, the members of the Company, accustomed as they were to working in secret, began to launch a veritable publicity campaign aimed at collecting funds and recruiting volunteers. Two leaflets were printed by them in May and August 1659. The second, entitled 'Summary of the Missions in China and

---

17. Henri Sy, *La Société des Missions étrangères: les débuts: 1653–1663* (Paris: Églises d'Asie, 2001), 137. This work contains a detailed analysis of the commercial dealings carried out by Pallu and the Company of the Blessed Sacrament and quotes many little known texts.

the sending of three bishops to the new Churches of this Empire' and attributed to François Pallu, skilfully played on two registers: while appealing to the religious zeal of its recipients, it took care to flatter their national pride.

> Since the discovery of so many new countries, various kingdoms of Christendom have been active in bringing the faith to these lands and have spared nothing in their efforts to do so; France alone, although having no less piety, nor zeal for religion, nor courage for business, nor an abundance of good workers, has only a small share in this great work of spreading the faith throughout the world. It is important for France to exercise its zeal in this most important work. God wishes it and generously offers it China, which includes the most civilized people, the most numerous and the most capable of entering into the mysteries of our faith. This is the portion of the world which Providence seems to have assigned to France. Can it not be said that the bishops whom France sends there will take possession of these new churches, as if they were a field in which the zeal of French missionaries will have a sort of preferential right, and a special blessing to cultivate this field well? In this way our France is going to commit itself forever to this flourishing Empire, joining the East to the West by a union of piety and zeal for the honour of God, the triumph of the Church and the salvation of souls.[18]

By addressing public opinion directly, the Company of the Blessed Sacrament laid down the operating principles of a missionary propaganda that would be popularised two and a half centuries later by the Annals of the Propagation of the Faith. Thus it was that this ambiguous discourse played on an amalgam of religious and secular motivations, an amalgam which, like the system of Padroado, would rapidly alter the evangelical purity of the missions. It is true that it was much too early to speak of patriotism or colonialism in France, but one can already glimpse, behind this pious and somewhat triumphalist enthusiasm, a germ of confusion that Louis XIV would be able to exploit perfectly a quarter of a century later with the Siamese embassies, and cause great harm to the missionaries.

---

18. Sy, *La Société*, 124–125. This glowing presentation of China reflects the optimistic image of this country drawn by the Jesuits of Peking (Beijing).

Carried along by these different interests, the project of a trading company for China took shape. In April 1660, a committee of shareholders led by the shipowner Lucas Fermanel, collected one-third of the funds needed to build two ships. The first, baptised the Saint-Louis, was soon under construction in the port of Amsterdam and its captain, named Philippe de Chamesson, was a former cavalry officer; as for the pilot, he was a Dutchman named Henri Jans. Meanwhile, in Rouen, where Lucas Fermanel was Colbert's correspondent, an association of merchants interested in overseas trade was formed to support the enterprise. However, in Rome the cardinals were becoming impatient and were beginning to think that their suspicions about the French were not entirely unjustified.

Pierre Lambert leads the way

Pierre Lambert, for his part, was certainly not totally unaware of these commercial projects, if only because of the quasi-familial links he maintained with the Fermanel family, shipowners of Rouen, very active committed Catholics and very much involved in all the major French maritime companies. But, being very busy in bringing to a conclusion the many works he had undertaken in Normandy, and respecting the instructions regarding discretion from Propaganda, he did not return to Paris until a week before his episcopal ordination. This took place on 11 June 1660 in the church of the Visitation Sainte-Marie. The Archbishop of Tours, Monsignor Lebouthiller, was the consecrating prelate. After a week's retreat, the new Vicar Apostolic left Paris on June 18, accompanied by a young Parisian priest and doctor of theology, Jacques de Bourges, his valet, Nicolas Legras, and a layman, Pressard, whom he sent away before setting off for Marseilles, realizing that he was not suited to the missionary life.

The Bishop of Beirut left with the greatest discretion, without taking leave of his archbishop, the powerful François Harlay de Champvallon, or of King Louis XIV, whose pressure he feared. On June 28, in Lyon, he fell seriously ill, remained unconscious for two days, then recovered sufficiently to continue his journey to Marseilles[19] where a final temptation awaited him. On his arrival, he found a letter from the Good Friends calling him back to Paris to deal

---

19. Marseilles is the largest port in France, situated in the south of the country on the Mediterranean Sea.

with some problems that were probably caused by the government's suppression of the Company of the Blessed Sacrament. But he refused this invitation, believing that if he turned back he might not have the courage to leave.

On November 27, he embarked on a ship bound for Alexandretta[20] in the company of Jacques de Bourges and a new missionary, François Deydier, originally from Toulon. In the last resort, therefore, giving priority to obedience to Rome rather than to French interests, Pierre Lambert showed that he had already assimilated the spirit of the Roman *Instruction* which he would have plenty of time to meditate on during the long months of his journey. In so doing, to some extent, he saved the reputation and the missionary future of the Church of France. For there was every reason to believe that any going back on his part would have angered Rome and may have discredited fatally a French missionary enterprise which was accumulating mistakes and whose many adversaries were watching for every opportunity to bring about its demise.

At that time, in fact, everything was going badly for the Parisian missionaries and, in the capital, triumphalist speeches were no longer appropriate. Since September, the Company of the Blessed Sacrament had been fiercely attacked in Normandy by both the Jansenist, Charles Dufour, and the Archbishop of Rouen, Harlay de Champvallon, and had been subjected to very close police surveillance; it was now meeting only in small committees. It gradually dissolved, thus depriving the French missionary enterprise of its principal support in human resources. Furthermore, the Saint Louis, seized at first by the Dutch authorities, sank with all its cargo during a storm which took it by surprise off Texel Island[21] on December 19. With it were destroyed months of effort, most of the funds collected for the missions and all hope of reaching Asia quickly by sea. This shipwreck provoked a sharp response from the Secretary of Propaganda, whose message transmitted by William Lesley sounded like a warning shot and a last admonition: 'He commanded me to write to you at length and to make it very clear that his idea was always that you should set out as soon as possible, without delaying to make so many preparations,

---

20. Alexandretta is a city on the coast of Turkey, a country at the eastern end of the Mediterranean.
21. Texel Island is off the north coast of the Netherlands.

nor for anything else that might hinder you, and that you should go by the Mediterranean Sea, and the rest of the way by land, following the example of Mgr Lambert; you must not think of going to China, except as an apostle.'[22]

The end of an era

When Pierre Lambert left Marseilles, the political, spiritual and moral universe in which he had been trained was disappearing. Three months earlier, in August 1660, Louis XIV had solemnly entered Paris accompanied by his young Spanish wife, Maria Theresa, the price of the provisional reconciliation between the two Catholic enemy nations. Mazarin died on March 9 of the following year, leaving the new king to exercise absolute power alone. One of the cardinal's last political acts was to obtain in December 1660 a decree from the Parlement forbidding any 'assembly, brotherhood, congregation or community without the granting of letters patent'. This measure was aimed essentially at the Company of the Blessed Sacrament, which continued to function clandestinely for some time until it was officially suppressed in 1664.

One of the most eminent members of the Company of the Blessed Sacrament, Vincent de Paul, died quietly in September 1660, at Saint-Lazare. His patron, the regent Anne of Austria, retired to the Val de Grace where she died in 1666. Blaise Pascal died at the age of thirty-nine, in August 1662, plagued by illness and regret for not having done enough for the poor. Corneille had lost the favour of the public, which was now enjoying the spectacle of human passions and improper conduct staged by the two new playwrights in vogue, Racine, a defector from Jansenism, and Molière, the libertine.

With the reign of the Sun King Louis XIV,[23] the day of a new nobility was dawning. Enslaved to the sumptuous and superficial constraints

---

22. Adrien Launay, *Documents historiques*. 264.
23. Louis XIV was born in 1638. He occupied the throne from 1643 to 1715, a period of 72 years. For Louis, the most important objective for a ruler was to seek glory for himself and for his country. He believed that he ruled by divine right and was an absolute ruler, i. e. free of all restraints, answerable to no one but God. He took almost complete control of church affairs, including the appointment of bishops. He chose the sun as his personal emblem; the sun gives life to all things. He was responsible for the building of the glittering palace at Versailles.

of court life, it no longer offered any political or intellectual resistance to royal absolutism. The great century of souls was disappearing, suddenly giving way to the Great Century. The powerful spiritual impulses that had lifted France and animated so many initiatives had definitely disappeared.

From now on, religious life, organized under the rule of the new king, became an instrument of power. Opponents and troublemakers, Jansenists, Quietists or Protestants, were eliminated without mercy. The bishops, who were brought to heel, ensured the supervision of a Church in France that had to be above all Gallican.[24] In this context, friction with Rome increased, and the mission of the Vicars Apostolic was progressively deprived of the support of the devout circles which had presided over its birth. It submitted to the pressure of the new power. The task of its protagonists, already singularly delicate, became all the more complicated.

---

24. The word 'Gallican' is derived from the word 'Gallia' (Gaul) which the Romans gave to the territory now known as France. In seventeenth century France, Gallicanism referred to the independence from Rome of the French king in temporal matters and the union of the king and clergy to limit the pope's action within France. It held that pronouncements of the pope were not infallible without the approval of the universal Church.

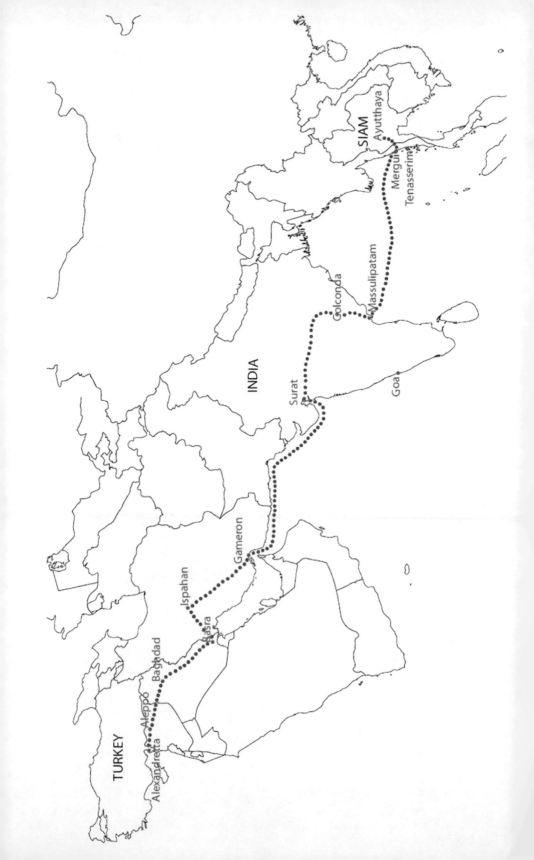

Chapter 3
The Discovery of Asia

The desert experience

Departing from Marseilles on 27 December 1660, Pierre Lambert, Jacques de Bourges and François Deydier arrived in Alexandretta on January 11, after stopping in Malta and Cyprus. They then went to Aleppo where they were received by the French consul who played the role of official protector of Christians in the whole of the Middle East, following the agreements concluded in 1536 between France and the Ottoman Empire. Thanks to him, the missionaries were provided with a place in a caravan that crossed the Syrian desert.

They left on 25 January 1661 dressed as Turks to avoid harassment from the Muslims. The journey, which was very trying for Westerners, lasted more than a month.'In the morning,' said Jacques de Bourges in his Relation de voyage (Journey Account) published in Paris in 1666, 'we mounted a horse or a camel, from which we did not dismount until evening, when we stopped to end our day and have supper, which was our only meal. Nevertheless, before setting out, we provided ourselves with biscuits and some dried fruit to sustain ourselves during the fatigue of the day's journey. It was only in the evening that we had our meal and had the leisure to light a fire and prepare food, which meant no more than the cooking of some rice with butter'. The winter climate obliged the travellers to travel during the day, under the constant threat of robber bands; the nights were so cold that often the tents froze 'so that we had to wait for the heat of the sun to melt the ice before we could fold the tents'.

Far from complaining about the harshness of the living conditions, Pierre Lambert accepted them wholeheartedly, for they fulfilled his ascetic desire for self-denial and abandonment. 'I have great joy in being able to keep and to imitate the Lenten discipline of the Minims more perfectly than when in France, at least on the fast days of the Church', he wrote to his spiritual director, Simon Hallé. 'We have begun to practice mortification before Lent from necessity, although we do so willingly and with pleasure. All this is very little. We find that habit takes care of everything: we are tired almost all day, we drink only water, we sleep out of doors, we hardly ever eat meat or fish by the wayside, and we have good reason to be afraid. Yet, we are not preoccupied by such hardships, and when we do reflect on them, we receive much consolation and we do so only to give very special thanks to Our Lord Jesus Christ.'

On March 4, the missionaries finally arrived in Baghdad where they lodged with the French Capuchins. Here they were able to regain some strength before taking a boat down the Tigris to Basra, the great international port on the Persian Gulf which was home to trading posts of the great European maritime powers, England, Holland and Portugal. In the stifling heat of this cosmopolitan city, people of all races and religions mingled: 'Jews, Muslims, Christians of different denominations, good people and idolaters.' Catholics were looked after by Italian Carmelites. The French missionaries were welcomed into their home and during their stay they were astonished to discover Hindu rites and a religious tolerance to which they were not accustomed, either among themselves or among others. 'Trade still attracts idolaters from India to Basra. The governor of the city, though a Muslim and consequently an enemy of idolatry which the Koran condemns in so many places, does not allow them to practice in public their wretched worship, which has been the cause of considerable astonishment and horror to us.'

The season not being favourable for navigation across the Persian Gulf, they decided to go north towards Ispahan where they hoped to find a road through the north of India, Nepal and Bhutan in order to journey as far as possible from the areas frequented by the Portuguese. After reaching Bandar Abbas on makeshift boats, they crossed the towering mountains leading to the Iranian plateau. They travelled in a caravan at night because of the heat, stopped at the Carmelite monastery in Shiraz and reached Ispahan on 11 June 1661 before sunrise. This detour marked a decisive turning point in the moral perception they had of their mission.

A lie with serious consequences

When they arrived in Ispahan, where Alexandre de Rhodes had died seven months earlier, the missionaries of Propaganda remembered the Report on the Persia Mission published under the name of the Jesuit from Avignon in 1659. This report described a religious situation full of promise thanks to the credit enjoyed by the Jesuits at the court of the Persian ruler, Shah Abbas. But the reality they discovered was quite different. The Catholic community was no more than a few families of artisans or foreign merchants, and the missionaries present there—Carmelites, Augustinians, Capuchins and Jesuits—were devoting themselves to linguistic and scientific studies without engaging in evangelization.

The French soon learned that this state of affairs was due to the untimely political activism of a Jesuit, Father Rigordi, who had appeared at court and thought he had won the favour of the ruler by a series of extravagant proposals: an alliance with France, the marriage of the Shah to Mlle de Montpensier, and the sending of a French fleet to Hormuz. But far from the expected result, this untimely intervention had provoked not only the expulsion of the Jesuit, but also an anti-missionary reaction which had affected the other orders. Since then, the situation had calmed down, but the Catholic religious had to keep a low profile and occupy their time with linguistic and scientific research without any apostolic results. The report of Alexander de Rhodes was therefore only an edifying fable written for the attention of devout French.

Worse still, the information gathered in this place suggested that the same was true of the other reports, including those from China, Cochinchina and Tonkin. The Bishop of Beirut immediately informed the secretary of the Propaganda of this disturbing discovery which called into question the very foundation of his own mission.

> I will tell your Excellency what I have noticed in this city. All the reports that the Fathers of the Society of Jesus have presented concerning the state of religion in this kingdom are false. This would be a small matter if the reports concerning the missions in China, Tonkin and Cochinchina were true. But if we are to believe all the missionaries of this city and others in the vicinity whom we have met, we can make the same judgment about these other missions as we do about

this one. For this reason, many trustworthy people of eminent piety have tried to divert us from our mission and would have us go further afield. But regardless of what they have told us, we believe that our determination to execute this work comes from God and we wish to carry out the order of the Holy Father and of the Sacred Congregation at the risk of our lives. That is why we are going to attempt in two weeks' time to go by a route that no European has ever tried. This is the route we are going to take: from here to Meched (Iran), Herat, Kandahar (Afghanistan), Delhi and Agra (India). It annoys me greatly to have to oppose the Fathers of this Society, but I cannot hide the truth and I do not want to be a party to any wrongdoing.

From the time of this break in their journey in Ispahan, the more-or-less precise warnings formulated by Propaganda before their departure took on a very real significance for the French missionaries, and the mistrust which had been recommended to them with regard to the Jesuits found its full justification. Pierre Lambert understood that he and his men would be considered intruders not only by the authorities of Padroado, jealous of their power, but also by the missionaries of the Society of Jesus, who had no interest in having embarrassing witnesses come to see for themselves the flagrant discrepancy between the real situation of their missions and what they proclaimed in Europe.

'In addition to this obstacle, we have still other groups who are all-powerful in the Indies, who have no liking for our mission since it is critical of them,' wrote Pierre Lambert to Pierre Fermanel. 'You know well enough who I mean. That is why we must avoid, as far as possible, the places where they are in control.' From now on, the Bishop of Beirut understood his mission to be a crusade for truth within the very heart of the European Church. He entered upon this internal struggle with all the ardour of his militant temperament; subsequent events contributed to confirm him in the correctness of his chosen path.

On the outskirts of the forbidden zone

On 26 September 1661, the missionaries left Ispahan in the company of the English agent who had offered to guide them. After a stop at the British trading post of Gameron, they embarked for Suali and finally arrived in Surat at the end of the year. There they were welcomed by two French Capuchins stationed in this city, Ambroise de Preuilly and Gilles de Bourges, who served as faithful contacts for all the missionaries of Propaganda.

Through these men they learned that in June an order from Lisbon had arrived in Goa requesting the arrest of the French bishops and their return to Europe. The mission of the Vicars Apostolic was taking on the appearance of a manhunt and it became more imperative than ever for the French to avoid direct confrontation with the agents of the Padroado as long as possible, whether they were civilians or religious. To escape the traps of the Portuguese, it was necessary to seek the assistance of the English or the Dutch, who were trying to outdo them in Asia. To avoid the opposition of the Jesuits, it was necessary to rely on the Capuchins, who had long been used to playing cat-and-mouse with them.

The French missionaries therefore decided to cross India from west to east through the territories of the Great Mogul and the King of Golconda, the great friend of the Capuchins who had wrested Ephrem de Nevers from the hands of the Portuguese. But Pierre Lambert was also concerned to find, in the longer term, maritime travel possibilities, at least for mail, and if possible for men. The main characteristic of the Dutch was that they were the most bitter enemies of Portugal, but their commercial greed made them unreliable allies: they opened the letters entrusted to them 'to see if there was anything that would disadvantage their own interests.' The English were more honest, and they had already given clear proof of their courtesy to the French missionaries. But nonetheless they were heretics and it was painful for the ultra-Catholic Lambert, a former supporter of the Fronde, to form an alliance with enemies of the Church. He would have preferred to solicit the help of the Spaniards in Manila, who were only seven or eight days away from China, although the route by sea from Europe to the Philippines—via Spain, the Canary Islands, Santo Domingo, Acapulco, and the Isle of Thieves—seemed to him difficult and dangerous. In actual fact, this route was the one taken in the opposite direction to that of Pierre Lambert by François Pallu when he was kidnapped in 1674 by the religious of Manila and sent to Europe.

Misled by his political convictions, Pierre Lambert placed too much trust in the Spaniards! However, the missionaries had to hasten their departure in order to avoid the rainy season which, from March to June, made the roads impassable. They left Surat on 25 January 1662, accompanied by two valets and six guards who were responsible for guarding their camp at night against robbers. The small convoy of four ox carts crossed the states of the Great Mogul through Oletabal, Noringabal and Beder, and stopped at Golconda, 'one of the most beautiful cities in India with the finest buildings which were as large as the buildings of Rome.' They arrived at Massulipatam on the Bay of Bengal on March 6. This journey, in record time, forty days instead of the forty-five provided for in the carters' contract, allowed the French time to enrich their religious knowledge of Asia.

Examples and counter-examples from religious in Asia

Their reactions were contradictory, a mixture of astonishment and incomprehension, but also of a certain admiration which clearly showed in their testimonies.' These idolaters are divided into several sects, whose differences and errors are difficult to explain. Although these peoples live in the deepest darkness of paganism, the skill with which they carry on their commerce shows that they are not lacking in intelligence. We were keen to talk to some of them, who seemed to us to have very good judgment.'

These first contacts, which could be described as 'interreligious', were far removed from the 'dialogue' advocated today, a dialogue that was inconceivable for Western Christians of the seventeenth century who had been raised since their birth in a climate of intolerance and religious struggles within Christianity itself. It is to be noted, however, that there was among our Frenchmen, a sincere esteem, mixed with astonishment, for the religious behaviour of these foreign people, which in certain respects was in harmony with their own religious sensibility.

In the course of their caravan journey, the missionaries had already noticed the sincerity of the Muslims who prayed 'every day in their own way, without any embarrassment, and in a manner that was outwardly more humble than ours'. Later, they would be impressed by the regularity, morality and asceticism of the Buddhist monks 'whose conversation seemed to us very gentle and honest. The morality they teach is quite in keeping with justice, such as doing no wrong to anyone, being merciful, keeping one's five senses in check lest the door be opened to sin, cleansing the soul of evil thoughts, devoting oneself to prayer, and above all keeping one's hands clean from animal blood. The life they lead is very simple and frugal: they eat only rice, herbs and vegetables.'

Regarding the Indian holy men, the bishop noted that,

> It is a surprising thing to see the blindness of these poor souls, the austerity in which they live, their simplicity, their superstitions and the belief that they are on the right path. Among them there are monks in the cities who live under a superior, who go about their lives in contemplation and are content to eat a little rice or herbs once a day. Others do extraordinary public penances, such as covering their flesh, hair and beard with ashes, letting their nails grow three or four fingers long, raising one arm continually in the air; others always keep their arms crossed or raised to heaven, and in the course of time they lose the use of these limbs, which are no longer able to regain their natural position.

In spite of their errors and excesses, the ascetic Pierre Lambert felt a certain sympathy for these Hindu monks. He could understand their taste for meditation, their austerity and the radicalism of their renunciation. Above all, he recognized in them a religious authenticity which only accentuated his feeling about the insincerity of secularized and corrupt Catholics.

From this attentive and, for the time, relatively benevolent observation of the religious practices of the Indians, there was born in Pierre Lambert an increasingly strong and damning conviction: although they were the depositaries of the revealed Truth, the Christians of the West were not living up to the demands of the faith they professed; their religious behaviour was inferior to that of the Orientals and constituted a counter-witness for them. Worse still, the responsibility for this situation lay particularly with the missionaries in the region, that is, those of Padroado, who not only failed to do their work of evangelization correctly, but, by their behaviour, damaged the credibility of the message they were supposed to deliver. By behaving like ordinary Europeans, as 'colonials,' they only provoked the rejection, contempt or jealousy of the natives, instead of providing an example of holiness of life which could touch the religious sensibilities of the Asians. Unable to take advantage of the religious tolerance that prevailed in these countries, they ruined the opportunity for evangelization by the counter-witness of their lives.

'It must be admitted that hearing about these things and seeing them were quite moving, but nevertheless what gave the missionaries the most pain was to see that there was complete freedom to preach our holy faith; the church of Massulipatam was as open as if we were in Europe, and it was the same in the Indies where missions were established. But, Infinite Goodness, you had no ministers who were preaching either by voice or by example; on the contrary, considering their guiding rules and their way of life, they were much more likely to confirm the Muslims and pagans in their idolatrous error than to draw them out of it.

However, there would be no remedy as long as the missionaries of these districts, or those who had acquired bad habits, were used; the loss of religious fervour was so great that a good man who wished to condemn the faults and vices found in the clergy and religious orders would be considered a public enemy and treated as such.

> If it were permitted to say openly what everybody in this country knows about the state of religious belief and practice in Goa and the other lands belonging to the Portuguese, it would be said that ignorance and vice prevail amongst the clergy, that religious no longer observe their constitutions, and that the bad practices that have been adopted exempt them from the obedience that they owe to their superiors. As for poverty, almost all the religious orders engage in commerce and, in lending money, are guilty of usury; there are even individual religious who have 10, 20, 30, 40, and even 50,000 ecus of their own. As for chastity, there is so much scandal among most of the religious that an honest man with a family would not dare to allow them frequent entrance to his house without defaming himself. It is certainly because of all these appalling disorders that one altar is set up against another, and that in public and solemn processions clergy and religious carry daggers and firearms under their clothes, which they sometimes use to cause great and scandalous massacres. It is true that the missions have failed to bear fruit because the superiors of the religious orders have preferred to see that the religious people they sent were at least as capable of maintaining the temporal affairs of their mission as they were for spreading the Good News of Jesus Christ.

Thus, to the grievance of lying and breach of trust already formulated by the Vicar Apostolic against the Jesuits of Ispahan, two others, no less serious, were now added which affected all the missionary personnel, but particularly the Jesuits since they were in the majority in Asia: moral laxity and financial speculation. For a man as passionately evangelical as Pierre Lambert de la Motte, trained in his youth to exemplary rigour by the French Jesuits, this was an immeasurable disappointment that was similar in many ways to a betrayal of love. He would never be consoled by what he felt was an inexcusable betrayal, the very negation of the missionary ideal that his teachers had instilled in him. And whereas his confrere, François Pallu, confronted a little later with the same painful evidence, always tried to relativise the situation, to differentiate responsibilities, to find excuses, the Bishop of Beirut, on the contrary, had a tendency to globalize the problem, to include all the members of the Society of Jesus in the same condemnation.

This overreaction sometimes prevented him from thinking clearly, caused him to exaggerate at times and above all discredited him immediately in the eyes of his Parisian partners who were incapable of detecting, behind the virulence of his attacks, the interior despair of a servant of the Church wounded in the depths of his soul by the defection of his peers, a despair which one day caused him to write this terrible confidence: 'The missionaries have often said that if they were not members of the Catholic, Apostolic and Roman religion, they would conceive a horror of it, seeing the enormous excesses of these fathers.'

He was thus without any illusion about the situation that awaited him in his mission, but also it was with a firm resolution not to compromise on evangelical requirements that Pierre Lambert embarked on March 26 on board a Muslim boat to cross the Bay of Bengal. On April 28, the ship docked at Mergui and, after the usual customs formalities, the French missionaries set foot on land at Tenasserim, in the kingdom of Siam, on 19 May 1662.

First impressions of Siam

The first person to welcome the French missionaries on their arrival in Siam was a Portuguese Jesuit, Father Jean Cardoso, who was in charge of one of the two churches in Tenasserim. Having sent them his boat when they got off the ship, he received them at his house for a few days before lodging them in the house of his recently deceased confrere. He even went so far as to ask Pierre Lambert, who had revealed his episcopal status to him, to administer confirmation. As in India, the apparent religious tolerance which reigned in the country awakened great apostolic hopes in the newcomers.

After a month's delay, the French left Tenasserim on June 30 aboard three small dugout canoes covered with palm leaves in which they had to eat and sleep. At the end of a final eventful stage, Pierre Lambert, whose boat overturned, narrowly escaped drowning by clinging to a tree trunk for a whole day while waiting for help. They arrived in Ayutthaya, the capital of Siam, on 22 August 1662, two years, two months and four days after leaving Paris.

Ayutthaya was then an important economic crossroads where all the commercial movements of Asia came together. Europeans came to buy and sell products coming from or going to China and Japan, whose ports were forbidden to them. More than twenty languages were to be heard there. Foreigners were welcomed and lived in 'camps' or reserved areas on the outskirts of the city. Chinese, Japanese, Cochinchinese, Pegouans, Malays and Macassars lived side by side with the Portuguese, who had settled in Siam in the 16th century. The Dutch and the English also had opened trading posts there in the early decades of the 17thcentury. Even four or five Frenchmen, from Dieppe and Honfleur, employed by the Company of Holland, were living there.

The Catholic clergy, comprised of eleven priests, was more than enough for a Christian community of two to three thousand people: Portuguese, mestizos and Japanese refugees who had survived the persecution. To the north of the Portuguese camp, the church of Saint Dominic was served by the Dominicans, while to the south, at the entrance to the city, the Jesuits had just rebuilt the church of Saint Paul, which was next to the small college of the Saviour.

The sharing of pastoral tasks resulted in plenty of leisure time for all these clerics whose rather free life and multiple secular activities immediately shocked our strict French ecclesiastics.' We found eleven priests in this city,' wrote Pierre Lambert to the Pope: 'three seculars who are quite rude and addicted to vice; four religious of the Society of Jesus, one of whom lives separately in order to carry on a private business; in the house of the Society itself the others are publicly engaged in commerce; in addition, two Dominicans who live in different houses and are engaged in secular business and other forbidden activities; finally, two Franciscans who also live outside their community and have come here to visit another mission country or to enter another monastery or for other reasons that we will never know.' 'As for the Christians, they are so bad that there is a great danger that their evil lives will be an obstacle to the conversion of the rest of the kingdom.'

Although they were very well received by the head of the Portuguese camp who found them lodging near his home, Pierre Lambert and his companions were anxious to dissociate themselves without delay from the habits of the local clergy, especially since the navigation season that had just ended stranded them in Siam until the following May. The bishop therefore decided to isolate himself for a forty-day retreat. The religious of Ayutthaya immediately understood this message of implicit disapproval. 'This solitude was seen in this place as something new and as a means of ending the friendship which they pretended to maintain after a fashion. From then on they avoided meeting with people who lived by rules different from those which were accepted in these districts.' By setting himself up as a silent example, Pierre Lambert provoked a distinct chill in his relations with the Portuguese clergy, who seized the first opportunity to openly express their animosity.

This invisible confrontation obviously entered into Pierre Lambert's long solitary meditation. As a man of action accustomed to assuming heavy responsibilities and to solving disputes, conscious of the importance of his mission and sure of Rome's confidence in him, he was in no way prepared to accept the slightest compromise with a missionary operation which he judged not only scandalous in itself, but also detrimental to true evangelization. As a mystic, however, he had to find spiritual means to rectify a situation whose complexity was far beyond his human powers. In the minutes of his prayers dated September 6 and 7, he formulated two key ideas that would guide his later actions. On the group level, it was the creation of a congregation of 'chosen people to make them true apostolic men,' a draft of the congregation of the Lovers of the Cross which he would define more precisely the following year. On the individual level, he decided to adopt a permanent fast from the moment he arrived at the place of his mission. These two projects, with a strong penitential colouring, bore the imprint of his formation with the Minims. In the face of the prevailing corruption, the external struggle, juridical or otherwise, would only be justified if it was based on a permanent asceticism and a spirit of sacrifice. To do penance for oneself, but above all for all those whose behaviour disfigured the face of the Church, such was the spirit of reform of Francis of Paola that Pierre Lambert adapted to his own situation.

Scarcely had he finished his retreat than, on October 10, the Vicar Apostolic, who had not yet received any news from France, hastened to write an important series of letters which he entrusted to the captain of a Dutch ship leaving for Batavia and the Netherlands. Although he had practically broken off all contact with the Portuguese, his relations were most cordial with the head of the Dutch trading post. The latter invited the French clergymen to his table and introduced them to two Cochinchinese who would teach them their language. It was through them that they began their apostolate with the small Cochinchinese community recently established in the city.

'We thought that this was an opportunity to begin our mission here,' wrote the bishop of Beirut to Mme d'Aiguillon. 'We made known to these good people who we were, who brought us here, and the happiness we wanted to bring them. With God touching their hearts at the same time, it did not take long to persuade them to hear the word of God. As we were very close to Christmas, I promised the Christians to have an altar set up in one of their houses. I went to the house that was willingly offered and celebrated midnight Mass, after which I gave them a short exhortation concerning the obligation to love God. This was given in Portuguese, which one of them, serving as my interpreter, explained in Cochinchinese. Since then we have been going there regularly three times a week to teach Christian doctrine to these good people, who often present their concerns publicly and depart satisfied with the answers that the good Lord gives through our words.'

The outbreak of hostilities

From the end of January 1663, the first baptisms were administered. This apostolic zeal, displayed with a certain ostentation before the eyes of the Portuguese religious, aggravated the tensions between the two missionary groups, who practically ceased all contact. In December 1662, the order came from Goa that the passage of the

French bishops must be stopped no matter what the cost. From then on, the Portuguese had an official reason to get rid of the intruders and they did not hesitate to use the most radical means, including a plot to poison the bishop, of which Bénigne Vachet gave an account worthy of a novel by Alexandre Dumas.

'To speak to a Portuguese about the power and authority of his king, is to make his heart swell with pride so that there is nothing he will not do under the impulse of his emotions.' In this situation, not only did hatred take the place of love, but not a day passed by without some new cause for anger. The captain of the Dutch trading post, who was on the other side of the river, knowing well that the lives of these gentlemen were not safe among the Portuguese, offered them his house as a safe retreat: but the Bishop of Beirut and his two companions did not think it appropriate to accept this offer, because, by retiring to the home of heretics, they would have given the Portuguese new reasons for complaint and indignation.

> Upon receiving this refusal, the generous Dutchman told the bishop and his two missionaries that at least they should be careful not to eat anything that was prepared in their house or that came from outside, and that he would take care to send them every day in a locked box all the food they needed. The Cochinchinese, who had their camp located a league higher up the river, having learned that the Bishop of Beirut was destined for their country and that he was in danger among the Portuguese, by a generosity natural to the people of this nation, came in the middle of the day to remove the Bishop of Beirut, his companions, their servants and their belongings, and lead them to their camp where they built them a house and a chapel on the banks of the river.

It was there that the bishop set up the permanent base of the French mission, which he named Camp Saint-Joseph.

In spite of the solicitude of the Cochinchinese, the atmosphere in Ayutthaya encouraged the apostolic vicar to leave the Siamese capital as soon as possible, although he still had no definite news of his two confreres, Mgrs Pallu and Cotolendi. He wished to meet them in order to discuss the attitude to adopt towards the missionaries of Padroado. He feared that they had been intercepted by the Portuguese, as well as all the mail coming from Europe, because he had received no news from France or Rome since his arrival.

But before leaving he had to inform the Roman authorities of the practically untenable position of the French mission. He therefore wrote to Cardinal Antoine, Prefect of Propaganda, an uncompromising letter in which he justified his own conduct and asked for a radical solution to remedy the situation: the pure and simple recall of the religious under Portuguese obedience. 'I feel obliged, because of the position you hold, to assure Your Eminence that everything I write to His Holiness and to the Sacred Congregation about the miserable state of the missionaries in all these places is so true that if commissioners are sent some day to obtain information, they will find the actual situation to be even more serious than the situation I have described. Certainly their bad example, their disregard for rules and their extreme slackness cry out for vengeance before God. If I had thought I could pass over this in silence, I would have done so willingly. But this cannot be done without prevarication. Now that I have given advice to the people who alone can remedy the situation, I can be at peace. I appeal to Your Eminence to let it be known that if the Sacred Congregation does not provide other missionaries, remedy the existing dreadful mess, and commission truly apostolic men to do this evangelical work, religion will be finished and the ministers of the Gospel will henceforth be a stumbling block for heretics, Muslims, and especially for good people.'

And he concluded this letter with an admission that indicated the measure of his dismay: 'I confess to Your Eminence that if I myself had not come to the end of the earth, I doubt that I would have believed the report of a good man who sent news of these things to Europe.'

The Jesuit Question

Very critical as he was of the behaviour of the Padroado missionaries in general, Pierre Lambert was particularly virulent with regard to the practices of the Jesuits in Asia, which recurred as an obsessive motif in the numerous writings he produced at that time. Having recalled the sad behaviour already stated (deceitfulness in relationships, relaxation of morals, and commerce), he revealed a mode of operation that refused all control and did not shrink from any means of coercion to ensure the survival of a system grafted onto Portuguese colonial power whose goals no longer had anything to do with evangelization.' The deceitful pretext that the members of this Society put forward to justify their actions is the maintenance of their mission and the provision of something with which to alleviate the poverty of a number of Christians. They allege that since commerce is carried out in good faith, the popes who forbade it on pain of excommunication were misinformed. No one should be so bold as to contradict these statements, any more than he should recall the abuses committed by these fathers in their missions and in the administration of the sacraments; otherwise a person places himself in a perilous position because in doing so, he sows the idea among the people that he is an enemy of the Portuguese nation, that he wants to introduce innovations and that he is not committed to the faith. There are only too many examples of such experiences in the lives of several great servants of God who were chained, poisoned, brought before the Inquisition and accused of heresy.

'These great crimes, which draw down upon them the consequences of a final blindness, can no longer remain unheard, and all Europe will soon be forced to believe by a just judgment of God that if the great St. Francis Xavier was one of the first to give birth to Christianity in the Indies by following the teachings of the Holy Gospel, his successors have destroyed it completely by their excessive ambition, their greed, their usury, their disgusting laxity and finally by their unfortunate prudence which has nothing Christian or moral about it. Having said this, it is not necessary to speak about the state of the missions or about the esteem in which the Christian religion is held. It follows from this that the people of the earth who do not know the sanctity of our faith and who know nothing of the splendid teachings of Jesus Christ believe that Christianity is a kind of paganism like their own and that what these fathers do is possibly not forbidden by the law they profess. They say, however, that the law of their priests is of a very different type of perfection altogether and that the pagans are much better than those called Christians because they have more mutual charity for one another and less vice. It is now easy to see why this Society has never wanted to admit anyone to the places where it is established and why an order came so quickly from Portugal to Goa to arrest the French bishops. This is a very notable example of the precautions that the Jesuit fathers have taken up to now to hide the abuses that they have committed and are committing every day in their work.

'Missionaries reflecting on the extreme difficulty for a religious of this Society to achieve salvation by coming to these countries have often regretted the misfortune of so many great subjects of Europe who ask with such great insistence to come here to sacrifice themselves in the work of the foreign missions in the interests of Jesus Christ. Scarcely have they arrived than they see that they are not only unable to do anything but, on the contrary, they are in the dangerous necessity of having to adopt the pernicious principles of this body of people or else, if they do not agree with them, they will be treated as scrupulous people attached to their own opinion, who are ignorant, and who will soon change their minds. If their fidelity to grace is strong enough to withstand so many attacks, they can be certain that they will never have either office or reputation in this society; this punishment, although very unjust, is nevertheless very favourable and even desirable for solidly virtuous people, but what makes it quite difficult is the continual fear that they have before their eyes of being expelled from the order. When an expulsion occurs, there are very few who are not stranded and do not surrender to the generally accepted way of life, because once they are expelled, they are abandoned by everyone, denounced, deprived of the necessities of life, without knowledge, three or four thousand leagues away from their home country and without any hope of being able to find funds to return to it.'

Faced with such a damning indictment, one question obviously arises: are these charges credible? In the excess of his pain, his fatigue and his dismay, has not the Vicar Apostolic lost all measure, all control of his thoughts? Is he not breaking down, experiencing a mental collapse? This is what some historians, and not only Jesuits, did not hesitate to imply. Moreover, Pierre Lambert himself recognised that, in the European context, his words were not credible and could only get him into big trouble. However, responding to criticisms made by the directors of the seminary, he protested the authenticity of the behaviour denounced. 'I am very grateful for the advice you have given me to be as accurate as possible in reporting what concerns the Jesuits. I have tried to follow your advice in this matter, having omitted nothing in order to know what the good Lord desires of me in this exchange. Therefore, in all that I have written I have done the best I can to express the truth in all its clarity and I hope to be able to assure you that there is nothing presented which can harm the trust which must be placed in a bishop and a Vicar Apostolic.'

Abusive denunciations or justified accusations?

How then, today, more than three hundred years later, can we verify the reality and the exaggeration of these denunciations which have always been modestly concealed by missionary historiography? Certainly, accusations of this kind are found in the writings of French people who travelled to the Orient at that time. The jeweller Jean-Baptiste Tavernier, for example, denounced the smuggling of diamonds by certain religious. Robert Challe, in the words of François Martin, who was in charge of the French trading post of the West India Company in Pondicherry, uttered an indictment of unparalleled violence against the Jesuits which repeated, in a much more aggressive way, the allegations of Pierre Lambert. Abbé Barthélemy Carré himself, in spite of his ecclesiastical status, denounced the wealth, the dubious dealings and the arrogance of the Portuguese Jesuits in India. He considered that 'often the religious, with their tendency to scheme too much and to control secular affairs, cause more trouble and harm than the accidents and setbacks of fortune, of which I have seen only too many examples in these oriental countries, which I will pass over in silence out of respect for religion.' Even if some of these authors could be suspected of some degree of anti-Jesuit feeling for their own personal reasons, at least from the repetition of grievances it is possible to get an idea of the bad reputation of the religious of Padroado in general, and the Jesuits in particular, from one end of Asia to the other.

But much more convincing evidence is provided by the recent work of a contemporary Jesuit historian, Charles Borges, who, in a book entitled The Economics of the Goa Jesuits 1542–1759: An explanation of their rise and fall, published in New Delhi in 1994, analysed the Jesuit economic system in Asia from archival sources found in Goa, Rome and Lisbon. The conclusion of his remarkably well-documented study would have been of considerable comfort to the Bishop of Beirut. For the author, in fact, the excessive financial power of the Jesuits was the main cause of their fall. 'At first the Jesuits established themselves in Goa in a humble way, but during the two hundred years of their stay they became a powerful force. Few people could govern or control them. Their generals and provincials called them to order through their various circulars, but a significant number of them did as they pleased. They believed that the situation in India was different and that it required a special economic system.'

Many viceroys and governors recognized that they could not talk to them, while the local people accepted their fate and hoped that one day the situation would improve. The numerous petitions sent to the Portuguese court by the Overseas Council, the clergy or the people, prove how bad the Jesuits' relations were with everyone. The Jesuits wrote at regular intervals to their superiors in Rome about themselves and their activities. It was often to their own advantage. They gloried in their successes, highlighted the injustices they had to suffer at the hands of the State and the people, and believed that they played a unique role in the conversion of the country to the Christian faith. Others also wrote about them. It is strange, but most often their reports describe the Jesuits as incorrigible tricksters, a blot on the overall picture. Nowhere do the writings of Jesuits show that they considered such criticisms to contain any truth; they pointed out the faults of their confreres in the descriptions they gave of each other, but they were united when an attack came from others than themselves.

'The Province of Goa kept regular records of its accounts for each of its houses. Since it was an internal matter with no external control, many believed that the figures certainly did not correspond with the wealth attributed to them. The difference between their income and their expenses always seemed very small. And yet the Province always had more than enough money to lend at five or ten percent interest. The State or the village communities borrowed large sums, and individuals also took small sums. There was no lack of money. The State had good reason to believe that the removal of the Jesuits from the scene would bring economic benefit to everyone.' The situation was not much different in Jesuit missions in other parts of the world. The reports that had been arriving for about two centuries in the Portuguese courts and offices convinced the government that the Jesuits must go. Although many reasons were presented, perhaps the most important reason for the fall of the Jesuits was their stranglehold on the entire economy. 'The Jesuits did not foresee the imminence of the catastrophe. Their reluctance to accept criticism had prevented them from assisting those who were suffering. They could have helped them by reducing their own economic control and thus compensated for the dangerous antagonism that was building up against them. When they did go, there were few who really regretted their departure.'

The key to the problem

It was not, therefore, the fear experienced by an overly scrupulous pious person, impressed by vague gossip, that drove Pierre Lambert to denounce the practices of the Jesuits to the Roman authorities, and also to all those in France who supported his mission. His dossier was very well documented and, even if his expression sometimes seemed to lack serenity, it was based on undeniable facts. Yet the Vicar Apostolic knew perfectly well that he would not be believed in France. Why? Quite simply because the Society of Jesus was emerging from a schizophrenic crisis that it had not known how to deal with quickly enough, and that would eventually lead to its demise.

From the end of the 16th century, a certain number of Jesuits, especially the French, including the eminent Father Coton, had sounded the alarm in the face of a growing secularization of their activities. In the excellent report requested by their General Aquaviva in 1605 about the state of the spiritual health of the Society of Jesus (*De detrimentis Societatis*), they deplored the lack of spiritual formation, the neglect of time for prayer and meditation, the exaggerated application to intellectual work and external success to the detriment of the practice of the virtues of fraternal charity, obedience, poverty, etc. However, no significant reform emerged from this important inquiry and the prudent General Vitelleschi, Aquaviva's successor, condemned the claims of the 'new spirituals' who were accused of distorting the spirit of the Society.

Now, Pierre Lambert was formed by the last heirs of this reforming or spiritual tendency dominated by the influence of a Louis Lallemant[1] or a Joseph Surin. But, the Jesuits of Portugal, because of the almost congenital links they had always maintained with the rulers of Lisbon, ended up identifying with the colonial power of their country, and even, in this period of decadence, controlling it, with all the abuses that such an assimilation implied. These were the two extremes of the wide range of possibilities for interpreting the Ignatian thought that were present, and therefore in opposition: the mystic Lambert, attentive to acting only under the movements of the Spirit, as opposed to Portuguese activists who were largely secularized. But these very

---

1. Louis Lallemant (1578-1635) was responsible for the training of many Jesuits. He emphasised the contemplative life over the active apostolate and was critical of some of his fellow Jesuits for their overly secular aspirations.

different interpretations were hardly known to the public, especially in France where the Jansenist crisis had provoked a reflex of the body. As a result, the Vicar Apostolic never succeeded in convincing his interrogators that it was possible to criticize a part of the Society of Jesus without siding with its adversaries.

Another factor worked against the Bishop of Beirut, who realized this too late: the fact that the French Jesuits in their turn were being drawn into an acceptance of the personal and authoritarian power of Louis XIV, who would use them to try to impose his own patronage on the missions entrusted to the Vicars Apostolic. Consequently, when Pierre Lambert died, a group of French Jesuits, sent by the same king and dominated by the equivocal personality of the amazing Father Tachard trampled on the fragile missionary fabric patiently woven for more than twenty years in Siam by Pierre Lambert and his men.

Pierre Lambert could not foresee this impending future, but he was convinced that heaven would not let the scandal provoked by the conduct of the missionaries of Padroado go unpunished. Soon he interpreted the successive episodes in the decline of the Portuguese Empire as divine warnings. 'I do not know', he wrote to Luc Fermanel, 'whether divine justice will stop here and whether divine anger will burst upon this Society and against this nation in Europe. I beg divine goodness to enlighten them, and me too, who live in extreme darkness in my vocation.' This cry of distress was also a warning of things to come. The Portuguese government, whether or not it was guided by the hand of God, was to precipitate the ruin of its former allies who had become embarrassing, and Rome had only to ratify the punishment. In 1773, the Society of Jesus was suppressed for reasons which, in the end, closely resembled the criticisms made a century earlier by Bishop Lambert.

However, even though he relied on undeniable facts, the Vicar Apostolic was aware that he was taking great risks in formulating such accusations, because, in Paris, it was the reverend Father Annat SJ, the personal adversary of Blaise Pascal, who was responsible for the formation of the conscience of the young Louis XIV. Any attack on the Jesuits could therefore be misinterpreted from a doctrinal point of view and have considerable consequences from a political point of view, and could even go so far as to call into question the official support that the king had given to the French mission. On the other hand, Pierre Lambert knew the complexity of Roman diplomacy and wanted to avoid creating a scandal by his public revelations that would be detrimental to the position of the Holy See. He therefore needed to know whether Propaganda approved or condemned his aggressive strategy.

It was undoubtedly in large part this need for clarification, combined perhaps with an understandable weariness, that led him to offer his resignation. In a letter in July 1663, in which he invoked his unworthiness and his inability to assume his office, he asked to be allowed to return to the rank of a simple missionary. He took this action in order to 'lead a penitential, hidden life, as one dead to the world, hoping to obtain the great mercy of the good God through the merits of Jesus Christ and the promises of his Gospel, and the efficacy of his prayers, and so to die out of love a violent death at the hands of an executioner'. Jacques de Bourges, whom he proposed as his successor, and who was given the task of carrying this letter to Europe, left Ayutthaya on 14 October 1663.

This tactic was clever, because it allowed the Vicar Apostolic to test the reaction of his superiors (the pope, and also the king of France) by forcing them to judge him. If they rejected him, they would accept his resignation, but if they refused it, he would be confirmed in his office. Having laid his cards on the table, the Vicar Apostolic let his superiors deal the cards again and offered them the possibility of excluding him without fear of disruption. But if he remained in office, he would interpret their choice as at least as tacit acceptance of his complaints and his policy. His authority would be strengthened and he would then be able to continue with more assurance to follow the hard line that he had drawn.

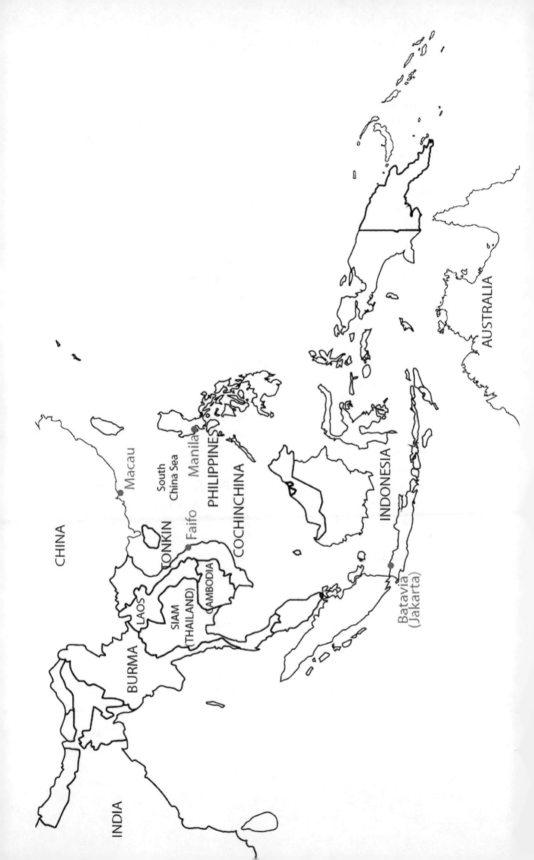

Chapter 4
Dialogue–the way forward

The first false start

While waiting for a response to his proposal to resign, Pierre Lambert continued to carry out fully his episcopal responsibilities. He took advantage of the navigation season to leave the minefield of Ayutthaya and resume his mission. On July 12, he embarked on a ship bound for Canton in the company of François Deydier.

After ten days of favourable winds in the Gulf of Siam, the missionaries' ship was caught in a storm as it entered the China Sea. For a day and two nights, with its sails folded, it drifted on a raging sea towards the coast, which was bordered by reefs. On board, there was panic as the ship began to leak and it was feared that it would break in two. In these dangerous conditions, Pierre Lambert and François Deydier busied themselves hearing confessions and consoling the forty or so Portuguese Christians on board.

With remarkable detachment, they undertook an astonishing analysis of their mental state. 'They used the rest of their time for prayer and tried to avail themselves of an opportunity which does not come along every day, that of seeing death before their own eyes without any hope of salvation. It was in these blessed times that they felt the struggles of the lower part of the rational soul and of grace. It was in these precious moments that they offered their sacrifices to the Eternal Father, illumined by the light that it pleased Jesus Christ to communicate to them. Finally, it was with joyful hearts in the midst of this peril that they offered up their acts of praise, adoration and joy to Our Lord, who mercifully spared them from being drowned at the bottom of the sea, happy in the obedient following of their vocation.'

Finally, the captain ordered his men to drop anchor three leagues from land and sent twelve men in a rowboat to seek help. But the boat broke up on the coast and its occupants decided to return to Siam by land. Meanwhile, on board, water became scarce and after three days the captain decided to go ashore himself in a makeshift boat made from ropes and planks torn from the sides of the ship.

François Deydier and five sailors accompanied him. When they reached the coast, they met a group of Cochinchinese, including three Christians who, learning that their bishop was in danger, offered, 'with the generosity typical of this nation', to go and bring him to land. But their boat broke up two-thirds of the way on their journey. In the boat, still waiting were the shipwrecked, who were reduced to drinking the water provided by two providential storms. Finally, after several days, a new boat arrived from Siam sent by the first group. The sea had calmed down and François Deydier found a new boat to join his bishop. The two missionaries were able to return to Siam where they arrived on September 15. After two months of maritime perils and wasted expense, they found themselves back at their point of departure to the great displeasure of the Portuguese, who did not delay in resuming hostilities.

Soon, in fact, a passing sailor, who claimed to be a relative of the King of Portugal, burst into the missionaries' house with great pomp and ceremony one Sunday after vespers. He summoned the bishop to show him the king's permission 'to come to the Indies, failing which', he threatened, 'I will treat you as a transgressor of his sovereign rights, and I will have you led, bound hand and foot, to the steps of his throne to make reparation due to his honour and to ask him for forgiveness for your temerity'. The situation became critical when a troop of Cochinchinese, 'dressed as warriors going into battle, that is to say, with horsehair caps on their heads, with their arms bare and swords in their hands,' burst into the room. Their leader grabbed the Portuguese by the arm, forced him to stand up and shouted at him in Vietnamese style: 'Get out of here, son of a dog that you are! Be grateful for the presence of my prelate, because, if it were not for the respect that I have for him, I would have already cut off your head.' In spite of the attempt of the bishop to intervene, the braggart was brought back military style to his boat 'having been contemptuously punched and kicked along the way.' He planned a bloody revenge, but the soothing intervention of the Dutch captain, 'who was wise and prudent', and especially the intimidating patrols of the Cochinchinese boats along the Portuguese quarter, finally calmed the hot headed Iberians. After a few days, calm returned. 'The poor Portuguese were so astonished', concludes the narrator, Bénigne Vachet, 'that for more than a whole month they did not dare pass in front of the camp of the Cochinchinese to carry out whatever business they had beyond, preferring to take a great detour by land. This is what put an end to an event that could only be regarded as sad and tragic.'

Impressed by the determination of these improvised bodyguards, the Portuguese in Ayutthaya no longer dared to attack the Vicar Apostolic physically and had to make do with legal arguments to contend with him.

Time for reflection

After these painful events, Pierre Lambert retired in October for his annual forty-day retreat. For some time his health had been deteriorating and his condition was becoming more and more critical, causing him to fear for his life. Despite the advice of those around him, the Vicar Apostolic took a bold decision that seemed like a spiritual provocation: refusing any treatment, he decided to begin the perpetual fast that he had been thinking about for a year and, against all expectations, he ended up being cured.

Soon he wrote to Jacques de Bourges: 'I am beginning to believe what I have always believed by faith, but which I could not morally hope for by reason, when you left: that I will die in the place of our missions. The reason why I believe this is because God has been pleased to restore me to good health thereby enabling me to hope for this happiness. This happened to me while I was at prayer one afternoon, when, considering the topic of living or dying, God, who loves me very much, prolonged my life which I had once asked of him when death seemed imminent. Then I resolved to abstain from meat and to fast for the rest of my days, except at Christmas, Easter and Pentecost.

This is what I had resolved to do as soon as I entered our mission territory, but the great obligations I have to Our Lord as well as the present situation in which I find myself, have made me anticipate this time. I see myself situated between these two inevitable extremes: that it is absolutely necessary either that I should love God forever with all my strength, or that I should hate Him in the same way, and that whatever way I choose depends on my fidelity to grace or my refusal of it. By this you can judge the commitment that I must bring to my following the attraction of the divine.'

Obviously such dispositions, would not encourage Pierre Lambert to adopt half measures in dealing with the problem that preoccupied him most, that of secularization, insubordination and the lax behaviour of missionary personnel. In an account of his prayer on November 3, he took up and developed the project of creating an apostolic congregation already envisaged the previous year, but this time more directly inspired by the memory of his first mystical experience as a child, when he dreamed of a contemplative community called the Lovers of the Cross. But from a religious congregation of 'perfect life' with a clearly contemplative vocation, the ideal project of the little mystic boy was transformed in the thirty-nine-year-old Vicar Apostolic into a missionary institute, without changing its spiritual orientation. In a daring synthesis, Pierre Lambert amalgamated the charisms of the principal spiritual schools he had attended (the intramundane commitment of the Jesuits, the spirit of prayer of the Carmelites, the penitential asceticism of the Minims) in order to conceive of an elite body with a specifically missionary vocation.

Placed under the authority of a bishop, this Congregation of the Lovers of the Cross would have all the authority to put in place the native hierarchy demanded by Rome. Also, this would make it possible to diminish the rivalries between orders and nations by welcoming into a unified structure all priests and religious truly called to a missionary vocation. Its members would be protected from the spirit of pride and the love of power and money by a life of asceticism and mortification, and would find in the assiduous practice of prayer 'in conversation with Our Lord, the means of attracting souls to a knowledge and love of him'. To experience this new life, the Vicar Apostolic persuaded his companion, François Deydier, to make a vow of perpetual abstinence and to devote several hours a day to prayer.

Pallu, a calming influence

The missionaries François Pallu met again when he arrived in Ayutthaya were very different from those he knew in France. He arrived in Ayutthaya on 27 January 1664 after a particularly trying journey in which he lost six of his ten companions. He had only two priests left: Louis Laneau and Pierre Brindeau, and a layman, Philippe de Chamesson, to whom were added, along the way, Antoine Hainques and Louis Chevreuil, the two survivors of the team of Bishop Cotolendi who had died near Massulipam on 16 August 1662. When the French Mission gathered in its temporary station in Siam, the band was reduced by more than a third of the number that had set out and totalled in all two bishops, six priests (one of whom, Jacques de Bourges, was on his way to Europe) and one layman.

After observing three days of thanksgiving without addressing the problems of the mission, the two bishops spent the entire month of February taking stock and evaluating their experiences. They had much to say to each other and the exchange between these two men with such different temperaments would have been difficult. Only their great humility and the deep respect they had for each other would have allowed them to agree. A former student at the college in Clermont, a founding member of the Good Friends, directed during all his years of discernment by Father Bagot, François Pallu, was in fact very closely linked to the Society of Jesus to which two of his brothers belonged. It was therefore with a certain amount of fear that he became aware, upon his arrival in Tenasserim, of the letters of Pierre Lambert. For the latter, not content with sending detailed reports to Rome, took it upon himself to provide information to all the French officials responsible for the missions. He wrote to the highest authorities of the State, including the king himself, to benefactors, to the directors of the Seminary of Paris, and to all the people of his acquaintance who had contributed in some way to the sending forth of the Vicars Apostolic in order to inform them, sometimes in very virulent terms, of the actions of the missionaries of Padroado, and especially of the Jesuits.

Horrified by the foreseeable consequences of these revelations on public opinion and in particular on the benefactors of the missions, the Bishop of Heliopolis took it upon himself to intercept most of the letters addressed to French recipients. At first, therefore, he felt he had to distance himself from the unexpected position taken by Pierre Lambert. Unlike the latter, he still wanted to believe in the possibility of cooperation based on goodwill. But soon the facts themselves, as much as the arguments of his colleague, opened his eyes. On 7 February 1664, he wrote to the prosecutors: 'Until now I have been suspicious of all those who spoke against this body which I like, and I became angry when I was told of their faults, although they were in full view for all to see and no-one doubted their existence. However, the love of truth must prevail. God forbid that we should betray our ministry through misguided love. All that has been said is only too true.'

However, in a spirit of conciliation, the Bishop of Heliopolis tried to convince his confrere of Beirut to temper his fighting spirit. It was certainly from the pressure he applied that Pierre Lambert addressed to several French Jesuits what looked like letters of justification, if not of apology. However, although he showed good will, Pierre Lambert was not easily disarmed. If he seemed to submit willingly enough to his colleague's advice concerning moderation, he had no doubt that events, with time, would prove him right. And, in fact, the newcomers changed quite rapidly. Around the month of May, the Bishop of Beirut was able to write to Michel Gazil: 'The Bishop of Heliopolis and all our dear brothers have the same feelings as I do, with this difference that they are perhaps more strongly irritated than I am by the incredible disorders which are now known to them. I attribute this advantage they have over me to the fact that their righteous anger is more recently acquired than mine, or that they have the interests of Jesus Christ more at heart than I do.'

Differences of opinion

Although their positions were similar in substance, the personalities of the two Vicars Apostolic were in reality too dissimilar to lead to perfect uniformity in action, and ultimately this complementarity in difference had positive effects. It was undoubtedly due to the reciprocal interactions of the one on the other that the impossible mission of the French succeeded. From this time on, the roles of each were defined and did not change much in the following years. Undoubtedly the intellectual and spiritual power of Lambert impressed Pallu, his force of persuasion convinced him and upset his incorrigible tendency to compromise. But Pallu remained sufficiently master of himself not to give in to Lambert's excesses, and was able to preserve a space for negotiation and conciliation. Lambert was a fighter, Pallu a diplomat and, in this particular case, while Pallu agreed in substance with the denunciations made by his colleague, he had reservations about the way in which the latter proceeded.

Many years later, in 1677, when he took stock of the relations between the Jesuits and the Vicars Apostolic, which had by then turned into a schism, the Bishop of Heliopolis recounted the course of these first debates and provided unpublished details which better explain, in retrospect, the behaviour of his confrere of Beirut:

> There was a small neighbourhood where a hundred or so Cochinchinese lived, to which Lambert came. Half of them had been baptised in Cochinchina by the Jesuit fathers, but they were as ignorant of the principal articles of our faith as the infidels themselves. It was known to them and to other Christians in China and elsewhere that they had been taught that there was only one God, but they did not know who Jesus Christ was, and that he had died for us on a cross. The Jesuit Fathers believed that it was enough for them to know the greatness and majesty of God without telling them about his humiliations. They did not consider them capable of understanding that a God would have been so humble as to allow himself to be hung on a cross like a criminal. But who would be capable of believing these truths without the gift of grace? It is expressly forbidden to give any worship except to God alone, and yet the Jesuits allowed these people to continue many idolatrous practices because they said that it was not possible to remove everything at once.
>
> They had never taught these people the commandments of the Church, claiming that they were not obliged to observe the positive law. They did not fast or keep the feasts, they did not feel obliged to attend Mass on feasts and Sundays, nor to go to confession and receive communion every year. They administered baptism without the customary anointing and ceremonies, mainly because of their modesty, they said. This was a clear statement of the doctrine of the Jesuit fathers in the missions they governed, but since they did not preach or convert in Siam, these things were only learned from the Christians. They became known later when they entered these kingdoms and these matters were only too obvious.

In retrospect, some of these adjustments may seem harmless to us today, or even perfectly justified by the popular concern for inculturation claimed loudly by Jesuit historiography to defend itself against the criticism of other missionaries who were accused in their turn of being reactionary and rigorist. Nevertheless, seen from this angle, the message they were transmitting seems to be reduced to very little, a kind of vague deism totally lacking the Christian announcement of salvation and evangelisation. More understandable now is Pierre Lambert's exasperation and the radical nature of his refocusing on Scripture and the Cross, but also the incredulity of the Parisian devotees who were incapable of conceiving the possibility of such a drift from the authentic Christian message. In reality, the situation of the missions described by the Vicars Apostolic only confirms the criticisms formulated by Blaise Pascal in the Fifth Letter of the Provincial Letters. The arguments of defence invoked by the directors of the Paris Foreign Missions Society, at the instigation of the Jesuits themselves, were precisely those which, ironically, the polemicist of Port-Royal denounced: 'These were the feelings of a few individuals which it was not fair to impute to the whole body.' The Jansenist quarrel falsified in France the perception of the very real decadence of the missions in Asia, and the Vicars Apostolic, with Pierre Lambert as leader, paid the price.

To prevent their missionaries from falling into a laxity that was difficult to avoid due to the ordinary conditions of European life in Asia, the Vicars Apostolic decided to convene a synod during which, with all their companions, they sought ways to preserve their spiritual and moral integrity. The Synod of Ayutthaya produced the famous *Monita ad missionarios*, the *Instructions to Missionaries of the Sacred Congregation of Propaganda de Fide*, a code of good conduct that served as a *vade mecum*[1] for all generations of priests of the Foreign Missions and which is still used as a reference today. This document constitutes a harmonious synthesis of the regulatory spirit of Pallu and the mystical inspiration of Lambert. It is a guide that is both practical and spiritual which completes and clarifies the *Instructions aux missionnaires de la S. Congrégationde la Propagande (1659)*. It advocates a life of prayer for missionaries and a pastoral ministry that is both demanding in terms of religious formation and respectful of people and cultures. Co-signed by the two bishops, the *Instructions* were judged by Cardinal Bona, Consultor of the Holy Office to be 'full of the apostolic spirit, inconformity with the orthodox faith and necessary for priests working in the missions for the salvation of the

---

1. 'Vade mecum' is a Latin expression meaning 'guide' in present-day usage.

infidels.' Published by Propaganda in 1669, which was a strong sign of Rome's support for the positions of its authors, it was regularly republished.

Provisional reconciliation

At the end of the synod, the Lenten season that was beginning gave the French the opportunity to begin a process of reconciliation with the Portuguese missionaries. They visited them several times and proposed a joint mission to the Christians of Ayutthaya in order to prepare them for confirmation, which Pierre Lambert had postponed because he felt that their instruction was insufficient.

The Portuguese religious rejected this project but nevertheless agreed to participate, on the first Sunday of Lent, in a procession involving all, after which Pierre Lambert finally conferred the sacrament of confirmation. They then responded favourably to an invitation from the Vicars Apostolic to celebrate the feast of St Joseph, a memorable day marked by a mixture of cultural elements, with the Portuguese band accompanying the prayer of the forty hours before the Blessed Sacrament exposed by the French. But the truce did not last much longer than the Easter season, because the gap between the two missionary groups was too deep and the occasions for disagreement too frequent. There was a complete lack of understanding between the newcomers and the old residents. The former proposed Sunday conferences between all the missionaries and asked that a religious who was notoriously licentious be forbidden to preach, but the old residents were not willing to change their ways and resisted any suggestion of reform. Meetings became less frequent once more. A relative peace maintained by the gentle spirit of François Pallu, lasted a few more months before new conflicts broke out.

At that time, the French still had hopes of reaching their mission region in the course of the year. In March, a ship from Cochinchina brought Pierre Lambert the replies of the Jesuits to whom he had written the previous year. The news was mixed. The fathers announced a resumption of persecution and the execution of four Christians, but they seemed to show great kindness towards the bishop of Beirut. In fact, it became clear later that, in spite of their apparent openness, these letters had no other purpose than to peacefully dissuade the Vicar Apostolic from proceeding to his mission. Although he submitted to this advice, Pierre Lambert was not totally deceived by its motives and it was only with reluctance that he postponed his trip and decided to send Louis Chevreuil on a mission of reconnaissance.

However, the news reported in April by the crew of a Siamese ship from Japan was even worse than that from Cochinchina. The persecution was still bad in the Japanese archipelago, and the inhabitants of Macau were dying of hunger in their city besieged by the Tartars. For the Bishop of Beirut, these events had a meaning: 'Perhaps by this great example, God wants to show to those who are sent to preach the Gospel that the silk of China, the silver of Japan, and the gold of Manila, which the Jesuit Fathers of these countries have sought with insatiable greed, have been the ruin of the Christian religion in these extremities of the world. Thus, this group of men will be disabused of the principles which it holds contrary to the Gospel, as well as all those who share this opinion, that there is nothing to be done for the conversion of souls unless one is very rich, very powerful and greatly feared.' In such circumstances, it was out of the question for François Pallu to enter China, so he decided to leave for Tonkin in the company of Pierre Brindeau, while it was the opinion of all the missionaries that Pierre Lambert should remain in Siam to centralize decisions in such an unpredictable context.

Louis Chevreuil left Ayutthaya on June 17 accompanied by Philippe de Chamesson who had to return to bring the news of his entry. He took with him 300 pounds and wine to help the Jesuits of Cochinchina who had expressed their need of it. A few days after their departure, a Portuguese ship from Goa and Batavia arrived in port. It brought other news which forced the missionaries to change their plans once again. The last three Jesuits from Tonkin who had been expelled from the country in the previous November had arrived in Batavia. The German superior, Father Onufre Borges, had died, but his two French companions, Fathers Tissanier and Albier, were on their way to Siam. They disembarked in Ayutthaya on July 29 and were warmly welcomed by François Pallu who, having given up the idea of entering Tonkin under such difficult conditions, hoped to be able to collaborate with these compatriots as Pierre Lambert seemed to be able to do with those in Cochinchina.

The two Vicars Apostolic still wished to believe that the French Jesuits, even if they were employed in the Padroado, had escaped the general decadence, could disassociate themselves from their

Portuguese confreres and would help them to open the eyes of the European leaders of the Society of Jesus. At first, indeed, this national collaboration took precedence over religious rivalries and the Bishop of Heliopolis succeeded in convincing the newcomers to take their side. At his request, Joseph Tissanier wrote a small booklet for his confreres in Ayutthaya, the Religiosus Negociator, 'in which he proved that the Jesuits could not engage in commerce for four reasons that were related to their status as priests, religious, religious of the Society of Jesus and missionaries.'

Accustomed to political and commercial intrigues, the Portuguese Jesuits in Ayutthaya were not fooled by the initiative of their confreres, which they interpreted, not without reason, as a French manoeuvre. As for François Pallu, it is difficult to discern whether his intentions were naively of good faith on the religious level, or were shaped by genuine political interests. For, unlike Pierre Lambert, who immediately judged that the two French Jesuits, 'although they are not corrupt like the others, have been infected with several maxims quite contrary to the apostolic life,' the bishop of Heliopolis had always experienced (and would always retain) difficulty in making a clear distinction between serving the interests of the Church and those of his nation. By allying himself with them, he placed himself in a risky political situation which other French Jesuits would later take advantage of in order to discredit the Vicars Apostolic and attempt to recover the mission of Siam for their own benefit.

The difference in perception between the two Vicars Apostolic appeared in a very significant way in the divergent interpretation they made of the events in Tonkin. For Pierre Lambert, the expulsion of the Jesuits was simply the logical, catastrophic and well-deserved consequence of an economic rivalry which the missionaries of the Society could have avoided if they had remained faithful to purely apostolic aims. François Pallu, on the contrary, made, officially at least, common cause with the unfortunate Jesuits who considered themselves victims of the rapacity and hatred of the Batavian heretics. When he returned to France, a few months later, he brought to the Jesuit authorities in France a genuine letter of accreditation, written by Tissanier and d'Albier, requesting the intervention of the King of France against the Dutch possessions in Asia. In his desire to preserve harmonious relations with the Jesuits at all costs, the bishop of Heliopolis made alliances which deviated dangerously from the instructions of non-interference formulated by the Roman Instructions, but which considerably reinforced his credit with devout French people, scandalized by the revelations of Pierre Lambert, whose reputation, on the contrary, crumbled.

And even if the two Vicars Apostolic continued to appear side by side and on an equal footing in official documents, only the first would henceforth be considered a valid representative by those in charge in Paris, while the second would be more and more openly accused of a lack of theological knowledge and of delusion. An official and politically correct rating of the founders was then put in place, which has not changed much to this day.

The Bourges mission

Already quite upset by Pierre Lambert's first letters, the directors of the Paris Foreign Missions Society had difficulty in accepting the return to France of Jacques de Bourges who arrived in Paris at the end of the summer of 1664. On November 14, Michel Gazil answered the bishop of Beirut on their behalf: 'I confess that here we are a little surprised by the strange things that have been written. Consequently, your friends think that there may be some exaggeration or a great deal of credulity on your part, as we find it impossible to believe your report of so much misconduct.

It is claimed here that the relaxation of morals is commonplace amongst heretics; that too much faith has been placed in enemies who are blinded by hatred; that many things are condemned without knowledge of particular reasons and specific circumstances; that it is not right to form vague, indefinite, general accusations to condemn the innocent with the guilty, something that is against all justice.

Moreover, it is uncharitable to arouse the hatred of a large number of malicious people against a body which is innocent of disturbances in the Indies and which has an unblemished reputation in France. It is a waste of time to stir up storms and tempests. Such action only produces discord and confusion, whereas missionaries should join together as closely as possible. Those who are wise should know how to correct others by behaving better than those they want to instruct. M. de Bourges, who is to return in March, will take care to explain all this to you.'

The position of the directors was indeed unenviable, for even if they were disposed to believe the accusations against the Jesuits, they were well aware that they had good reason to be afraid reprisals from them. 'I am sharing with you the reflections of prudent people on Bishop Lambert's actions,' wrote Michel Gazil two days later to François Pallu. 'Everyone here is convinced of his virtue and the high ideals which motivate his actions, but it is impossible to understand why he did not consider the consequences of what he wrote. For it seems that he and his missionaries wanted to create a general storm of opposition against an order that ought to be highly respected, an order that is to be feared, which has authority and a good reputation and which most certainly has competent people wherever it establishes itself. Certainly, to put something in print can be unbelievably dangerous since those who are criticized know very well how to justify themselves.'

'They say', he concluded after enumerating the traditional justifications invoked by the Jesuits when confronted by their detractors,

> that it is the ultimate ingratitude that missionaries whom they believed to be their friends, from their first steps in the missions, should have aligned themselves with their enemies, that they should have borrowed all their venom from them in order to spread it everywhere, and that they should have filled letters with it which they have dared to take to the courts of the most august and most holy authorities. When the faults and failings of some individuals are discovered in the Indies, it is advisable to conceal such information rather than to discredit the culprits for their misfortune and weakness.
>
> It must be remembered that superiors do what they can to counsel and correct their subjects, but because of their distance from such remote places it is not surprising that many things escape their notice. In short, they are quite convinced that division will lead to the failure of the enterprise. The Gospel has no greater enemies than factions within the ranks of missionaries, so that if they continue with these insults the Jesuits will be obliged to defend themselves and show the weakness of those who have allowed themselves to be convinced by the reports of their enemies.

True to their custom, the Jesuits did not consider it advantageous to justify themselves and responded to the accusations of the Vicar Apostolic with the same answer as to all those who criticized them, that of the conspiracy theory. Fortunately, in this critical situation, the directors found comfort in the conduct of Jacques de Bourges who, moderate by nature and aware of the storm his arrival had raised, was careful not to overstep the simple role of messenger entrusted to him by his bishop. Michel Gazil was clearly grateful.

> M. de Bourges arrived in this city with various letters that were distributed in part. Some people were alarmed. Some religious in particular believed that he had come only to denounce them, but they experienced the opposite, and everyone was satisfied with the moderation that he showed. He has been sensitive to our feelings; he has seen for himself how important it is to maintain peace; he will provide you with reasons for this. In short, we are edified by him; he has seen all the friends of your mission, especially Mgr the Prince of Conti and the first President. Whether he returns as a bishop is a matter about which I have no knowledge.

Thus, in Paris, there was a great temptation to accept Pierre Lambert's proposal of resignation and to appoint his designated successor, M. de Bourges, in his place. It was undoubtedly with this hope in mind that Jacques de Bourges was allowed to leave for Rome in November 1664. At the same time an official report for the Assembly of the Clergy of France was prepared in order to reassure the devout French.

The report was as follows: 'As a result of the loss of Bishop de Metellopolis and four clergymen, the Bishop of Beirut decided to send to Europe Sieur de Bourges, one of his clergymen, to inform the pope of the spiritual needs of the mission, to obtain a third bishop and to invite others to devote themselves to this missionary work. The said Sieur de Bourges, after nine months at sea, went to Rome and explained to the Holy Father the state of the mission in China.'

> His Holiness not only received him favourably, but granted him various graces for the good of these new churches, and provided him with the necessary powers for the consecration of a new bishop, the choice of whom he left to the other two bishops on the spot. The Holy Father acted thus all the more willingly since this mission, as one of the most important in

the whole Church, is very close to his heart, and also, touched by the zeal shown by these first three bishops, he is willing to attach it to our nation, as the one most capable of providing the necessary workers. The opportunities for bringing the faith to all these kingdoms have never been greater than they are today, especially to China, where there is complete freedom to preach, and where people are increasingly willing to embrace the faith. It is the lack of workers alone that delays progress, which the Holy See wants to remedy promptly by sending the aforementioned bishops, so that they can establish these churches as soon as possible by ordaining local priests, thereby giving our religion the means of sustaining itself and of growing.

This text is obviously in conformity with the expectations of pious people and does not risk disturbing those in power. Unfortunately, it contains three lies: the first is by omission, meaning that there is no statement of the main reason for Bourges' trip, which is the denunciation of abuses; the second lie is by the erroneous assertion of successful evangelisation: the mention of persecutions is absent, whereas almost all the missionaries have been expelled from the territories concerned; third, the preferential attribution of these missions to France, whereas the Jesuits of Padroado still considered themselves to be the only ones legitimately responsible, since Rome had not stated otherwise. A mixture of religious and national propaganda, this official version illustrated well the ambiguous position of the directors of the young Paris Foreign Missions Society and their inability to accept the radicalism of a Vicar Apostolic determined to defend the truth. And soon the arrival in Paris of an important Jesuit personality, Philippe Marini, procurator of the Province of Japan, heightened their fears even more, since he, as an outspoken defender of the 'exclusivist' line which had governed the Province of Japan since Valignano, did not conceal his opposition to the French missions.

The thorny issue of trade and other material necessities

Fr Marini favoured the Portuguese. Because of his rank in the Jesuit hierarchy, he had access to the most important people at court and could put pressure on his confrere Father Annat, confessor of the king, to act against the Vicars Apostolic. In this game of influence and privilege, the directors were not well placed and therefore had to avoid false moves in order to keep their royal protection that depended more on their political submission than on their religious sincerity. However, what interested the king at this particular time concerning the missions, was not the means used for the conversion of the infidels but the diplomatic advantages that he could gain from the presence of French Vicars Apostolic in the principal countries of Asia. In 1664, when Colbert created the (French) East India Company, France was preparing to join the Portuguese, Spanish, Dutch and English in the great game of commercial and maritime competition in the East. In his study *Les Relations politiques et commerciales entre la France et la péninsule indochinoise au XVIIe siècle*,[2] Frédéric Mantienne analyzed the ambiguity of the role of the Paris Foreign Missions, which sought to use the Company of the East Indies for religious purposes, and their share of responsibility for its bankruptcy. Unlike the previous short-lived Company of China, the East India Company was founded for purely economic and political reasons. It is thus easier to understand why, in such a context, Pierre Lambert's fulminations against trade by religious seemed particularly unwelcome and why the directors put so much pressure on François Pallu—who, let us remember, was distantly allied with the Colbert family—to straighten out the situation and keep the missionaries in a frame of mind that was more in keeping with national interests.

The bishop of Heliopolis applied himself to this task with remarkable patriotic zeal, multiplying reports and other efforts in favour of the interests that he wanted to be common to the French East India Company and the missionaries. However, the differences in attitudes of the two Vicars Apostolic towards trade should not be exaggerated. For if Pierre Lambert categorically refused to allow clerics to practice it on their own, he saw no problem with missionaries and French traders helping each other.

At least this is what is implied in a letter written to M. Fermanel, assuming that it was not dictated to him by Pallu to mitigate the devastating effects of his first correspondence.

> We find so many advantages for religion in this kingdom that we have resolved to make it the centre of our mission. Although I am not a businessman and cannot be one, I do not

---

2. *Political and Commercial relations between France and the Indochinese Peninsula in the 17th Century.*

hesitate to make you aware that the profits that are made in all these areas are immense. I am writing this to you after being well informed about it and for two reasons: the first is that if people were convinced of this in France, they would certainly come here to trade, and this would be a wonderful opportunity for us, making it much easier to bring missionaries here in the future. Obviously I am interested in such an outcome. The second reason is that I am very happy to give this advice to our nation to use for its own advantage and take the place of the poor Portuguese who no longer have any power here and who have strayed because of their pride and their vice. I know that the Dutch are extremely afraid of this eventuating, even though they are witnesses that we only trade in the conversion of souls. They understand very well that through the advice we can give our countrymen, the French will come here to trade, especially when they see that we are established in this kingdom, and in a short time in Cochinchina, Tonkin, and China, and if it pleases God, within a few years, I hope, in Macassar, Achem, Bantan and Pegu.

Thus, despite his intransigence and his sincere desire to distinguish God from Caesar, the Bishop of Beirut did not escape the ambiguity inherent in his position, an ambiguity that would only become more pronounced with Louis XIV's growing interest in Asian affairs. And his mystical inspiration, burning brightly as it was, would never erase in him either the rigor of the jurist unable to come to terms with the deviations, the disobedience and the abuses of power by religious, or the sense of duty of the senior civil servant concerned with the interests of his country. In reality, his position was neither that of a visionary nor that of an opportunist. Pierre Lambert, who knew the world of finance very well since, in civilian life, he was highly successful in that field, simply believed that, while the search for profit was legitimate and useful for lay people, it was harmful for missionaries, because it diverted them from the only attitude that was appropriate to their state, the total gift of themselves to God and therefore total abandonment to Providence.

Pallu returns to Europe

While in Europe, Jacques de Bourges bore the full brunt of the opposition of the Society of Jesus towards the Vicars Apostolic. Meanwhile in Siam, Pierre Lambert and François Pallu continued their consultations. While they had no trouble in agreeing on the principles of conduct set out in the *Monita*, the two Vicars Apostolic had more difficulty in agreeing on the project of a congregation to be known as the Lovers of the Cross. At first, François Pallu was resolutely opposed to it, judging it too demanding on the ascetic level and unrealistic on the spiritual level. When examined closely, it can be seen that these contradictions and reciprocal disagreements between the Vicars Apostolic and the Parisian directors were undoubtedly due less to the opposition of personalities, even if individual sensibilities diverged, than to differences in function and situation. Such differences lasted for some time within the Paris Foreign Missions Society and only disappeared when it was decided to appoint only men with mission experience to the direction of the Seminary. Indeed, while in Paris the directors, whose task it was to ensure the supply of personnel and equipment, devoted all their energy to the establishment of these human resources, the men in the field, constantly confronted with precarious situations, attached only relative importance to the conditions of material well-being and were more concerned with what could maintain their interior strength. This is the feeling that Jacques de Bourges expressed in the letter he wrote to Luc Fermanel when he had just learned that Father Annat, in retaliation for the denunciations of Pierre Lambert, persuaded the King to refuse to grant pensions to the Vicars Apostolic.

'I bless Our Lord, since now we have all the more reason to abandon ourselves to the divine and most loving Providence, being deprived of this help which was undoubtedly, humanly speaking, very important; I ask you in this spirit to pray for Father R. P. Annat. If only we could learn the hidden riches of holy dependence on God in all things, if only we could feel something of the privileges of poverty which are suffering and contempt, how happy we would be and how indebted to those who brought about this happiness. Yes, may God be blessed, and I say this with all my heart. We are missionaries who have imitated gentlemen a little too much. May it please God to have mercy on us now and forever.'

'The bishop of Beirut has a great influence on all those who approach him, and he persuaded them to do whatever he wanted', he confided one day.

However, there was still some doubt about the relevance of the project, which risked being misunderstood in Europe. 'If I am not mistaken, this is what God intended for our little association. But he has deferred giving enlightenment', Pierre Lambert himself acknowledged. And although he personally proposed this commitment to a life of perfection to a few companions who seemed to him capable of embracing it, among them his brother Nicolas and Jacques de Bourges, he sometimes seemed disoriented, even overwhelmed, by the superhuman demands it implied. Aware of the limits of his human discernment and anxious to set an example of obedience, Pierre Lambert, although he had won the support of his confreres for his project, did not want to decide anything definitively without the agreement of Rome. Moreover, since he still had no news of Jacques de Bourges, he did not know if the latter had reached his destination. A second fact-finding mission to Europe was therefore necessary, but on questions so important that they required the support of a bishop. Now François Pallu was in much better health than his colleague. And above all, his moderation and familiarity with the Jesuits would make the denunciations of missionary abuses more credible. After much deliberation and without enthusiasm, the Bishop of Heliopolis, with his usual availability and dedication, agreed to retrace his steps less than a year after his arrival in Ayutthaya.

On 17 January 1665, he left the Siamese capital in the company of Philippe de Chamesson. During his trip, which was marked by many setbacks, he wrote numerous reports to his Parisian and Roman authorities in order to justify the conduct of the Vicars Apostolic. He was at that time in complete agreement with the thought of his confrere. Thus, he wrote to Pierre Lambert, 'I will look to you and respect you all my life as my father, since Our Lord used you to withdraw me from the thick darkness in which I was shrouded and to give me entry into the life of his divine Spirit; I beg you to count me among your children, and to take care of me as a good father.'

In Ayutthaya, Pierre Lambert was once again alone, taking responsibility for all the operations on the ground. For years, he would have to fight simultaneously on two fronts: first, against the missionaries of Padroado, seculars and regulars who did not intend to give up any of their rights of patronage over the whole of the Asian continent; and second, against the Jesuits, Portuguese or not, who claimed exclusive control over 'their missions' of Cochinchina and Tonkin and would do everything to prevent the envoys of the Propaganda from gaining a foothold in them.

Chapter 5
Consolidations and Fractures

News from Cochinchina

After the departure of his confrere, François Pallu, Pierre Lambert found that his position was strengthened. He had four missionaries with him, François Deydier, Louis Laneau, Antoine Hainques and Pierre Brindeau, all of whom had adopted the ascetic way of life of the Lovers of the Cross, no doubt following the example and the advice of François Pallu. It was therefore the responsibility of Pierre Lambert to direct all operations in the field as long as he did not know Rome's response to his request to resign. He was a bishop who was determined to do everything possible to keep the French mission in place, a man who had nothing left to lose, since he had sacrificed his life and his reputation in this cause.

At the end of one of his usual forty-day retreats, the Vicar Apostolic set his men two priority tasks that would keep them busy without causing too much friction with the other missionaries: the instruction of youth and attempts at evangelization in the villages around the capital, with Louis Laneau providing guidance, for he was a man already dedicated to Siam.

On 7 April 1665, the three Jesuits from Cochinchina disembarked in Ayutthaya having been expelled after a persecution at the end of the previous year that had left more than forty dead, including the best catechists. After a difficult time in Cochinchina, the three missionaries had been brought together by the persecution. Imprisoned in the same residence, before being expelled one after another, they were helpless witnesses to many apostasies (in particular among the Japanese of Faifo) but also to some heroic cases of resistance. Out of 5000 Christians, about 4000 gave in to threats.

The disembarkation of the Jesuits was followed five days later by the arrival of Louis Chevreuil, who also had to leave the country. Louis Chevreuil brought back two certitudes. First, the persecution of the Christians was above all political, its principal motive being the fear felt by the King of Cochinchina that 'our holy religion, which the Portuguese say is theirs, was the pretext used by the fathers to make his vassals revolt against him and to put the King of Portugal in possession of his kingdom when the number of Christians surpassed that of the infidels.'[1] Secondly, the number of apostasies was due to the poor formation of Christians and their abandonment by religious, who led a comfortable existence in the cities where 'their table was one of the best in the country.'

This confirmed an impression that the French had since their arrival in Asia: the decadence of Christianity in these regions was not due to the lukewarmness or fickleness of the Asiatics, but to the laxity of unworthy European missionaries who no longer did their work and were content with superficial conversions without deep roots, often obtained by harmful concessions. Moreover, the exemplary fidelity of some martyrs, such as the young Lucie, delivered to the elephants at the age of fifteen, whose head Louis Chevreuil brought back as a relic, attested on the contrary that these Asian Christians could be compared to the martyrs of the early Church and deserved dedicated pastors who were ready to make any sacrifice. Obviously, these two observations, made visually by a witness previously well-intentioned towards the Jesuits, strengthened the resolve of the Bishop of Beirut in his fight against those he considered to be the main adversaries of Christianity: the Portuguese and the Jesuits. They also increased his desire to go to the mission assigned to him in order to support his flock in their ordeal. These were the sentiments he expressed in a letter full of solicitude and respect that he sent to the Christians of Cochinchina through the intermediary of a newly baptized Cochinchinese sailor: 'Do not reflect on the disgrace that may befall me. My life is yours and I will be happy to endanger it and lose it for your benefit. I will therefore wait here for your letters or for someone from you who will tell me what you want from me and what I can do to console you in the extreme need in which you now find yourselves.'[2]

---

1. *Relation du premier voyage de M.Chevreuil en Cochinchine*. AMEP, volume 733, 103ff. Published in A Launay, *Histoire de la mission de Cochinchine 1658-1823. Documents historiques*, 1.1.14, 19.
2. Mission Journal, AMEP, volume 0001/01, 156–159.

First exchanges with Phra Narai

Perhaps it was also the situation in Cochinchina that prompted Pierre Lambert to make contact with the court of Siam, in order to differentiate himself, in the eyes of the king, from the Portuguese missionaries and their secular activities. The king of Siam was then Phra Narai. Having ascended to the throne in 1656 thanks to the armed support of the foreign residents of Ayutthaya and in particular the Portuguese who had helped him to overthrow his uncle and predecessor, Sirisuthammaraja, the sovereign enjoyed absolute power over his subjects. He was also the main trader in the kingdom. Benefiting from a certain number of monopolies, he sought to promote trade to develop the economy of his country and he knew perfectly well how to play on rivalries between Europeans. Between 1661 and 1664, he was at war with the Dutch who blocked the port of Ayutthaya and imposed a commercial treaty that was very unfavourable to the Siamese. While there were frequent conflicts between him and his close neighbours, the sovereign readily used the skills of foreign auxiliaries whom he incorporated into his administration, sometimes in very high positions. So it was that his principal advisers were Persians, while Turkish, English and Portuguese governors were appointed in certain cities. In Ayutthaya, it was the Portuguese Jesuit, Tomaso Valguarnera, who directed the construction of the ramparts.[3]

It is therefore not surprising that the king was interested in the French, newcomers who began to care for the sick and to educate young people. Without perceiving the religious motivation of their presence in his states, and after having sent a mandarin on a reconnaissance mission to them, he asked them to take in a dozen young Siamese to teach them Western science, which was highly prized by all Asian rulers. Seizing this opportunity, Pierre Lambert then wrote a request to the king, both to thank him for his confidence and to propose that he consolidate his project by establishing a college 'in his royal city, or wherever he wished, in order to teach the sciences that are necessary for a state to distinguish it in the eyes of all the nations of the earth.'[4] He did not forget his apostolic duty

---

3. Fr. Tomaso Valguarnera (1608–1677) was originally from Sicily. He arrived from Macau in 1655 and remained in Siam for fifteen years.
4. Mission Journal, 146.

and took advantage of the opportunity to address a true profession of missionary faith to the sovereign, which was also a way of distancing himself from the ambiguous position of the Portuguese religious and of asserting his opposition to them. This text, a succinct summary of the principal evangelical principles in perfect conformity with the Roman *Instructions*, contained nothing that could worry a sovereign or offend a Buddhist soul and could explain, apart from any calculation of political interest, the unfailing favour that Pierre Lambert enjoyed with Phra Narai until his death. From this first contact, the Vicar Apostolic, by expressing himself sincerely and clearly, was able to ensure that both his office and his religion were respected.

> You will know that we left the country of our birth, our parents, our friends and our jobs, only to better fulfil a commandment of the law we profess, which obliges us to love every man in particular as ourselves without enemies. We are not able to give more evident and advantageous signs of our love for your subjects than by communicating to them the knowledge and enlightenment we have received from God. With this in mind, we offer to Your Majesty the presence in this kingdom of two French fathers who will be continually occupied with this work. Moreover, because it is important that Your Majesty should be informed of the main purpose of our religion and way of life, we declare that we claim nothing else in this world than to adore, love and serve God with all our heart and to love our neighbour as ourselves, and because our souls are immortal, we believe that they will receive an eternal reward or punishment, according to their good or bad deeds. Hence, we hold that the one who has loved God the most, who has had the most charity for his neighbour and who has done the most good deeds will be the happiest throughout eternity. 'It is with this in mind that we lead an austere life of continual penance, that we do not meddle in affairs of state or in temporal matters except to help the poor, visit the prisoners and assist the sick. These, Sire, are the motives which have brought us to these parts. If your Majesty accepts the offer we make of our services, we hope from your royal magnificence—and this is the only favour we ask of you—that you will give us a temple in which to pray daily to the almighty God whom we worship, for the preservation of your Majesty's health and the prosperity of your States.[5]

---

5. Mission Journal, 148.

It is apparent that the bishop had retained from the important responsibilities he held in France the art of finding words that touched the hearts of Great Ones.

Comings and goings in the port of Ayutthaya

However, this letter did not reach its destination until the end of the year, due to the illness of the mandarin who was to deliver it. In the meantime, other important events occurred following the arrival of a patache from Macau. This sailing vessel brought to Ayutthaya three ordinands sent by the vicar general of the Portuguese city of Macau to be ordained by the Bishop of Beirut, as well as the provincial of the Jesuits in person, Manuel Rodrigues, who had come 'to remove the grounds for complaint against the religious of the Society'.[6] The latter gave the Vicar Apostolic a blank cheque signed by the visitor, Louis de Gamma, and proposed to remedy 'several intolerable abuses which have caused the extreme disorder that everyone sees in the provinces of India and Japan'. In fact, the French soon guessed that this visit was only due to the insistence of the vicar general and the governor of Macau, as well as the leaders of other religious orders in the city, all of whom were experiencing some difficulty with the Jesuits, and who wished, despite the Jesuit opposition, to invite the Bishop of Beirut to their homes.

Judging that the three ordinands were not ready for the priesthood, Pierre Lambert retained them for further formation with three other native candidates, including a young twenty-two-year-old Indo-Portuguese mestizo from Meliapur, François Perez. Declining an immediate response to the invitation of the religious of Macau, he sent Pierre Brindeau on a journey of reconnaissance. He left on June 23. He brought to the captain general of Macau a very kind letter from Pierre Lambert in which the latter protested his political neutrality.

> Your letter gave me as much joy as I had displeasure in believing until now that I was not well thought of by the inhabitants of Macau. The basis for this belief came mainly from the letters I had received on my arrival in the Indies, which said that there was an order in Goa to arrest the French bishops who would pass through the lands subject to the crown of Portugal. The

---

6. Mission Journal, 150.

harm this has done has prevented me from doing the good and providing the service that a nation that is a great friend of France could have and should have expected of me. Without examining the reasons for acting in this way, nor making complaints, I will be happy to have a meeting with you. This will give me the opportunity, with your help, to assure all those who are in Macau and all the other subjects of the king that they will always be as important to me as if they were French; for even though I am French by birth, the rank I hold in the holy Church obliges me to regard all Christians as equal, in whom there is no difference except in virtue.[7]

Two months later, Antoine Hainques and Louis Chevreuil left Siam for Cochinchina where no missionary had been living for nearly six months. They embarked on 11 August 1665 on a small boat bought by the mission and piloted by Cochinchinese Christians from Ayutthaya. This departure provided the occasion for a new quarrel. This time it was with the Jesuit provincial, Manuel Rodrigues who, not being able to bear Louis Chevreuil's refusal to draw up a certificate attesting that 'the Jesuit fathers had always fulfilled their duties well in the mission of Cochinchina,' drove from his room the two missionaries who had come to greet him. He became 'so angry that he said that the pope could not send missionaries to that place without the permission of the King of Portugal. The good Lord allowed this father's anger, or rather the expression of his feelings and those of his Society towards the missionaries, to be such that they were always on their guard against their evil designs.'[8] This was the conclusion of the Mission Diary, summarizing the opinion of the French. Thus, each side dug in its heels and mistrust developed on both sides as hostility grew, auguring badly for what might happen when the two parties met on the ground.

Shortly before Christmas, a Spaniard who arrived on a Dutch ship from Tonkin delivered to the French a letter from the catechist Raphael de Rhodes dated 24 October 1665, acknowledging the receipt of the letter sent by François Pallu the previous year, and assuring them that the situation had improved. The king would like the Jesuits to return to revive trade and the Christians were eagerly awaiting priests and the arrival of their Vicar Apostolic.

---

7. Letter of Pierre Lambert to the captain general of Macau. AMEP, 1665, volume 121, 595.
8. Mission Journal, 165.

Two days later there was another piece of good news: a courier from Tenasserim brought a package of letters from Europe announcing the establishment of the Seminary of Paris. Finally, the missionaries received a favourable response from the King of Siam who granted them a piece of land of their choice and promised to provide them with the materials to build their residence. They settled near the Cochinchinese camp in a large field on the edge of the river where they built 'two rooms of wood, covered with tiles to protect the books and church ornaments from fire.'[9]

On 31 January 1666, the small boat that had taken Antoine Hainques and Louis Chevreuil to Cochinchina returned to Ayutthaya. The journey of the two missionaries had been made difficult by bad weather and illness. Hainques was able to enter Cochinchina but Chevreuil, 'suffering from a continuous fever', was entrusted to the good care of a Cochinchinese Christian family in Cambodia. At the end of March, other ships brought new letters from Cochinchina. Several were from Antoine Hainques who arrived at Faifo secretly ministering to the Christians on the way. He was well received by the founder, Jean de la Croix, who passed him off as his brother-in-law to the authorities, and advised him to buy a boat and a cargo of rice and, dressed as a merchant, to go and visit the Christians far from the capital. Two other letters were written by the Christians of Cochinchina who thanked their 'very great father' the bishop, for his concern, and awaited his coming, but they had not yet found a way to bring him to them without danger. Pierre Lambert replied with a message of encouragement and, fearing that access to the country would be closed to foreigners for a long time, asked them to send him a few people who would be suitable for ordination to the priesthood.

Finally, at the beginning of April, Siamese ships arrived from Macau with a group of new ordinands sent by the vicar general. Through them and the messages of Pierre Brindeau which they carried, the bishop learned that his emissary had been well received by the captain general and most of the religious of the city, Augustinians, Dominicans and Franciscans, with the exception of the only Jesuit visitor 'who told him, with tears in his eyes, that the French missionaries were coming to their district to destroy the missions of the Society'.[10] While learning the Mandarin language, Brindeau

---

9. Mission Journal, 182.
10. Mission Journal, 201.

preached, confessed, 'occupied himself with a thousand good offices of charity' under the authority of the vicar general and very quickly became involved in the rivalries that undermined the missionary clergy in Macau as elsewhere.

At the request of his bishop, Brindeau also collected a certain number of testimonies intended to constitute a dossier of proof that could be used to support the accusations of the French missionaries against the Jesuits. Among the pieces of evidence he gathered, the most formidable was an apology of the Friars Minor against the Jesuits of Ceylon, a damning indictment denouncing various exactions and a shameless exploitation of the islanders by the missionaries of the Society of Jesus.[11] This explosive document, which far exceeded the scandalous revelations and the worst charges of Pierre Lambert. Its violence can only be explained by attributing it to a settlement of accounts between two rival orders. Since it constituted an invaluable argument for Pierre Lambert, he had it translated into French and sent at once, with some other pieces of less importance, to his colleague Pallu. It cast a glaring light on the practices and relationships within the missionary clergy of that time. It was calculated to shock current attitudes used to an inoffensive writing of history. Unfortunately, it also confirms many of the 'horrors' denounced by several secular authors who were contemporaries of the events and who, in respectable circles, would be accused of anticlerical exaggeration.

Having relied too exclusively on 'edifying' letters, historians of the missions often missed the less edifying, but nevertheless very interesting reality contained in this kind of unofficial testimony,

---

11. Translation of the apology of the Friars Minor of the East Indies, in which they show the fruitfulness of their labours in the conversion of the infidels and how little reason Dom Mires dao Saldanha, viceroy of the Indies, had for giving letters patent to the Jesuits permitting them to be installed on the island of Ceylon in place of the Friars Minor. From this defence, it is clear that he was misinformed and it shows the reasons which obliged him to act in this way. (AMEP, volume 114, 21–60). A copy is included, probably by Lambert himself, 61–84. To avoid any dispute, Pierre Lambert scrupulously sought to verify the truth of the facts recounted in this apology, as he wrote to Pallu: 'There was one thing that pained me, reading this apology, which was that the author said that there were no Christians amongst the Madurese. But having clarified this point for myself, I learned that he was telling the truth at the time he was writing and that there are now Christians from the coasts of Pêcherie, Travancor, Cap de Comorin etc. who have withdrawn to Maduré since the Dutch war.' (Letter from Pierre Lambert to François Pallu)

which was discreetly buried in ecclesiastical archives and therefore was more difficult to discover. It is undeniable that the propaganda effect, initiated by *The Jesuit Relations* in the seventeenth century and perpetuated by the *Annales de la Propagation de la Foi* (largely fed by the writings of the Paris Foreign Missions) in the nineteenth century, falsified the history of the missions. Pierre Lambert was the first, and one of the few within the Church, to speak out officially against this distortion. His aim was not to defend the historical truth, nor even simply the interests of the Church, but, more fundamentally, the credibility of the Gospel message. For this reason alone, and for whatever excesses he was reproached with, he certainly deserved a little more understanding, a little more trust and a little more kindness, at least by his own people.

The forces at work

In the new and terrible battle that began in the spring of 1666 between the French missionaries and those of the Padroado, the Vicar Apostolic was generally accused of abuse of power. The image forged by his adversaries of a Pierre Lambert seeking to impose himself at any cost, even at the price of irreparable ruptures, has prevailed among practically all historians. And it is true that the complexity, the dispersion and sometimes the contradiction of the sources make it very difficult to reconstitute the gigantic trial of strength that took place between a handful of French missionaries and the all-powerful Lusitanian-Jesuit[12] coalition in Asia. A totally disproportionate fight led by the strategist Lambert assisted by the negotiator Pallu. There can be no doubt that it was a dirty war, one that was not very flattering to the external respectability of the Church; it was a conflict that claimed three victims in the French ranks: Louis Chevreuil who lost his reason, and Antoine Hainques and Pierre Brindeau who lost their lives. However, it resulted in the legal discomfiture of Padroado and the irreversible installation of the bases of the native clergy in Asia. It was a costly victory for European Christianity, but a precious one for the universal Church, that perhaps only a jurist as subtle, a fighter as fierce and a mystic as detached as Pierre Lambert, supported by the unwavering devotion of his companions, could win.

---

12. The name 'Lusitania' comes from a province of the Roman Empire. It corresponds reasonably well with modern Portugal.

Before entering into the details of this confrontation, it is useful to recall, at the risk of repeating certain points, the positions of each party. On the one hand, the politico-religious infrastructure of the Portuguese Padroado was centralized in Goa, the administrative and ecclesiastical capital of the East Indies, where the viceroy and the archbishop resided, and where the Inquisition officiated. At the eastern end of the empire was Macau, an important trading post, the seat of a bishopric that was vacant at the time, and also the headquarters of the Jesuit province of Japan, which included the missions of China, Japan, Indochina and the East Indies. To the south, Malacca, another episcopal city on which Siam depended, was captured by the Dutch in 1641. Its ecclesiastical governor, Paul d'Acosta, had taken refuge in Cambodia, in Colompe, on the banks of the Mekong River, with a community of 500 Portuguese and Malay Christians.

From 1662, all the civil and religious representatives of Padroado, who only recognized the decrees of Rome if they were validated by Lisbon, had been ordered to oppose by all possible means the entry of French missionaries into their missions. The most numerous and most active in this opposition were the Jesuits, mostly Portuguese, but also French, Italian, German and Belgian. As holders of numerous privileges which they did not want to be dispossessed of by an ordinary ecclesiastical jurisdiction, they had always and everywhere found it difficult to live alongside bishops and had an almost congenital reluctance to share missionary work with any other congregation. This possessiveness was particularly strong with regard to China, where they had succeeded in positioning themselves in spheres of power. So too, with regard to the missions of Cochinchina and Tonkin, of which they considered themselves to be the fathers with the sole right of possession. However, it was precisely these three territories that were entrusted to the apostolic vicars, who were consequently considered undesirable, even usurpers. The French missionaries, for their part, were only nine: two bishops assisted by six priests and one layman. Three of them, Pallu, de Chamesson and de Bourges, were still at sea, somewhere between Europe and Asia.

The battle was all the more unequal because the position of the supervisory authorities was very ambiguous. In Rome, Propaganda unconditionally supported the Vicars Apostolic, but the Padroado had never been officially denounced (the Portuguese were therefore at liberty to defend their rights) and the Holy See, which had a difficult relationship with Louis XIV and had been struggling for years with the Jansenist affair, did not want to poison its relations with Portugal. On the other hand, the Jesuits benefited from many powerful supporters in Roman circles. In Paris, the directors of the Seminary refused, as much from personal attachment as from political prudence, any questioning of the Jesuits and tried to obtain from the king the diplomatic protection of the French missionaries against the demands of Portugal, one of the few European nations friendly to France. On the human level, the confusion of political and religious interests placed the envoys of Propaganda in a dead-end situation. Only their hope in the grace of God, their sense of Church and the ineradicable feeling of the legitimacy of their mission enabled them to hold out and, in the long run, win.

The first skirmish occurred, as we have seen, in August 1665, between Louis Chevreuil and the Jesuit provincial Manuel Rodrigues, who, when all his men had been expelled from Cochinchina and Tonkin, could not bear the thought of the French returning there alone. A little later, in Macau, relations quickly became strained between Pierre Brindeau and the representatives of the Society of Jesus. Everywhere, the latter found that far from being intimidated or seduced by their threats or their superficial kindness, Pierre Lambert had taken the audacious decision to disperse his meagre troops in order to occupy the whole region with the five men who remained with him. No sooner had he learned of the arrival of Antoine Hainques in Cochinchina than, against all human prudence, he sent his oldest companion, François Deydier, to Tonkin. The latter left on 20 June 1666 disguised as a sailor on a Chinese boat, a perilous situation for an isolated European, who risked being deprived of his luggage and thrown into the sea at any time. As for Louis Chevreuil, before settling down in Cochinchina, he was ordered to carry out a confidential mission: to go to Cambodia to find Governor Paul d'Acosta and to ties with the clergy of Ayutthaya. To thwart the traps of the regular clergy, Pierre Lambert decided to rely on the secular clergy from whom he hoped for greater loyalty. This decision proved to be soundly based since, in the end, and with a few exceptions, the French missionaries enjoyed relative kindness from the latter. Finally, the last missionary, Louis Laneau, continued his integration into Siamese society, while the Vicar Apostolic continued to wave the red rag in front of the eyes of the religious of Ayutthaya in order, perhaps, to divert attention from him and to make it clear to everyone that he had no intention of backing down.

The Fragoso affair

An excellent opportunity to assert his authority was given to Pierre Lambert in May 1666 by one of his Dominican neighbours, Louis Fragoso, who was also a commissary of the Holy Office, and who appeared before him on the day of confirmation with a rich inhabitant of Macau, for whom he was to be godfather. The bishop was well aware that as a religious, Fragoso did not have the right to perform this function, but, out of prudence, he granted him a dispensation 'because of the possibility of important consequences'.[13] However, François Deydier, with his title of Doctor of Theology, pointed out that he did not have the right to exercise this function. A few days later, Fragoso responded with a letter in which he defended himself by invoking the authority of a famous Spanish jurist, Quintanaduenas, a man approved by the Inquisition. A juridical duel, characteristic of the customs of the time, began between the Dominican and Pierre Lambert, who, relying on a more recent treatise by Vericelli, had Louis Laneau draw up a censure against two proposals by Quintanaduenas and he sent it as information to Fragoso on May 31. The latter, after having consulted the Jesuits who also felt threatened by this questioning of their privileges, summoned the Vicar Apostolic, in the name of the Inquisition, to show the powers which authorized him to carry out this censure. Pierre Lambert replied on June 9 that, as a bishop sent by Propaganda, he was accountable to no one but the Holy See. Matters remained as they were for the time being.

A few months later, just after All Saints' Day, when he was just recovering from a serious bout of nephritic colic, the affair took a new turn when the ecclesiastical governor of Malacca, Paul d'Acosta, sent a reply to Ayutthaya, granting the Vicar Apostolic the use of his powers in the territory of Siam, and to his priests the right to administer the sacraments. This letter was transmitted to the bishop through the intermediary of a Portuguese cleric who, learning of this decision, immediately warned the religious who, fearing that he would use it to reform the abuses and disorders, tried to prevent him from using these powers and spread rumours questioning his suitability as bishop and threatening him with the Inquisition.

On November 26, a clergyman sent by Fragoso presented himself before Pierre Lambert to summon him to show his credentials within

---

13. Mission Journal, 205.

two days. The bishop answered 'that he had never refused nor would he refuse to show anyone letters indicating his identity, but that a more respectful tone of voice should be adopted in making such a request'.[14] He then asked for the request in writing.

This was a good response, because the Portuguese, not wanting to provide any evidence that could be used against them, were content to send their emissary back the next day, accompanied by armed servants, to repeat their request. The Vicar Apostolic did not deign to receive them and sent a servant to them to tell them 'that he stood by the answer which he had already given and complained about the futility of what was being done'.[15] The reply was not long in coming, and it was scathing: Louis Fragoso had a defamatory statement written against Pierre Lambert and his missionaries. This document, countersigned by the Jesuit Louis Vaz, accused the Vicar Apostolic of opposition to the Holy Office, declared him suspect in matters of faith and forbade all Christians to associate with him and his missionaries. It was displayed at the door of the Dominican and Jesuit churches on the feast day of St. Francis Xavier. This was done in spite of a last-minute concession by Pierre Lambert who, unable to produce his bulls as Vicar Apostolic because of Rome's prohibition, sent a copy of d'Acosta's letter of authority to Fragoso on December 1.

The effects of this defamatory statement on the Christianity of Ayutthaya were disastrous. The seminarians from Macau whom the bishop was to ordain were 'ordered not to communicate with Dom Pedro Lambert, called Bishop of Beirut, nor with his clerics',[16] and to return home. Likewise, several Christians left the parish of Saint Joseph, but the Cochinchinese, the new Siamese converts and the main Japanese faithful, as well as an eminent Portuguese personality, took the side of the French. On December 24, Pierre Lambert sent a summons to Louis Fragoso, enjoining him to send his defamatory statement to Rome. In response, the Dominican had one of the two Siamese Christians carrying the message arrested and put in irons on the ship to Goa. The unfortunate man was freed eighteen days later by officers of the King of Siam, much to the annoyance of the Portuguese who felt that the political wind was changing.

---

14. Mission Journal, 233–234.
15. Mission Journal, 233–234.
16. Mission Journal, 233–234.

Meanwhile, the Vicar Apostolic prepared his defence, gathered the various documents attesting to his dealings with Father Fragoso and sent them in quadruplicate to the Pope, the Inquisitor and the Archbishop of Goa, and to François Pallu. Rome took its time to send an answer, but its verdict was unequivocal. On 4 August 1670, the cardinals of Propaganda approved the censures brought by Lambert against Fragoso and Quintanaduenas and sent their author a letter of encouragement. In 1671, the Holy Office ordered the Inquisitor of Goa to recall Fragoso. However, the latter did not comply with the order until three years later, in 1674, after the publication of another writ excluding the territories entrusted to the Vicars Apostolic from the power of the Inquisition.

The 'Fragoso affair' remains a fine example of the effectiveness of Pierre Lambert's offensive strategy, despite the fact that Lambert's critics generally tended to attribute responsibility for conflicts to his intransigence in asserting his rights.

All is grace

This firmness, however, cost the Vicar Apostolic dearly, and he had to redouble his precautions. For from now on, the Portuguese understood who they were dealing with, and accordingly they multiplied their efforts to cut him off from his bases and render his efforts ineffective in every way possible: 'They always wish that misfortune may befall us and I have been warned from a reliable source that they want to harm me more than ever', he wrote to François Pallu, 'and in revealing my thoughts to you on this subject, I can say that I rejoice at finding my life to be in danger'.[17]

This prospect, far from frightening him, inspired him to engage in a new and extremely provocative tactic, which was well in keeping with his general line of conduct. Instead of adopting a low profile or throwing in the towel, as the first two Vicars Apostolic sent to Asia had done a few decades before him, he chose instead to stand his ground, even if it meant pushing his opponent to the limit, to use a sporting term. For he became convinced that, in the present state of affairs, perhaps only an act as serious as his own murder would finally lead to an investigation and thus reveal to Europe the truth about the real state of the missions:

---

17. Letter from Pierre Lambert to François Pallu, 4 November 1666. AMEP, volume 876, 571.

> I often tell God, when absorbed in prayer, that the sacrifice of my life would be very appropriate. I believe that by such a sacrifice I would contribute greatly to the reform of the religious missionaries. I even believe that it would be more profitable for the Church if I died for the faith in this way in the lands of our missions rather than at the hands of an executioner. With this in mind, I will remain here this year hoping to be the recipient of this blessing. Therefore I do not intend to enter the places of your jurisdiction any sooner than next year.[18]

In fact, there is no indication that the Portuguese sought to physically eliminate the Vicar Apostolic at this particular time. They preferred to attack his flock. All Christians who had dealings with the French were obliged to obtain permission to do so from Father Fragoso, who brandished the threat of the Inquisition in front of them and censored the few Portuguese and Siamese who remained in their parish. The limits of this tactic of intimidation became obvious enough quite quickly, since sides were quickly chosen. Then the religious clergy tried a more effective weapon, that of defamation, by attacking the bishop about his morals.

> Father Louis of the Rosary, now the vicar of the Jacobins (Dominicans), said openly that I was not as was thought, that he knew on good authority that I was a man of loose morals in the company of women, that he was very aware of the excesses I had committed on my way to Tenasserim, in the Portuguese and Dutch camps and that, in a word, I had only left those places to come to this one, in order to continue my dissolute ways more easily. This report made by the oldest religious here surprised people. The Jesuits spoke of it to several people as if they were astonished.[19]

---

18. Letter from Pierre Lambert. to François Pallu, 571.
19. Letter from Pierre Lambert to François Pallu, 31 January 1668. AMEP, volume 876: 571–575. This information is corroborated by Louis Laneau: 'We are made to look like villains and infamous people who, in order to do their evil work more easily, have withdrawn from among them and have gone to live in a district far from them, and this from the mouths of people I can hardly bear to name. Our people are imprisoned and it is said that they would imprison a person of importance; they would even imprison Monseigneur.' Letter from Louis Laneau to his brother, 2 September 1667. AMEP, volume 858, 137–139.

This moral attack did not seem to alter the confidence of the Vicar Apostolic any more than the physical threats, since he reacted very skilfully by appealing to the judgment of the pope to whom he wrote by the first available means, in October 1667.

> It is the prerogative of Your Holiness to have me judged so that, despite my profound unworthiness, I may at least benefit from the authority of the Vicar of God. Several years ago I asked to be replaced, driven to take this step mainly by the consciousness of my weakness. But now, when I am accused of such serious faults, there is good reason to ask why I am not removed, willingly or unwillingly, because of my inadequacy to fill such an office? May I be permitted, therefore, most Holy Father, to withdraw from society to a place where I can spend the rest of my life in prayer and penance atoning for my sins.[20]

On the spiritual level, Pierre Lambert turned this new trial to his advantage by considering it in the pure light of the Beatitudes to be a fruitful grace for his mission.

> This news having been reported to me, I wept with joy, not only on seeing myself accused of such great evils, but also because I believed that on the information that was put forward against me, I would be sent to Goa and found guilty of these charges. Your Holiness can see how God in his goodness is treating me in allowing me to be declared suspect in matters of the faith and accused of being a man of very dissolute behaviour in this place. I do not know if I am mistaken, but it seems to me that it is difficult for a Vicar Apostolic defending the interests of Jesus Christ to receive any greater honour. Since I have been graced with these great favours, I feel a greater strength to carry the cross of Jesus Christ, which I desire so much. I receive more blessings from heaven, and our work is going well. We have built a strong and suitable house during this storm.[21]

---

20. Letter from Pierre Lambert to Pope Clement IX, 19 October 1667. AMEP, volume 876, 487.
21. Letter from Pierre lambert to Francois Pallu, 31 January 1668. AMEP, volume 876, 571–575.

Indeed, in the midst of this sordid controversy, the mission grew stronger and more prosperous. In Ayutthaya, while the conduct of the religious continued to be the subject of much publicity and dissension arose among them, the king showed himself to be more and more favourable to the French. After the release of their messenger, he offered them his legal protection against the Portuguese. The answer of Pierre Lambert, stated in evangelical terms, was clever nonetheless. With the simplicity of a dove, the cunning of a serpent and a consummate sense of diplomacy, the bishop rejected an intervention of the Siamese secular power in missionary affairs while positioning himself before the sovereign as the leader and official representative of the Christians. To the officer who came to discuss his grievance he replied 'that being superior to all the religious and spiritual father of all the Catholics who were in Siam, he considered all the disputes that had occurred were of minor importance, such as happen in families and they should remain unknown to others'.[22]

Royal favours and great projects

This royal favour, however, as well as the hope of seeing new missionaries arrive soon, prompted him to undertake the work he had postponed the previous year, the construction of a permanent French residence. He was encouraged to do so by the king who, eager to consolidate the position of the missionaries, offered to provide them with materials for the building. Public works held no secrets for Pierre Lambert, who had supervised the construction of several large buildings in Rouen. On a piece of land measuring forty metres square, raised by two metres and walled on the river side to protect it from flooding, the bishop had a brick building erected in pure Siamese style. The first floor consisted of six rooms with a room 'for consecrated people' while the second floor housed the chapel. The cemetery which extended all around, was bordered by a garden. The complex, surrounded by some houses inhabited by Christians, was named Camp Saint-Joseph in honour of the mission's patron saint.

In these new premises, which were completed in August, the 'seminary' was gradually repopulated. Louis Laneau taught several children of different nationalities, encouraged by their parents, before

---

22. Mission Journal, 249.

soon receiving the catechists sent from Cochinchina and Tonkin by Antoine Hainques and François Deydier. The king, who, like all his Asian colleagues, did not distinguish between the religious teaching and the secular teaching of the Westerners, even wished to send a 60-year-old mandarin to learn from them.

Taking advantage of this growing interest of the sovereign in the 'science' of the French, Pierre Lambert sent him a customised pedagogical aid, 'a collection of images in intaglio printing of all the mysteries of the life and passion of Our Lord, of the twelve apostles, the four evangelists, the founders of the principal religions and the two most illustrious saints of each order and of the four last ends. We had this work bound in France, with blank sheets between each image, in order to write there what they signified.'[23] The desired effect was immediate. Two or three days after receiving it, the king asked for the meaning of the work. Louis Laneau, who had learned Siamese and Pali from the monks, spent two months writing the text of this first Thai catechism, which would have been the delight of researchers if it had been preserved.

During this time, Pierre Lambert, encouraged by these favourable circumstances, drafted great projects. In addition to the extension of the seminary, transformed into a true international college which would require at least two additional teachers and a master to teach manual work to young boys, he planned the creation of a community of little virgins supervised by 'two or three virtuous ladies from France' and a hospital managed by 'two people zealous for the service of the poor and who had some knowledge of surgery and medicine'.[24]

Even the budget was already planned: for 2,500 écus of rent on a capital of 50,000 écus from France or 12,000 écus in Spanish reals invested in Siam 'at twenty-two and a half per cent, which is the lowest rate in the kingdom', Pierre Lambert planned to be able to maintain one hundred seminarians and about the same number of little virgins and sick people. Obviously the preoccupations of the former wise manager of the general hospital of Rouen reappear here in the writings of the Vicar Apostolic: formation of the clergy, popular education of boys and girls, care of the sick and especially of

---

23. Letter from Pierre Lambert to François Pallu, October 1667. AMEP, volume 857(1), 221.
24. Letter from Pierre Lambert to François Pallu, October 1667.

the most neglected. Freed for a short time by the grace of Phra Narai from the vagaries of the struggle for survival that pitted him against the missionaries of Padroado, Pierre Lambert rediscovered his true face, that of a remarkable figure of charity and a very great servant of the Church.

While the Vicar Apostolic was organizing Ayutthaya as an important centre of the French missions, his men, scattered in other countries, continued their work under difficult conditions, though they seemed to be fairly well accepted by the ordinary ecclesiastical authorities where they existed, that is, in Macau and Cambodia. On the other hand, in Tonkin and Cochinchina, where the French were alone, the Jesuits, before being expelled, had made it known to the Christians 'that whoever comes to announce the Gospel there if he is not a member of their Society must be considered an antichrist'.[25] Consequently, Deydier and Hainques had some difficulty in being recognized by the catechists. Nevertheless, they had great apostolic success with the people who appreciated their dedication and the holiness of their lives. Antoine Hainques sent one of his catechists, Luc Ben, to Ayutthaya to be ordained and François Deydier announced the arrival of four of his men. In short, in the midst of so many trials, the six French missionaries present in Asia faithfully accomplished, with exemplary devotion and zeal, the task entrusted to them by the Holy See. And their mission, which one might have thought was doomed from the start, achieved an astonishing range in a short time.

An unfortunate initiative

During the month of July 1666, Louis Laneau completed the translation of the Siamese catechism which was given to the king. The king communicated it 'to the greatest and most important doctors of his court' who gave their verdict. The missionaries judged it to be favourable, but that above all, it testified to the traditional and benevolent Buddhist neutrality. They declared that 'the Catholic religion was good and that the religion the king professed was also good'.[26] And even though it was reported that Phra Narai said 'that this religion pleased him,' even though he redoubled his attention to the

---

25. Mission Journal, 250.
26. Mission Journal, 250.

French, Pierre Lambert, being a fine politician, noticed that the king listened just as attentively to the Muslim ambassadors of the kingdoms of Aceh and Golconda. He also saw that while the construction of St Joseph's Church was being completed thanks to royal generosity, the Muslims had obtained permission to build a mosque and public baths. For the apostolic vicar, who could not understand the logic of the universal tolerance of Buddhism, it was a sign that a race against time was under way between Islam and Christianity to obtain the conversion of the sovereign and thus of his kingdom. And he feared that he would not be able to compete with the great means deployed by his rivals. He noted with concern 'that not long ago the queen of Aceh, which is the most important kingdom of Sumatra, asked the king of Siam to embrace the Koran. The king gave a welcoming reception to her ambassador and ever since then it was noticed that he gratified many who belonged to this unfortunate sect.'[27]

To win the game, the bishop, taken by surprise, thought that it was essential to have political support. At the same time, he forgot the advice of prudence from Rome and conceived the unfortunate idea of appealing to his own sovereign, Louis XIV. It was a tragic error of judgment by this man, usually so detached from political interests who, in all good faith and guided by his only concern, which was to serve the Church, intended to introduce a wolf into his own sheepfold by opening to the King of France the doors of the mission of Siam! In October 1666, he wrote to François Pallu:

> It is necessary, Monseigneur, that I inform you of an idea I have which you may use as you please. Having learned of the great plans of our generous monarch for the establishment of trade in the Indies, it seems to me that since this city is a very advantageous place for such business, we could suggest to our king that he send an ambassador to this court, following the example of the Dutch who have succeeded well here, in order to deal with the king about the trade that can be done in this kingdom. Furthermore, His Most Christian Majesty could invite this king to embrace our religion as being very holy and the most suitable for making the princes who profess it reign in supreme authority, because it obliges Christians by its laws to be faithful and obedient to their sovereigns, on pain of

---

27. Letter from Pierre Lambert to François Pallu, October 1667. AMEP, volume 857 (1), 221.

being damned. Moreover, while representing to him that he owes the prosperity and greatness of his states to the Catholic religion which he and his predecessors have happily professed for so many centuries, his belief that all religions are good will make him react favourably to our proposals.[28]

This simple suggestion, relayed by a French state agency actively solicited by François Pallu, was to have catastrophic consequences and undoubtedly constituted the most serious, albeit unintentional, mistake in the career of this exceptional man. Indeed, as he struggled with difficult negotiations with the directors of the Seminary, the Bishop of Heliopolis would obviously seize this opportunity, which was timely and perfectly in line with his own convictions, to show that the Vicars Apostolic could also be useful in supporting national interests. Immediately, he set in motion the heavy machine that would lead, twenty years later, to the lamentable fiasco of the Siamese embassies.[29] If François Pallu was the main architect of this project, if he allowed it to take on a quasi-colonial dimension that his colleague did not envisage, it is no less true that it was Pierre Lambert, blinded, for once, by naivety and the desire to do the right thing, who was responsible in the eyes of history for this unfortunate initiative.

The pastoral letter against the trade of the clerics

It must be admitted, however, in his defence that, at the very moment when he conceived this unfortunate idea, the bishop of Beirut was quite disturbed by the unexpected arrival in Ayutthaya of one of the most devious adversaries of the French missionaries, the Jesuit Philippe Marini,[30] whose manoeuvres in Rome had greatly worried Jacques de Bourges. He left Goa on a vessel loaded with a cargo of sulphur and saltpetre. He intended to use these commodities to negotiate with the King of Tonkin for permission to return to his former mission and, at the same time, to expel François Deydier. He was diverted to Siam by bad weather and was obliged to spend the

---

28. Letter from Pierre Lambert to François Pallu, October 1667, 221.
29. For several years during the reign of Phra Narai embassies from Siam visited France and embassies from France visited Siam. Opposition to Phra Narai by the Siamese court and Buddhist clergy led to his death and a revolution in 1688, which saw most of the French driven out of Siam.
30. Philippe Marini was a missionary in Asia from 1640 to 1682, based in Macao for the most of this time.

winter there. Pierre Lambert vaguely hoped that he would bring him news from Paris, where the directors of the Foreign Missions had showered him with marks of respect and solicitude. But the Jesuit ignored the Vicar Apostolic who, learning the nature of the goods he was trading, feared the disastrous effects of this trade on the mission of Cochinchina. Indeed, the two Vietnamese kingdoms were living then in a state of perpetual war. Between 1627 and 1672, the armies of the north attacked those of the south seven times without success. If the King of Cochinchina learned through one of his subjects in Ayutthaya that missionaries were selling ammunition to his adversary (although he himself was recently supplied with guns in Macau through the Jesuits), he would consider that the European religious had changed sides and would take his revenge on the Christians in his country, where Hainques was still operating in perilous secrecy.

To counter this danger, Pierre Lambert saw only one solution: to disavow dealings of this kind clearly and in the most official way possible, by making public in all the places of the missions entrusted to the French the bull of Urban VIII of 22 February 1653. The bull 'forbade absolutely any trade by all missionaries, and specifically by the religious of the Society of Jesus, under the heaviest possible penalties, namely the penalty of excommunication incurred ipso facto and the deprivation of active and passive voice, of functions, grades and dignities whatever they might be, and even the disqualification from acquiring them'.[31] On 15 October 1667, Pierre Lambert wrote a pastoral letter which denounced in very violent terms the greed of religious orders. It recalled the contents of the bull of Urban VIII against trade by clerics, and ordered that the letter be translated into the vernacular, posted at the doors of the churches and communicated twice a year before the assembly of the faithful, as well as before and after the arrival of ships in Siam and in all the places subject to his jurisdiction.

This measure amounted to a public condemnation in the eyes of Christians of the Procurator of Japan himself,[32] as well as of all religious, and especially of the many Jesuits, who were engaged to some extent in commercial activities. Whatever the good intentions, the blow was enormous. Whatever his good intentions, the blow

---

31. Pastoral Letter of Pierre Lambert forbidding religious to engage in commerce, 15 October 1667. AMEP, volume 876, 483.
32. Philippe Marini.

was enormous. Clearly it provoked the outraged fury of the Jesuits against the Vicar Apostolic and alienated even the most moderate elements of the Society, such as his former regent of Caen, Jacques Le Faure, who until then had been quite cooperative. This initiative immediately led to a scathing riposte from Thomas Valguarnera who took advantage of the occasion to settle the serious dispute that had been going on between the Vicar Apostolic and himself for years. On November 1, he wrote a memorandum to Rome on the mission of Pierre Lambert, Bishop of Beirut, listing twenty-two charges against the head of the French missions. These responses had the desired effect in Rome, where the pastoral letter was considered an inappropriate provocation and the Bishop of Beirut was considered to have gone too far in his public denunciation of the Jesuits in his desire to enforce the regulations without any concession.

Seven years later, in 1674, Charles Sevin, sent by Pallu to the Holy See to negotiate new rights in favour of the Vicars Apostolic, noted that 'something else of great importance would have been achieved if the pastoral letter of Bishop of Beirut had not ruined and entirely changed the plans of the cardinals, as can be seen clearly in the letter of the Congregation written to the Vicars Apostolic. This letter was generally disapproved of by everyone, without exception.'[33] Pierre Lambert, for his part, did not seem to be aware of the enormity of his act, nor very worried about its consequences. On 23 November 1667, he wrote to the Capuchin Ambroise de Preuilly about the arrival of Father Marini: 'I have not seen him and I don't expect to, judging by the way these religious are behaving towards us. If it were not for the welfare of our missions, which may suffer from these misunderstandings, I would not worry about it, as I can do without this Society. Since our maxims are more evangelical than theirs, they have come off second best in everything they have undertaken against us until now. I hope, with God's help, that it will be the same in the future.'[34]

Indeed, on the ground, the affair seemed to settle down quickly enough. In 1675, Louis Laneau tried to reassure the directors, who were greatly distressed by this story. 'As for this pastoral letter, I don't know how much disturbance it caused in France, for in these regions it is as though it has scarcely been heard of and it has been completely

---

33. Letter from Charles Sevin to François Pallu, June 1674. AMEP, volume 5, 303.
34. Letter of Pierre Lambert to Father Ambroise, Capuchin, 23 November 1667. AMEP, volume 876, 539.

hushed up for several years.'[35] The following year, taken to task by his Parisian correspondents, the bishop of Beirut agreed to justify his actions by revealing that a falsified copy of his letter had been used to orchestrate a campaign against him in France. 'Allow me, sir, to touch on this matter of the pastoral letter which has caused such an uproar and which is not to be found in the original which is in the seminary, nor is it in the one written by my hand, of which the Bishop of Heliopolis has drawn up a copy. Moreover, there is nothing that is not true, and even though it is not always good to tell all kinds of truths, the main reasons that led me to do so were that no credence should be given to people who made us out to be heretics, who said that our bulls were false and who taught many things that would lead to the loss of souls.'[36]

False hopes involving the court

If Pierre Lambert seemed to attach so little importance to this new duel, which he no doubt considered to be just another episode in the intermittent war of attrition that pitted him against the Padroado religious, it was perhaps also because events much more important to him were taking place at court. The king's younger brother, who was paralysed, had read Laneau's catechism and had summoned its author to him for an explanation. Like his elder brother, he found the religion of the Westerners attractive, but above all he hoped to be able to obtain healing from their God who was presented as all-powerful. This was an unprecedented phenomenon and an unhoped-for godsend: a Buddhist who, in this particular case, would like to believe in miracles. During the month of November, Louis Laneau was received in audience three or four times by the prince, who eventually invited the bishop in person to Louvo, the king's country residence, where the court had moved for a tiger hunt. On December 1, the prince declared to the missionaries 'that he recognised only one God, the creator of heaven and earth, whom he adored several times a day'[37] and he repeated the same declaration on January 16 at the royal palace in Ayutthaya.

---

35. Letter of Louis Laneau to the directors of the Seminary, Siam, 19 October 1675. AMEP, volume 858, 315.
36. Letter of Pierre Lambert to the Président (?), Siam, 6 September 1676. AMEP, volume 858, 365.
37. Mission Journal, 264–65.

Thus Lambert and Laneau found themselves in direct contact with the ruling class of the kingdom without having made any great effort to achieve this.

> Here is the means which God's goodness was pleased to use to open the door of this Louvre to the French missionaries and to preach the unity of God, the Trinity of the divine persons, the mysteries of the incarnation, the birth, the life, the passion and the death of Jesus Christ on a cross for the redemption of humanity,' the bishop wrote in his diary.[38] He was therefore fully aware of the gap between genuine faith and the rather self-serving profession of faith of the prince and an authentic commitment to the Christian message. And in circumstances where some, less cautious, would have been tempted to claim victory, he showed himself to be extremely careful. 'As the success of this great opening to the Christian religion depends purely on God, only he knows what the outcome will be. However, the missionaries firmly believe that because of their little faith and their little merit, this affair will not succeed.[39]

Meanwhile, at the beginning of January, the seminarian, François Perez, returned from Surat after having escaped from the attempts of the Portuguese to kidnap him. On the other hand they had just arrested Pierre Brindeau in Macau and were plotting dark schemes against the French missionaries throughout Asia. François Perez, brought letters to his bishop from François Pallu and Jacques de Bourges announcing the answers given by Rome to his requests made in 1663. The authorization to ordain native priests who did not know Latin was extended to six years and the Vicar Apostolic had the right to ordain priests from the dioceses of St Thomas of Meliapur, Malacca and Funai. His resignation was not accepted. He was granted an extension of his jurisdiction over Champa and Cambodia, but not over Siam, where his authority could only be exercised over Cochinchinese residents. This decision weakened Pierre Lambert's position even more, since Paul d'Acosta, the ecclesiastical governor of Malacca, had already terminated his powers without warning upon his return to Goa the previous April, thus depriving the Vicar Apostolic of all legal authority. The balance of power within the

---

38. Mission Journal, 264–65.
39. Mission Journal, 264–65.

missionary clergy of Ayutthaya was reversed and Pierre Lambert was forced to adopt a much more discreet attitude.

Restricted in his efforts in Siam, Pierre Lambert then made arrangements to reach Cochinchina as soon as possible where no one could rightly contest his legitimacy. It was there that Antoine Hainques was overburdened with work. On 31 May, while he was still waiting for the boat chartered by the Christians to pick him up, he ordained the first Cochinchinese priest, Joseph Trang, a catechist sent to the seminary by Hainques the previous year, and also François Perez, who left shortly afterwards on a mission to Tenasserim. In April, the Vicar Apostolic had the joy of baptizing the first converted Siamese mandarin and his wife, keeper of the king's wardrobe. But the mandarin, seriously ill, died fifty days after his baptism and his wife was not able to obtain the authorization necessary to have him buried in the cemetery of Saint-Joseph. This was an opportunity for the French to understand that while missionaries and foreigners enjoyed great religious freedom in Ayutthaya, the government did not trifle with Buddhist traditions when it came to Siamese subjects.

Also in April, a ship from Tonkin arrived with two catechists and two seminarians sent by François Deydier. The first two, Benoît Hien and Jean Huê, judged to be worthy 'disciples of the early Church,' were ordained after only two months. In spite of their desire to continue their seminary training, they were sent back to their country on June 19 to assist Deydier whose strength was stretched to the limit. In the meantime, on May 8, a Cochinchinese boat arrived, piloted by five Christian fishermen and their catechist, who were to take the Vicar Apostolic to his mission country. Among the departing boats, Father Marini's boat, with its cargo of sulphur and saltpetre, left the port with great pomp and ceremony, but it was forced to return a month later in a damaged condition.

Lacking authority over the Portuguese religious who were regaining confidence, the bishop also experienced a setback in his relationship with the royal palace. Urged on by his 'first soothsayer', Phra Narai asked the missionaries for a miracle that would convince him of the truth of their religion, that is, the healing of the prince. Pierre Lambert and Louis Laneau felt compelled to accept this ambiguous proposal and spent long hours in prayer before the Blessed Sacrament to ask for this grace. They were without too many illusions however, protesting 'that they did not doubt that they would be heard; their only doubt was about the faith of those who asked for miracles, more for their own interests and to satisfy their curiosity than for any desire for conversion. With God's help, they would soon know this to be true.'[40]

The position of the missionaries was delicate, for they did not want to tempt God by too obvious a bargain, nor to displease the king on whom, in their minds, the conversion of the whole kingdom depended. The outcome of the affair, as recounted in the mission diary, is rather confusing.

> The blood began to circulate in the veins of the legs of this paralytic prince, and the flesh began to grow little by little in the sight of the whole court. When this news was reported to the missionaries, they gave thanks to God and said that this was enough to show the omnipotence of God, that moreover they believed that this situation would remain unchanged until the prince had fulfilled his side of the bargain with God, which was to become a Christian at the first extraordinary sign that appeared. It was then that it became clear that it was a question of a general change of religion throughout the kingdom, and that this matter was of the utmost consequence. This was the reason why everything came to a stop and the reason why the correspondence which was between the court and the missionaries on the subject of religion ceased entirely.[41]

Prudence and reason prevailed on both sides, and in the end the Vicar Apostolic emerged unscathed from a situation that was becoming somewhat difficult on both the spiritual and human levels. No doubt this unfortunate experience would have shown him the dangers involved in resorting to the supernatural, especially with people who were culturally unfamiliar with distinguishing between faith and magic and would have made him more realistic in this area. Henceforth, the relations with the court remained cordial, but were limited to the diplomatic field until the French embassies, after the death of the bishop, revived the plan to convert the king.

Thus, for a few months, the illusory hope of a conversion of the leadership, in the Constantinian style, diverted Pierre Lambert from

---

40. Mission Journal, 279–280.
41. Mission Journal, 279–280.

the straight line he had so scrupulously followed until then, that of the absolute refusal of all human means. Perhaps it was the awareness of this deviation that inspired him to write the *New Views on the Congregation of the Lovers of the Cross*, which radicalized the initial rules defined with Pallu by making them obligatory for all missionaries and by introducing the practice of corporal mortification.

In the course of the summer, the Bishop of Beirut informed the Bishop of Heliopolis, François Pallu, of these modifications. At the same time in Paris, the bishop of Heliopolis experienced some very difficult moments with the directors of the seminary who were fiercely opposed to the project. Never, without a doubt, had the gap been so wide between the missionary conceptions of Pierre Lambert and those of the seminary directors. While the bishop, again limited on all sides in his actions after a few months of optimism, had no other recourse than the interior life of prayer and sacrifice. In France the laborious beginnings of the Company of the Indies, the interests of the king and the increasing pressure of the Jesuits, united as one in the defence of their Society, incited the Parisian leaders to a political realism that they tried to impose on a courageous, loyal and kindly, but very uncomfortable François Pallu.

The return of Jacques de Bourges

In November 1668, Pierre Lambert learned that a group of French missionaries, led by Jacques de Bourges, had arrived in Tenasserim. He then decided to leave Siam, where there was nothing to hold him back, leaving Louis Laneau in charge of Camp Saint-Joseph. On December 11, he boarded the Cochinchinese boat with the new priest Joseph Trang and a local cleric, Luc Ben. His intention was to join the French in Pipeli, to consecrate Jacques de Bourges in place of Ignatius Cotolendi so that he could go to Tonkin or China as a bishop, and then he intended to join Antoine Hainques in Cochinchina. But he had to wait several days before finally seeing the arrival on 5 January 1669 of a group that had been severely tested by a journey of almost three years.

During this journey Nicolas Lambert had died off the coast of Brazil on June 24 in the preceding year. Faithful to his resolution of absolute detachment, the Bishop of Beirut expressed nothing in his writings of the feelings he must have felt on learning of the death of this younger brother, whom he had so insistently called upon to come and join him and whom he did not even know had left France. On the other hand, it is clear that his death affected Jacques de Bourges deeply, and no doubt also the directors of Paris who had been counting on his influence to moderate the radical positions of his elder brother. The sadness of all was further aggravated by the death of François Savary, three days after his arrival, while Guillaume Mahot and Claude Guiart were in very bad shape. Only Gabriel Bouchard, one of the newcomers, was in reasonably good health. Then there was Pierre Brindeau, who joined the group in Massulipatam on foot after having been taken to Goa by the Portuguese and then released after a few weeks for lack of a valid reason for a conviction. He was already a man of experience and seemed to have endured his misadventures well. After three days of prayer and recollection, the missionaries, as was their custom, held a conference. Jacques de Bourges tried to convince his bishop to change his plans and return to Ayutthaya where his presence was considered indispensable to supervise the placement of the new personnel.

On 22 January 1669, having taken stock of the situation, with evident indignation, de Bourges addressed a particularly firm letter to the directors in Paris reproaching them for their attitude toward the Vicar Apostolic.

> You can imagine the joy we felt in finding the Bishop of Beirut here after having been separated from him for so many years. In Massulipatam I had received several packages of letters from France for the Bishop of Beirut. I was surprised to see that after having clarified things as I did when I was in Paris, you continue to treat him in the way you do. I know very well that he has not the slightest inclination to resent or complain about this treatment. That is why I am complaining on his behalf, not about you, because your letters were nothing but fair, but the truth is that there have been others, whom I will not name, who have gone a little too far. In writing things that are either false or based on bad information, they judge a person for whom they should have more respect and they should not be so quick to condemn his conduct. It is difficult for them to understand before writing how prudent his Excellency is, so that they can be excused for their reckless condemnation. You should understand that all these letters will not have an adverse effect on the Bishop of Beirut, because he knows how to make use of crosses from wherever they come, but I beg you to understand the impression they would make if they were intercepted along the way. I hope that after the Bishop of

> Heliopolis has spoken to you and to our friends, and after his Excellency has explained everything to you orally, they will change their attitude and their way of acting.[42]

Thus, five years of separation and very different experiences had not altered the mutual understanding and esteem of these two men with radically opposite temperaments. So, despite his haste to return to his mission, the Vicar Apostolic was of the same mind as his earliest companion. After having conferred priestly ordination on Luc Ben and having sent him with Joseph Trang to Cochinchina, he agreed to return with Jacques de Bourges to Ayutthaya where bad news awaited him. Indeed, a few months after the arrest of Pierre Brindeau in Macau, Antoine Hainques was the victim of a kidnapping attempt in Hué that he narrowly avoided. The procedure used by his adversaries, the Italian Jesuit Fathers Fuciti and Sassi, was particularly abhorrent. After pretending friendship for the Frenchman, they prevented him from meeting the founder, Jean de la Croix, who had welcomed him, alleging that they were following orders from the vicar general of Malacca. Then they tried to lure him into a trap by calling him to visit a sick man who was supposedly dying. Warned by the son of the founder, the missionary managed to escape by boat.

At the same time in Cambodia, Louis Chevreuil was experiencing serious difficulties with a fugitive Capuchin from Tonkin, where he had caused François Deydier quite a few problems, and had joined forces

---

42. Letter from Jacques de Bourges to Michel Gazil, Pipeli, 22 January 1669. AMEP, volume 858, 147–149. Generally speaking, the newcomers, once in the field, took Pierre Lambert's side and made this known to the directors. This is the feeling of Claude Guiart, who mentions 'a letter from M. Mahot, the meaning of which is that the Bishop of Beirut has written nothing but the truth and that they must be careful not to suppress any of his letters to Rome, it being of great importance that Rome should be informed of everything he sends; that he does not find it strange that they have difficulty in Paris in believing these things, since they all had the same difficulty at Massulipatam with regard to M. Brindeau. Some of them, perhaps, had written to have the letters suppressed, because none of them could believe him because of their lack of experience. But they all changed their minds when they had first-hand knowledge of such things. 'A copy of a complaint in the name of the Jesuits was sent to the Bishop of Beirut at the end of June, signed by Father P. Marini, and a copy of another less extensive complaint which he had sent in the month of April. As this Father sent this complaint to Rome, the Bishop of Beirut sent his reply and a complaint from M. Hainques whom the Jesuits wanted to remove from Cochinchina.' Letter from M Guiart to the directors, 18 November 1669. AMEP, volume 857, 50–51.

with the Jesuit Charles Delia Rocca to harass him. Finally, in April, Pierre Lambert received at Saint-Joseph's a copy of a manifesto written against him to Propaganda by Father Marini. This text denounced the 'invasion' by the French missionaries of the missions of Cambodia, Cochinchina and Tonkin which were founded by the fathers of the Society of Jesus. From Goa to Macao, Jesuits and Portuguese, united in a merciless struggle against the French missionaries, had only one watchword: all foreign clerics circulating without the authorization of the King of Portugal or the Viceroy of India were to be arrested and handed over to the Goanese authorities.

It was then that a patache flying the French flag arrived in the port of Ayutthaya. It belonged to a merchant from Massulipatam, M Junet, who had already rendered great service to the missionaries. This ship was returning from Manila and had to take refuge in Siam where its arrival provoked the anger and jealousy of the Dutch and Portuguese. To avoid reprisals, Pierre Lambert negotiated with the Siamese authorities to allow him to anchor in front of Camp Saint-Joseph, an exceptional privilege for a foreign ship because of the proximity of the royal palace. In exchange for this service, the merchant felt obliged to give in to the proposals of the missionaries who saw this as a unique opportunity to travel to Tonkin without having to avail themselves of foreign ships whose quality was unknown to them. 'Moved partly by the hope of profit and partly by his desire to serve the mission,'[43] Captain Junet agreed to attempt a commercial expedition to Tonkin and to take on board Pierre Lambert, who would act as chaplain, as well as Jacques de Bourges and Gabriel Bouchard, who would pose as employees. The Vicar Apostolic's plan was to consecrate Jacques de Bourges as bishop so that, in the company of Gabriel Bouchard, he could enter China, with all the powers of the late Bishop Cotolendi. Meanwhile, Pierre Lambert would go to support François Deydier in Tonkin. As for Guillaume Mahot and Claude Guiart, still not fully recovered from their trip, they would stay with Louis Laneau and see to the smooth running of the house. On 18 July 1669, Pierre Lambert and his two companions embarked on the first French merchant ship bound for Tonkin. Unwillingly, and although his intentions were pure, the Bishop of Beirut entered personally into the game of national economic interests. The Jesuits did not fail to draw compelling arguments from this action, and to use them against him.

---

43. Mission Journal, 205.

Chapter 6
Pastoral visits to Vietnam

François Deydier in Tonkin

When Captain Junet's ship arrived in sight of the Red River estuary on 30 August 1669,[1] after a forced and eventful stopover at the island of Hainan, it was met by François Deydier who had been leading the Tonkinese Christian community alone for three years. He had accompanied Pierre Lambert from France in 1660 and shared the pastoral concerns of his bishop whose influence still remains today in the organization of the Church in this country. Born into a noble family of Toulon, he was destined for a career in the army and the navy, but while finishing his studies in philosophy, he chose the ecclesiastical state after the death of his parents. François Deydier was the holder of a doctorate in theology, a man who spoke Portuguese and Vietnamese perfectly, and who distinguished himself by his liveliness and strength, both intellectual and physical.

This future Vicar Apostolic with the appearance of a musketeer, of whom the archives of the Foreign Missions have preserved a vivid portrait, was scarcely able to conceal beneath a colourful and somewhat 'square' temperament a very great emotional sensitivity, a paternal and merciful heart in spite of the strictness of his decisions, an ardent faith, an untiring devotion, a spirit of scrupulous obedience and a total abandonment to the divine will.

The account he gives of his first steps on Tonkinese soil is quite picturesque. In the first village where he disembarked, dressed as a sailor and having cut his beard, he found himself surrounded by a crowd of curious people. 'They made many shameless requests of

---

1. The Red River, the second longest river in Vietnam, flows into the Gulf of Tonkin.

me, and invited me to engage in unchaste acts, but I rejected their invitations. I said to some that I had my wife in the royal city, that she was so pretty that I needed no one else, that she was greatly praised, and that it was therefore not appropriate to defile myself with immoral women. To others I said that such actions were forbidden by the ordinances of my king; to others that I feared I might contract an incurable disease, by which I meant 'sin.' These poor people were satisfied with these reasons, but the sailors, who had the ladies every night on the ship, were not so reasonable and waged a much more cruel war; I could not defend myself from them in any other way than by abandoning my customary friendliness and resisting them strongly, so that in the end they believed that I was too honest a man to wish to engage in any way with these immoral women."[2]

This missionary from Toulon arrived at a mission in Tonkin, greatly influenced by the action of its founder, Alexandre de Rhodes, who had met with tremendous success during the three years he stayed there, from the time of his arrival from Cochinchina in March 1627 until his final banishment in May 1630. Very popular among the working classes of the port of Than Long (ancient Hanoi) where he disembarked from a Portuguese trading ship and where his eloquence as an orator resulted in a huge number of conversions, the Jesuit also knew how to curry favour with the Chua, Trinh-Trang, who, charmed by his company, had a splendid mansion built for him near his palace. This proximity to the court enabled him to obtain many conversions, but soon the jealousy of the concubines, eunuchs and mandarins as well as the resumption of hostilities between Tonkin and Cochinchina, brought about his disgrace and exile.

Before his departure, Alexandre de Rhodes had time to organize this nascent Christian community through the formation, as in Cochinchina, of a team of catechists who were to become the true backbone of the Church of Vietnam in those times of sporadic persecution. In order to ensure the continuation of their work, he made them promise not to marry, not to possess personal wealth and to obey their appointed superior until the arrival of new missionaries. His successors kept this original organization while interpreting it in their own way. While the first catechists insisted on formation

---

2. Journal of M Deydier. AMEP, volume 666, 1 ff, quoted in A Launay, *Histoire de la mission du Tonkin, Documents historiques*, 1658–1717, t. I, 22.

and dedication to pastoral work, those who followed stressed the importance of the hierarchical framework in order to keep the catechists in strict dependence on the Fathers of the Society of Jesus who all possessed an unshakeable conviction that they were the only legal owners of this very promising mission. A direct consequence of this split between the general interests of the Church and the particular interests of the Society of Jesus, was the refusal by the Jesuits of any episcopal jurisdiction. This conviction was reflected in the welcome given by the Tonkinese Christians to the French whose mission was authorized by Rome, the first of the French being François Deydier.

Thus Raphaël de Rhodes, a Cochinchinese 'adopted' in the past by Alexandre de Rhodes and who occupied the function of interpreter at the Dutch trading post of Than Long, was prepared to use all his influence and his fortune in the service of the newcomer, François Deydier. On the other hand, the other dominant personality of the Christian community, the Japanese Paul de Abada, who was well regarded at court because he had offered his daughter as a concubine to the Chua, refused to recognize him on the grounds that he had not been given any authority by the Jesuits.

It took several weeks for François Deydier to gain acceptance by the majority of the catechists and to re-establish a unified discipline in this very fervent Christian community, which was disorganized by persecutions and the all too frequent turnover of an unstable missionary staff whose last members had to leave the country in 1662. In spite of these initial predictable difficulties, the missionary succeeded in gathering all the catechists for a synod that was held between October 11 and 15 at Than Long in the boat that Raphael de Rhodes had given to the young catechists so that they could earn a living by engaging in small business. Deydier chose to keep the Jesuits' administrative staff, directing them towards a priority goal, the formation of local priests. 'I cannot refrain from telling you at this time,' wrote François Deydier to his bishop François Pallu, 'about the complaint that the King of Tonkin has often made, that the other nations use Tonkinese as priests for their gods, each according to its own religion, and that it is only the Portuguese who are unwilling to elevate them to the same status as their own.'[3]

---

3. Letter from François Deydier to François Pallu, 4 April 1667, quoted in Launay, *Relation de la Mission du voyage du Tonkin* (Paris: Pierre Le Petit, 1674), 135–136.

He therefore decided to keep with him in Than Long the two oldest and most experienced catechists, Jean Huê and Benoît Hien, in order to give them an initial formation before sending them to Ayutthaya; Pierre Lambert ordained them priests in 1668. The other old catechists were sent to the provinces, each assisted by a young man capable of helping him fulfil his duties. As for those who, because of their age and competence, were able to learn Latin, they too stayed with Deydier and formed the first floating seminary of Vietnam in their boat. Soon there were fifteen students receiving literacy instruction, a necessary prerequisite for any theological training. 'One thing that surprised me,' the missionary remarked, 'was that no one knew how to speak Portuguese, nor how to use our alphabet; they told me that the Jesuit Fathers forbade it.'[4]

Unlike the Jesuits and in accordance with the model established by Pierre Lambert at the seminary of Ayutthaya, François Deydier was anxious to maintain strict equality among all and to make no difference between himself and those whom he considered to be future confreres. He abolished the privileges of the old catechists and convinced each one to 'lead a community life, and more importantly an apostolic life'. 'We ate together', he wrote in his diary, 'each one read and served in turn at the table; I did not exempt myself from this any more than did the youngest of my seminarians.'[5] To further strengthen the system of community material property, he gave his personal money to Raphael of Rhodes who became, as it were, the general bursar of the mission. These rules of conduct having been fixed by mutual consent, each one set about his work with renewed zeal.

François Deydier, who alternated between staying at Raphaël's house and in the seminary boat, divided his time between the clandestine administration of the sacraments, journeys into the provinces, and the formation of future priests. Periodically, he had to face new outbreaks of persecution, the most serious of which was caused, in the spring of 1668, by the revolt in the province of the

---

4. Journal of M Deydier, 28. François Deydier, who interpreted this ban of the Jesuits as a deliberate desire to keep the Tonkinese catechists in a state of dependence, adopted a diametrically opposed attitude and demanded total transparency with regard to the Tonkinese. Thus, when in 1669 the Jesuits landed again in Tonkin, he asked them to 'write in Tonkinese words, albeit with our characters, so that my dear confreres Benedict and John with all the former catechists will be witnesses of all that happens between us.' Journal of M Deydier, 60.
5. Journal of M Deydier, 26.

Levant of a faction led by Christians whose services he had used during one of his journeys. Thanks to the discreet intervention of high-ranking Christians, the situation calmed down politically, and by the end of 1668 the king seemed to have adopted a kind of benevolent indifference towards religion. François Deydier finally began to hope for a brighter future when an event occurred which not only revived the persecution, but also tore apart the Church in Tonkin for many years.

The arrival of Pierre Lambert

On April 19, a ship arrived from Macau with two 'official' Jesuits on board, Fathers Philippe Fieschi and Balthasar da Rocha, who brought gifts to the king in the hope of being admitted to Tonkin again. But it also carried two 'clandestine' Jesuits, an Italian father, Dominic Fuciti, and a Tonkinese brother, Ignace Martin, who disembarked discreetly, wearing secular dress in order to remain anonymous in the country in case their confreres' approach did not succeed. This precaution was wise, for, as Deydier recounts, 'as soon as the king was informed that these religious had dared to return to his kingdom in spite of the prohibitions he had issued against them, he became very angry and ordered these religious to withdraw. He had them locked up in a house, rejected all their gifts, burned all their images, medals and other objects of piety that they had brought, and ordered the renewal of the edicts against the religion of the Christians, who were known in this country almost exclusively by the name of Portuguese. Five or six hundred churches were torn down.'[6] Three edicts of persecution

---

6. News written from Tonkin on 9 October 1669 by M. Deydier, priest and vicar general of the Bishop of Heliopolis. AMEP, volume 653, 41–45. For the French, this persecution was not so much due to an aversion to Christianity on the part of the authorities as to the behaviour of the Jesuits: 'The rank that these religious want to hold everywhere; the extreme respect that they demand from the Christians who accompany them in crowds when they walk through the streets, the contests in their house by day and by night, the quantity of gifts that they receive from the faithful which made the king say that the Christians had two taxes to pay, his own and that of the Jesuits; their political and suspicious intrigues, their great trade which gave them the opportunity to make several enemies, the promises that they made to the king which they did not fulfil, the bad reputation of the Portuguese nation which the king regarded as a deceitful and wicked nation: these were the reasons for banishing them from this kingdom. Mission Journal, 331.

were promulgated on May 13, June 24 and 29. Fathers Rocha and Fieschi, having been released, were sent away on the boat to Macau, but were soon forced by a storm to return to Phô-hiên to wait for a lull in the storm.

It was in these critical circumstances that Captain Junet's ship arrived, whose French flag, unknown in this part of the world, initially provoked the mistrust of the Tonkinese authorities. An official message written in Portuguese was sent to the king by a mandarin intermediary. Captain Junet presented himself as a delegate of the French East India Company wishing to establish himself in the country. When questioned about the number of priests on his ship, he presented Pierre Lambert as his chaplain, which justified the presence of religious objects on board, while Jacques de Bourges and Gabriel Bouchard, dressed as sailors, blended in with the crew. Meanwhile, thanks to a Christian marine pilot, François Deydier was able to inform his bishop of the religious situation.

The king showed himself at once quite well disposed towards these new arrivals but the Dutch, who had supported Deydier until then, turned against him. Fearing commercial competition, they denounced the French stratagem, and only the skilful intervention of Deydier's protectors at court persuaded the Chua (Chua: 'prince' or 'governor') that the French nation was far more powerful than that of the Dutch and that it was therefore in his interests to welcome the new arrivals. As a result, Captain Junet, his officers, and no doubt his chaplain as well, found themselves invited to several lavish banquets as well as entertainment, military exercises and elephant fights. To avoid drawing attention to himself, Pierre Lambert refrained from visiting the Christians personally, but he had the catechists warn them of his arrival, and he administered confirmation to those who, taking advantage of the commotion at the port, managed to climb aboard his ship without being noticed. Finally, the king offered the French a piece of land to establish a trading post in Phô-hiên since, following the unwelcome arrival of the ship carrying the Jesuits, foreign ships were no longer allowed to go to Than Long.

Unfortunately, this favourable official reception upset the plans of the Vicar Apostolic, whose initial intention was to consecrate Jacques de Bourges as a bishop and send him to China with Gabriel Bouchard. However, access to the Middle Kingdom, i. e. China, was still impossible, and Propaganda only authorized the consecration of a new bishop on condition that he go immediately to his mission. In addition, François Deydier was too exhausted to continue to face alone the needs of the Christian community of Tonkin, disorganized by the new persecution. Finally, the cover offered by a French commercial establishment would allow the missionaries to enjoy a certain freedom of movement and enable them to carry out their work in secret and in relative security.

This was moreover, the solution that François Deydier, a man of considerable experience, had recommended for a long time. It was therefore decided that Jacques de Bourges would remain in Tonkin as manager of an alleged trading post of the East India Company, into which he would integrate François Deydier. This unsatisfactory solution must have obviously upset Pierre Lambert, whose principles of non-interference of clerics in commercial affairs it rather undermined. But it was the only possible way forward, and it was only a façade, since it was well understood that the missionaries would never trade by themselves but would be satisfied to prepare for the arrival of a hypothetical French ship which they would await for a very long time.

Although an agreement was reached with the Tonkinese authorities, relations with the Jesuits remained very tense. The clandestine presence of Dominique Fuciti promised to make life difficult for the French. The Italian Jesuit was indeed one of the most bitter opponents of the presence of Propaganda missionaries in Vietnam; he had strongly opposed Chevreuil in Cochinchina a few years earlier. While Pierre Lambert was out of action due to a new illness, Father Fuciti worked to rally the Christians who longed for the Jesuits whom Deydier's strictness had repelled. He encouraged rumours insinuating that 'the bishop who had recently come to this kingdom was a fugitive from France because of his crimes; he had no power, and there was reason to doubt whether the priests ordained by him had the power to absolve.'[7]

To try to stop the schism that was taking shape, Pierre Lambert instructed Deydier to invite Father Fuciti and the main leaders of the Tonkinese Christian community to a 'public' (although clandestine) conference during which the missionary would show the Pope's writs providing evidence of the legitimacy of the French. This provoked

---

7. Mission Journal, 340.

the fury of his rival. Sometime later, the Jesuit refused Deydier's proposal to let him have the exclusive administration of one or two provinces, claiming that he had received the authority of vicar general over the whole country from the bishop of Macau. Pierre Lambert answered these claims with detailed legal argumentation which did not change Father Fuciti in the least. For fifteen years, he maintained his opposition in spite of warnings from Rome. It was not until 1684 that he left the country to continue his struggle against the French jurisdiction from Siam.

As for his two colleagues, Rocha and Fieschi, they came to pay the French a visit which, although courteous enough, only made the disagreements clearer. When questioned about the reasons for their refusal to recognize the Vicars Apostolic, they simply invoked their vow of obedience *perinde ac cadaver* to their superiors, which dispensed them from any such personal recognition. From then on, any negotiations became impossible and a division developed. This state of affairs, so tragic and scandalous, undermined the church in Tonkin until the end of the century.

Ordinations and synod

These painful incidents did not prevent Pierre Lambert and his companions from engaging in activities of a more constructive nature. In January 1670, the bishop summoned the candidates preselected and formed by François Deydier to Than Long to prepare them for the priesthood. At the end of a retreat, he ordained as priests four catechists of the first rank and three of the second: Martin Mat, 68 years old; Antoine Qué, 56; Philippe Nhan, 52; Simon Kien, 60; Jacques Chieu, 46; Leon Tru, 46; and Vite Tri, 30, the youngest of the group, who was granted an exemption from the age requirement due to his exceptional skills.

The selection criteria were indeed quite strict and, despite the urgency of the needs, the Vicar Apostolic did not give in to the temptation to prefer quantity to quality. A certain maturity was required of the postulants, and above all they had to show by their conduct, solidly established moral virtues.

If Pierre Lambert was so demanding of the local priests, it was because he did not consider that they should be relegated to a secondary role, as mere substitutes for the French missionaries. On the contrary, the priestly dignity conferred by ordination being the same for all, he entrusted them with equal responsibilities, taking into account only the time needed for some of them to adapt, especially with regard to the use of Latin and the learning of the liturgical formulas, which were more difficult for some than for others.

On February 14, just before his departure, he gathered his three missionaries and the nine Tonkinese priests at Dinh Hien to hold the first synod of the church of Tonkin during which the rules of 'ordinary' operation were defined. The country was divided into nine districts, each of which was administered by a native priest residing in a fixed parish, assisted by a senior catechist. Each community would be directed by a person assigned to organize the worship, to see to the good conduct of the Christians and report to the administrator, who would in turn report to the Vicar Apostolic or to the missionaries who represented him. All goods would be pooled in a central fund at the mission headquarters. Each province, however, would have its own budget for alms, with profits and deficits being absorbed by the central fund at the end of each year. The financial transactions would be entrusted to one or two receivers in each province, subject to the control of the administrator, while Raphael de Rhodes was confirmed in his function as general treasurer.

The main task of the vicar general and the missionaries would be the formation of seminarians, whom the local priests were to recruit from among the children whose religious education they would provide with great care. All priests were required to maintain a uniformity of conduct compatible with the dignity of their state. They should not engage directly or indirectly in commerce under pain of excommunication. They should see to the edification and good behaviour of their flock without tolerating abuses or particular arrangements introduced by the Jesuits, especially in the administration of the sacraments. As for the religious, they could not claim any special power without the authorization of the Vicars Apostolic. In this regard, article 32 stipulated that 'in prayers to God, and especially in the holy sacrifice of the Mass, a spirit of submission will be asked of God for the Jesuits of these districts who do not want to recognize the Vicars Apostolic; thus, with this great obstacle removed, work can be carried on advantageously for the conversion of souls.'[8]

---

8. Launay, *Histoire Tonkin*, 99.

Disputes between Christians were to be settled by the priest administrator with the possibility of an appeal to the bishop or his missionaries in serious matters, or in matters of doctrine, sacraments and cases of conscience. The relics of Saint Julian and Saint Mellitus, brought from Rome by Pierre Lambert, would be exhibited in the churches of the Resurrection and the Nativity of Than Long, and the choice of Saint Joseph, chosen as patron of the kingdom by Alexandre de Rhodes, was confirmed.

In this first organisational scheme of the Church of Tonkin, the personal touch of the great ecclesiastical administrator, the Bishop of Beirut was clearly recognizable. But no more than in Rouen some fifteen years earlier, was it a question of a creation *ex nihilo*, or of disregarding the past. The Vicar Apostolic relied here on the remarkable preparatory work accomplished by François Deydier with the help of the catechists who were themselves trained by Alexandre de Rhodes and his successors. And as in Rouen, Pierre Lambert catalysed energies and skills into a dynamic synthesis whose three pillars—service of neighbour, spirit of prayer, asceticism—integrated the most human and material necessities with the highest spiritual demands.

The Lovers of the Cross

It is on these three pillars that rested one of his most original and fruitful creations, the congregation of the Lovers of the Cross, fruit of the meeting between the high ideal of religious life that he had carried within him for years and a group of Tonkinese women aspiring to a radical commitment of which no one until then had been able to give them a model.

When he arrived in Tonkin, Pierre Lambert had already been practising the ascetic rule of the Lovers of the Cross for five years. Several of his companions, including François Deydier, had followed his example and the Vicar Apostolic wished that this way of life should be integrated into the discipline of life of the local priests, and even extended, at least in spirit, to the catechists and to the most highly motivated Christians, as testified by Article 21 of the synod: 'The administrators, catechists and attendants will exhort the faithful to follow the narrow way, leading them to devote themselves to mental prayer, at least on the holy days of obligation, and especially to meditate on that day on the passion and death of Our Lord Jesus Christ. They will propose to those judged suitable that they should become members of the Congregation of the Lovers of the Cross, and live according to the regulations that have been drawn up."[9] Deydier himself, in full agreement with the thought of his bishop, insisted strongly in his teaching and preaching on the importance of prayer, and the first two Tonkinese priests, Jean Huê and Benoît Hien, voluntarily embraced perpetual fasting. Among the catechists, the oldest remembered the example of Alexandre de Rhodes whose rigour, modelled on the discipline of the Marian congregations, was similar to that of the Bishop of Beirut.

When, at the end of 1669 or at the beginning of 1670, François Deydier presented Pierre Lambert with the request of some thirty women, girls and widows already accustomed to a very austere existence, who asked for a rule to live in common, the latter saw in them a providential sign, the embryo of the feminine branch of the great institute that he always had in mind. He wrote to them at once:

> Since my arrival in this kingdom, one of my principal occupations has been to inform myself of the state of this church. In the account given to me, I learned with great joy that you are consecrated to God by a special vow; as this commitment is an obvious mark of God's special mercy on you, it is only right that you should be more grateful to him than those on whom he has not bestowed such a great grace. It is with this thought in mind that I intend to propose to you a way of life which seems to me will result in the greater glory of God. I am able to relate this to you with all the more confidence, since I can assure you that before knowing you or ever having heard of you, I was asked a long time ago to draw up a rule for the benefit of some souls who are loved in an extraordinary way by God.[10]

In the goals he set for the first institute of local nuns in Asia, Pierre Lambert applied the most advanced spiritual intuitions of his time and went beyond them by indissolubly uniting contemplative life, missionary vocation and charitable action, the three main axes

---

9. Launay, *Histoire Tonkin*, 97.
10. Launay, *Histoire Tonkin*. Circular letter to those who have taken a vow of chastity and who have lived in common for several years, 101–102.

of European Catholic progressive thinking of the 15th and 16th centuries. At the same time he adapted them to the particular conditions of the Church in Vietnam (clandestinity, persecution, absence of ecclesial structures), with the spirituality of the cross as their distinctive characteristic. 'The end of this institute will be to make a special practice of meditating daily on the sufferings of Jesus Christ as the most profitable means of coming to know and love him.'[11] In accordance with this spirituality, the contemplative and ascetic life was a priority and had to precede any missionary action. 'The first task of those who embrace it will be to unite their tears, their prayers and their penances continually to the merits of the Saviour of the world, to ask God for the conversion of the unbelievers who are in the three apostolic vicariates and especially those of Tonkin.'[12]

But the Bishop of Beirut was all too aware of the immense needs of the Church in Vietnam to confine his daughters to a purely contemplative life. On the contrary, he would bring them out of the secluded life they had led until then to put them at the service of their neighbours. With his extensive experience in charitable organizations, he knew how to identify the priorities, i.e. the needs of the weakest and most neglected. He noticed that in Vietnamese society, women, and in particular poor women, had many handicaps (multiple pregnancies, total submission to men and mothers-in-law, hardships that were the direct consequences of famines and civil wars) and that it was only other women who could help them. It was therefore towards them that he directed the service of the Lovers of the Cross.

In the seventeenth century, in France, this idea had been popularized by St Vincent de Paul, but in the Asian social context, it was a real revolution. Another surprising rule, but very much in line with his action in Rouen, was that the tasks of training and education were given priority over the care of the sick. The first charitable occupation of the Lovers of the Cross was to 'instruct young girls, both Christian and pagan, in matters that people of their sex should know; that if, because of the pressing matters in which religion finds itself, this cannot be accomplished, they will remember that when they are able to do so, it must be one of their principal occupations.'[13]

---

11. Launay, *Histoire Tonkin*, 102.
12. Launay, *Histoire Tonkin*, 102.
13. Launay, *Histoire Tonkin*, 102.

Once again, this text shows the evangelical universalism of Pierre Lambert's thinking and his remarkable sense of the dignity of persons. He had long understood that social or simply human progress was impossible without a minimum of knowledge and education. He also knew that mothers could not bring up their children properly if they were kept in a state of ignorance that nourished servitude and misery. In this necessary promotion of the female condition, the Vicar Apostolic made no distinction between pagan and Christian women, because education should not be a reward or a privilege granted to those who are converted; it is a fundamental right of the human person. In the same way, he had asked his missionaries in Siam to give priority to prisoners held in degrading conditions.

For him, the first missionary act consisted in concretely manifesting the solicitude and love of God for all people, 'without distinction of sex or condition,' while giving priority to the most disadvantaged. Neither were Christians and pagans distinguished in the second task assigned to the Lovers of the Cross, 'the care of sick women and girls, whether Christian or infidel, in order to use this work to deal with them in matters of their salvation and conversion'.[14] Here, the apostolic concern for conversion was more clearly expressed, and it was not by chance: it is when people are weakened by illness, distressed by the prospect of death, that they are most receptive to the message of salvation and eternal life. It is also at this time that the need for conversion, and therefore for baptism, is most urgent. This was also what motivated the third task of the nuns, a common one, the baptism of children in danger of death. Finally, the last task proposed for the nuns 'will be that they should do everything possible to rescue women and dissolute girls from their immoral lives,'[15] one of the common preoccupations of the French reformers of that time.

The formulation of the rules of the Lovers of the Cross revealed clearly the thought of their founder. Compared to those of the European institutes of the same period, they were very few in number. Pierre Lambert knew that in a nascent Church condemned to partial or total clandestinity, he could not overload the nuns with detailed obligations. He had to allow them the opportunity to adapt to circumstances and to evolve. The conditions of admission were

---

14. Launay. *Histoire Tonkin*, 103.
15. Launay, *Histoire Tonkin*, 103.

classic: the three vows, preceded by two years of probation. The time of prayer was concentrated in the morning, after rising at four o'clock. It included, in addition to vocal prayers, an hour of meditation on the Passion, but no Mass because of the lack of priests. On the other hand, Pierre Lambert did not exempt women from the discipline, while praying the Miserere and the Respice.[16] In the evening, they should spend a quarter of an hour on the examen and the same amount of time on vocal prayer. The rosary and half an hour of spiritual reading would occupy the time of the Sunday rest.

This schedule freed the Lovers of the Cross to be totally available during the day for the service of their neighbour, which also required great freedom of movement. Dispensed from the cloister, dressed in secular clothes, they could go out in pairs, with the permission of the superior. Their moments of freedom were devoted to manual work to ensure the material needs of the community were taken care of. These needs were to be reduced to a minimum. Pierre Lambert's egalitarian attitude towards women led him to believe that they were as resilient as men, and therefore there was no need to relax the diet he had set for them: two meals a day, perpetual abstinence from meat (except at Christmas, Easter and Pentecost), and fasting on Fridays.

Charged with a specific missionary task in the same way as their confrere priests, the Lovers of the Cross were, like them, subject to the authority of the bishop or his representative regarding both temporal and spiritual matters. Circumstances also required that the communities should be small, separate and mobile: no more than ten 'at the present time'. Pierre Lambert did not want to block a later evolution, when conditions were more favourable. Finally, he recommended a measure that had already been adopted by Jean Eudes in his refuge in Caen: repentant women could be received into the institute on an equal footing with the others, but to avoid corruption of others by possible relapses, they would live separately under the authority of superiors 'who have never failed'. The former director of

---

16. The discipline is a small scourge or whip, used by some members of Christian denominations as a form of penance. The capuchins pray the Miserere and the De Profundis during this flagellation. The *Miserere* is a penitential psalm, Psalm 51, in which there is an acknowledgment of sin and a petition for mercy. The saying, *Respice finem*, invites people to reflect on their end and act with appropriate caution.

the general hospital in Rouen had not forgotten the trouble caused by some women who were not genuinely repentant.

In writing such rules, Lambert showed great confidence in the capacity for endurance and self-denial of the first Tonkinese nuns. He demanded of them the ascetic austerity of the Carmelites, and the work of charitable women like that of the Daughters of Charity, all of this undertaken in the precarious situation of missionary life. Such conditions could be considered excessive and discouraging for postulants, but the opposite was true. Communities multiplied in Tonkin and soon in Cochinchina. Later, Pierre Lambert also established Lovers of the Cross in Siam, among Vietnamese immigrants.

The first two Lovers of the Cross, Agnes and Paula, pronounced their vows on Ash Wednesday 1670 in the presence of the Vicar Apostolic who had to leave Tonkin the same day. A week later, when his ship was unable to move for lack of wind at the bar of Tonkin, he reminded them in writing of the essentials of their vocation.

> I am writing these words to remind you that you are no longer your own, and that you belong to Jesus Christ, to whom you have given yourselves totally, in order to devote yourselves to know and love him alone by meditating on and imitating his life and by applying yourselves to the obligations of your institute. I exhort you with all my heart to be faithful to the observance of your rule, knowing full well the great benefits you will receive by doing so and the benefits you will bring to the whole Church.
>
> I also recommend that you take very special care of your novices, whom you should consider as sacred repositories that God has placed in your hands. Remember to teach them frequently the principal end of your institute which is to continue the sufferings of Jesus Christ in their lives and to ask him every day, by your prayers, your tears, your labours, your sacrifices, for the conversion of unbelievers and unfaithful Christians. Moreover, it is extremely important to make it your practice to do all things in the place of Jesus Christ who, desiring to undertake certain works himself and being unable to do so, makes use of certain chosen people whom he fills with his spirit. In this way he continues his life's journey and sacrifice until the end of time. You see by this, my sisters, the

nobility of your vocation and that you have died to the world, that is to say, to the senses, to nature and to human reason, in order to live henceforth only by the maxims, the practices and the life of Jesus Christ. Reflect well on this, I beg you, and do not forget me before God.[17]

At the end of the year 1670, a report from Jacques de Bourges stated that the original community had split in two to avoid being discovered, and that a third group had formed in another village under the leadership of a widow named Line. Moreover, the missionaries had received a number of requests which they had to reject in order to avoid establishing overly conspicuous groups that might stir up persecution.

Tensions in Ayutthaya

Having established this fruitful and promising foundation, Pierre Lambert returned to Ayutthaya in April 1670. During his absence, the situation had remained calm. Louis Laneau, more attached than ever to the Siamese world, continued his apostolate in the capital and its surroundings. Aware no doubt of the obstacle constituted by the politico-religious system of Theravada Buddhism, he chose, in an evangelical spirit, to 'begin this mission to the most abandoned', the outcasts of Siamese society, in particular 'the prisoners who are so poorly nourished and so harshly treated in this kingdom that they cannot live long in their misery'.[18] Laneau thus baptized about forty adults and, encouraged by these results, sent François Perez on a mission to the Tenasserim region.[19]

With the authority of pro-vicar conferred upon him by Pierre Lambert before his departure, Laneau also asked Claude Guiart, the designated procurator of the mission, to study the Siamese language, although Guiart did not share the enthusiasm of his superior for the conversion of the local people. He would have preferred to follow the example of his companion Guillaume Mahot, who learned Vietnamese from the Cochinchinese of Ayutthaya, in order to enter

---

17. Letter from Pierre Lambert to Sisters Agnès and Paula, 26 February 1670, in Launay, *Histoire Tonkin*, 104–105.
18. Mission Journal, 375–376.
19. The Tenasserim region is the narrow southern part of Myanmar (Burma).

their country as soon as possible. There was a certain amount of uncertainty in Camp Saint-Joseph where the absence of the bishop had created a great void.

Louis Laneau, whose spiritual qualities were undeniable, did not have the charisma of a leader, and with him in charge, the two newcomers had difficulty in finding their feet. For the first time, among the missionaries in the field, a division appeared that would last for centuries between the minority supporters of the evangelization of Siam and those who aspired above all to join the more successful and prestigious missions in Vietnam and China. Upon his return, Pierre Lambert took control of the situation and supported Laneau's initiatives all the more firmly since events had made him certain that entry into China would remain impossible for a long time. No doubt he also felt a special sympathy for this last member of the pioneer group whose love of contemplation and tireless evangelical dedication he shared, this gentle and peaceful man who remained his closest and most faithful disciple until his death and who would then receive his spiritual inheritance. He is 'one of the most noble souls I know', he confided to the directors.[20]

In October, Pierre Lambert wrote for the first time to Pope Clement IX, newly elected in June 1667, to inform him of the latest events and to give him a detailed account of the situation in Tonkin. Since he had become aware that one of the greatest obstacles to the ordination of local priests, especially from a certain age, was their difficulty in learning Latin, he asked that the brief granted to the Jesuits in China by Paul V in 1615 authorising Chinese priests promoted to the priesthood to celebrate Mass in the Mandarin language be granted to the Vicars Apostolic. He also wrote a terse and rather cold letter to the directors of the seminary, reduced to strict material considerations. Even if they continued to work together for the advancement of the missions, the moral rupture was now complete between the Parisian leaders and the Vicar Apostolic who was deeply wounded, in spite of his protestations of indifference, by their incomprehension and especially by their obstinate refusal to take his advice into account so as not to displease the Jesuits.

---

20. Letter from Pierre Lambert to the directors of the seminary, 12 October 1670. AMEP, volume 858, 185.

On November 5, a delegate from the chapter of Goa, Nicolas da Motta, arrived at Camp Saint-Joseph. He brought to Pierre Lambert an ordinance of this chapter, written on 20 August 1669, apparently at the instigation of the religious of Ayutthaya, which required him to present his patents and bulls of appointment within ten days, under penalty of excommunication and a fine of 200 silver coins. In order to avoid aggravating a local situation that was still as tense as it had been since the clashes of 1666, the Bishop of Beirut, who had resisted all such pressure until then, complied. He produced the requested documents, accompanied by a formal letter of protest. Nicolas da Motta only noted the authenticity of the pontifical documents, which did not imply their validity in the eyes of the Portuguese since they were not ratified by Lisbon. He left Ayutthaya with the outcome a draw, and as was his custom, Pierre Lambert sent a copy of the file to Rome.

Four very suspicious deaths

Shortly afterwards, the Vicar Apostolic fell seriously ill again. The king sent to him his best Chinese doctor, who succeeded in curing him. He had just begun his convalescence when the sinister news arrived in Ayutthaya of the sudden disappearance of Antoine Hainques and Pierre Brindeau, who had died within a month of each other in December 1670 and January 1671. Although the mission diary did not mention it, the circumstances of these deaths were more than suspicious. Bénigne Vachet reported that the two missionaries, who enjoyed excellent health and a great reputation for holiness, 'fell ill almost on the same day, only five leagues apart, and were unable to help each other. The two men, as well as the Christians, believed that they had been poisoned, and that the culprit was a miserable servant of Jean de la Croix who fled after he had carried out this foul deed. There was no doubt about it after their deaths, for all the indications of poison appeared on their bodies. Men may be mistaken, but God alone knows the truth.'[21]

This suspicion was confirmed the following year by Claude Guiart who, brought to Cochinchina by Pierre Lambert himself in order to replace the priests who had passed away, collected corroborating evidence where they had lived.

---

21. Bénigne Vachet, *Vie de Pierre Brindeau*. AMEP, volume 733, 219–230.

> I will repeat what has already been said, without having regard for the suspicions of several people, that there was evil at work in the sudden deaths of Fathers Hainques and Brindeau. We know that some people who were opposed to the deceased and who reviled the Cochinchinese priests boasted that they had found a way to break the two sticks (that is how they referred to our two dear missionaries) which were the supports of the two Cochinchinese priests, but that afterwards they had gone to Siam to deal with a stronger cane which was not easy to bend, but that the other sticks had been broken easily; that Joseph and Lucas (this is how they speak of the two Cochinchinese priests out of contempt without any title of honour) would be trodden on and pounded like mortar.[22]

Later, in 1673, the testimony of an English ship's captain provided further support for the theory of poisoning.

Undeniably, therefore, and although some ecclesiastical historians tried to hush up the affair, this double death was part of a generalized offensive by the Padroado, who, through the Jesuits and their followers, decided to use diabolical means to get rid of the envoys of Propaganda. Thus, at the beginning of 1670, Louis Chevreuil was kidnapped in Cambodia and then, after four months of imprisonment and harassment in Macau, he was transferred to Goa where the inquisitor had him released without, however, granting him a document justifying his innocence. After that, he was placed under house arrest with the Theatine Fathers by order of the viceroy.

However, as Guiart pointed out, the French missionaries were not the only ones targeted. In March 1671, two months after the death of Pierre Brindeau, two Tonkinese priests, Jean Huê and Philippe Nhan, fell ill after a meal with dissident Christians. The first died six days later; suspicious spots were found on his neck and chest. The second, who had taken an antidote, survived for more than a year before succumbing in his turn on 27 October 1672. Two Cochinchinese priests, Luc Ben and Joseph Trang, were well aware of the danger

---

22. Letter from Claude Guiart to the directors, Cochinchina, 6 February 1672. AMEP, volume 733, 409–410. Eleven years later, a Belgian Jesuit, Father Thomas, gave an ecclesiastically correct version of this double death by trying to prove in an Apology of the Society of Jesus that the two Frenchmen had died from drinking unsanitary water, *cf* J Guennou, *Les Missions Etrangères de Paris* (Paris: 1986, 171).

because, after having baptized several pagans who had spontaneously converted following the death of the two Frenchmen, they decided to seek help from their bishop and soon disembarked in Ayutthaya.

News from Rome

At the beginning of the summer of 1671, events at Camp Saint-Joseph moved along quickly with the arrival on July 4 of two new missionaries, Bénigne Vachet and Pierre Langlois, accompanied by the ever-faithful lay companion, Philippe de Chamesson. They brought with them several decrees published by Rome in 1669 that were intended to consolidate the position of the Vicars Apostolic against the claims of the Padroado and its religious: the bulls *Sollicitudo pastoralis*, which confirmed the prohibition of clerics engaging in commerce, and *Speculatores domus Israel*, which submitted religious to the authority of the Vicars Apostolic, as well as the brief *Cum sicut accepimus civitas*, which granted jurisdiction over Siam to the apostolic vicar of Nanking, that is, to the successor of Ignatius Cotolendi.

The comfort that Pierre Lambert drew from such favourable decisions was, however, largely compromised by the only refusal that Rome ever made to his requests, that of the official recognition of the Congregation of the Lovers of the Cross. François Pallu, however, loyally defended the project which, on the other hand, the directors in Paris vigorously opposed.

A few years later, on 28 August 1678, a Roman decree granted indulgences to the communities of the Lovers of the Cross created in the vicariates of Cochinchina and Tonkin without distinction of sex and it is this text which founded the legal existence of the Lovers of the Cross for three centuries. The male communities disappeared, in fact, but the female communities multiplied and enjoyed a success that is well known.[23]

It was not, therefore, for their substance that Pierre Lambert's missionary conceptions as revealed in the project of the Lovers of the Cross were censured, but for their form: on the one hand, because they contradicted the usual functioning of the Church (by mixing regulars and seculars), but above all, because they set the bar too high

---

23. In the twenty-first century, autonomous congregations of the Lovers of the Holy Cross are to be found in Vietnam, Thailand, Laos, Cambodia, and the US.

to allow for a sufficiently large number of recruits, because they were only applicable to a spiritual elite. This is the opinion of the very wise Jacques de Bourges who believed that 'if a large number of Saints Paul and Francis Xavier had been found, a truly apostolic congregation could have been formed and given these ideas for its rules.'[24]

The French missionaries accepted this change, of course, with a perfect spirit of obedience, although some at least had regrets. François Pallu was the first to indicate his submission by eating meat and drinking wine on the very evening that the Pope approved the advice of Propaganda, but he wrote to François Deydier: 'As for myself, I confess to you that I have never experienced more grace and mercy and been more conscious of the protection of God than at the moment when I made my first vows. God forbid that I should want to justify our conduct by this and maintain what has been very justly censured. I see very well where we have gone too far, and what there is to retain and to reject.'[25]

Like his confreres, and just as he had committed himself from the beginning, Pierre Lambert submitted to the decision of Rome to the great amazement of the newcomer, Bénigne Vachet, who recounted, with his usual loquaciousness, his first meeting with the Vicar Apostolic.

> He took me to his room where two places had been laid at the table. This was the first surprise. When I saw that we were served a fricassee of chicken and that a bottle of wine was brought, I was almost lost for words and did not know what to say. The bishop, who noticed this, said to me, laughing, 'You didn't expect to have such good food, did you!' I admitted quite simply that what I saw contradicted the idea I had been given of him, since I was sure that no meat was eaten, no wine was drunk, nor was lunch served in the seminary, and I saw now that the opposite was true. 'You have not been deceived,' he replied, because for more than three years we have been leading a life here that is much more strict than that of the most austere religions; we had believed that it was suitable for missionaries and we had committed ourselves to it wholeheartedly. But from the moment that the Supreme

---

24. Launay, *Histoire générale de la Société des Missions étrangères* (Paris: Téqui, 1894), t. 1, 173.
25. Launay, *Histoire générale*, 177.

Pontiff, the cardinals of the Congregation and our friends in Paris refused to approve it and rejected it, as the Bishop of Heliopolis wrote, I did not hesitate for a moment to accept their ideas, and I am, as you can see, the first to condemn myself. I have already given orders for meat to be served at dinner, a change that our gentlemen may have some difficulty in accepting, but I hope that they will imitate my example.[26]

A perilous expedition to help the Church of Cochinchina

In the immediate future, however, Pierre Lambert had little time to dwell on what appeared to be a personal disavowal and a victory for the directors, for another problem, more serious and extremely urgent, preoccupied him: the fate of the Cochinchinese Christians who had been abandoned since Luc Ben and Joseph Trang, disoriented and frightened by the death of Hainques and Brindeau, fled their country to seek help in Ayutthaya and to bring to their bishop messages of distress from his flock. Having consulted his entire team, the Vicar Apostolic decided to accompany the two Cochinchinese priests in person and to include two French confreres, Guillaume Mahot and Claude Guiart. The first would travel with him and would enter secretly while the second would present himself openly but in civilian clothes, as the assistant of a French apothecary, M. Maurillon, who, while passing through Ayutthaya, decided to undertake a small commercial expedition in Cochinchina.

After having obtained, not without some difficulty, the authorization of the king of Siam to leave the country, the bishop, dressed as a secular, embarked on a boat 'without a nail, without any rope, without metal fittings, without canvas and without a pilot'.[27] The boat almost disappeared in the wildest of storms.

> To prevent the boat being suddenly submerged by the waves, each of us positioned himself on the edge of the boat with an oar in his hand, in order to support it and to prevent it from being struck on the side thereby causing the loss of everything. I observed Mgr de Beirut two or three times; to all outward appearances he was as serene and as cheerful as ever, and

---

26. Memoir of Bénigne Vachet. AMEP, volume 110, 166.
27. Launay, *Histoire de la mission de Cochinchine. Documents historiques* (Paris: Téqui, 1923), 79.

when he noticed that I was astonished that he should appear so calm, he said to me with a little smile, which was a good indication of his state of mind and the tranquillity of his heart, that our current situation should not worry us because it was one of the consequences of our vocation, and he added: 'All that should occupy us is that we are doing the will of God.'[28]

After having escaped the fury of the waves and then the rapacity of Chinese pirates who pursued them for several days amongst the islands of the Gulf of Siam, the frail boat landed on Cochinchinese soil where two no less formidable dangers awaited its passengers: persecution by the government and ambushes by Christians who remained faithful to the Jesuits.

Cochinchina was then a narrow strip of land stretching along the China Sea between Cape Varela and the Dong-hoi wall. Introduced in 1615 in the region of Tourane by refugees from Japan, tolerated intermittently until 1645, Christianity was officially forbidden there from that date and several Christians paid with their lives for their attachment to the new religion. At the time of Pierre Lambert's appointment as Vicar Apostolic, the Jesuits, by playing on the king's interest in trade with Macau, and especially his interest in the arms trade, succeeded in maintaining three residences in Tourane, Faifo and Hué, and some thirty chapels. Since the arrival of Louis Chevreuil in 1664 and their banishment in 1665, the last three fathers of the Society of Jesus did not give up their efforts to regain their place in the kingdom and to drive out the French missionaries. Following Dominique Fuciti, who entered and was expelled in 1668 after having tried, as we have seen, to have Antoine Hainques kidnapped, Ignace Baudet in 1669 and then Pierre Marquez in 1670 made the same attempt to enter.

On 1 September 1671, Pierre Lambert set foot for the first time on his mission land, in the region of Nha Trang. He arrived at night, with the assistance of the local Christians who took him hidden in a net to a house where the faithful were gathered. Vachet and Mahot walked beside him, in Vietnamese clothes, hidden in the midst of a group of men who carried fig tree trunks for the governor's elephants.

More than eight hundred people came to visit the bishop who confirmed two hundred children and some adults who had previously

---

28. Launay, *Histoire Cochinchine*, 80.

been to confession to the Cochinese priests, because neither he nor Mahot knew the language well enough. It took them a little more than a month learning the language for them to be able to communicate adequately with their flock. Soon, a Christian mandarin came to advise Pierre Lambert to report his presence to the governor of the province who, although pagan, was not hostile to Christianity. Far from taking advantage of this opportunity to harm the missionaries, he came to pay them a secret visit and gave them a pass that would be very useful during the remainder of their journey in helping them avoid police checks.

The governor's feast

The Vicar Apostolic also received an excellent welcome from the governor of the neighbouring province of Nharou who invited him to his home and provided him with ample provisions to continue his journey. The bishop was now accompanied only by Bénigne Vachet and Joseph Trang, having left Luc Ben and Guillaume Mahot to care for the south of the country.

Things became complicated, however, when he arrived in the province of Quinhon, whose governor had just returned from the court accompanied by Barthélémy d'Acosta, the new Jesuit who had recently replaced Pierre Marquez. Of mixed parentage with a Portuguese father and a Japanese mother, this loyal defender of the rights of the Padroado had won the confidence of several dignitaries thanks to his medical skills, which put him in a position of strength in relation to the Vicar Apostolic. Although Pierre Lambert's presence was to be kept secret, he nevertheless intended to assert his authority and to gain recognition for his rights which had been recently confirmed by Rome. There are two contradictory versions of the story of their meeting, or rather of their confrontation, both attributed to the pen of Bénigne Vachet. The requirement of historical honesty obliges us to quote them both.

The first, published in the very official *Relation des missions et des voyages des Evêques et Vicaires apostoliques ès années 1672–1675*, is supposed to be taken from a letter of Vachet. No copy of this text, either in original or in copied form, appears in the archives, so it is impossible to prove its authenticity.

We learned that Fr. Barthélémy d'Acosta, a Jesuit, Japanese by nationality, was only four leagues from us. This news gave us great joy, as we hoped that we would be able to see and support him. As soon as he knew that Monseigneur de Beirut was so close, he came to pay his respects, and after several polite exchanges on both sides, this father told us that they were in serious trouble. A ship that had left the previous year for Macau, and on which Father Marquez had embarked, was rumoured to have been shipwrecked This accident was a matter of great concern because the King of Cochinchina might use this event as a pretext to persecute Christians, having entrusted 10,000 ecus to Father Marquez to use for some commissions. Since this order had not been complied with, Father d'Acosta believed that no one had dared to send a ship from Macau that year, and that a ship might not come for a long time, for fear that the King of Cochinchina would confiscate it to compensate for the sum he had given Father Marquez.

The seriousness with which we regarded this problem prevented us from rejoicing in other blessings as much as we would otherwise have done; the fervour of the Christians who came from all parts, and the intense desire they had to benefit from our presence, gave us great joy. However, this joy was soon followed by an overwhelming sadness because of the extreme suffering experienced by Mgr de Beirut. In spite of the resolution he had taken not to stay long in this place, he was obliged, in spite of himself, to remain there for more than six weeks while his illness lasted. Everything contributed to the weakening of the patient: the delicacy of his temperament, the violence of the fever, the rainy and foggy weather in a place surrounded by mountains, marshes everywhere, the lack of medicine and his inability to take food. To make matters worse, I found myself unable to help him, because I was attacked by a burning fever before he was.[29]

The second version given by the same Bénigne Vachet in his *Mémoires pour servir à l'histoire ecclésiastique de la mission de Cochinchine*, written in France in 1692, testified to a completely different story.

---

29. Launay, *Histoire Cochinchine*, 87.

Mgr de Beirut received the news that Father Barthélémy d'Acosta had arrived from the court in Nharou with the governor, who had been baptized as a child and who had married a Christian woman, from whom he had a son, now some years old. Both mother and son were good Christians, but the father was unworthy of his religion because he kept three or four concubines in his own house. Upon hearing this news, Mgr de Beirut, I can say, thought that he should seize the opportunity to visit the Jesuit Father d'Acosta in order to appeal to the governor in a gentle manner. We were only a day away.'

'Mgr de Beirut had a catechist, who was the governor's physician, give him notice of his intentions the day before his arrival; it was enough to make Father d'Acosta leave, which he did with incredible haste to return to John de la Croix.'[30] The governor then met the bishop, promised him to mend his ways and invited him to dinner with Vachet. Here is the rest of his story: 'We entered a room where we found a very nice light meal; he wanted to serve us himself. First he put candied Chinese orange on two porcelain dishes in front of us; it is the best and most delicious food that is eaten in the country. The prelate ate about half of it and served me the rest. The governor urged us to spend the night at his house, but he could not persuade us to do so; he had us taken safely to the church where we were staying. Two hours later, we fell into a deep sleep; we were lying on boards covered by a mat.

'About midnight I awoke with a frightful headache; I felt a devouring fire burning inside me, and it seemed to me that the room was turning upside down. I thought I heard the voice of the Bishop of Beirut as if he was far from me, although we were lying side by side; I tried to ask him if he was calling me:"Yes," he answered, adding that if I was sufficiently awake, I should search in the bottom drawer of his chest, and that I should bring him a small porcelain jar where there were some pills. I found what I was looking for; he took one and gave me two which I swallowed. After a while we fell asleep and I rested for a good two hours. I woke up and of necessity dragged myself into a courtyard where I was violently ill. Fortunately, a servant of the catechist who was passing by saw me; I had fallen down and was unconscious. They cleaned me and took me to sleep in another

---

30. Launay, *Histoire Cochinchine*, 92.

place. The doctor, with the help of a little alcohol, enabled me to return to full consciousness, but nonetheless I suffered from a violent fever which lasted all day without any let up; the exuberance of my temperament helped me greatly to pull through. Nevertheless, I was inconvenienced for eighteen months by a flow of blood and by severe kidney pains which I felt sometimes by night and sometimes by day.'

'As for the Bishop of Beirut, the fever did not torment him so much, but it lasted twenty-four days, gradually losing its strength; all of our hair fell out and the nails of our hands were as yellow as the purest gold; we were in this situation when M. Guiart and M. Maurillon arrived. The latter, who was a good apothecary and who had provided Mgr de Beirut with the above-mentioned pills, assured us that we had been poisoned and that the external signs were incontestable proof of this.

Before leaving this province we learned from Father Luc that a fire broke out in the governor's room, from which he escaped badly burned, screaming to high heaven because of the appalling pain he was suffering. Fr Luc Ben, the Cochinchinese priest, was called to whom he confessed in the presence of his wife, his son, the doctor and some servants, that he recognized that God had laid his almighty hand on him to punish him for the crime he had committed of having poisoned the bishop and the clergyman, his companion, with candied oranges from China. This was done at the instigation of a person whom he named, but it is too shocking to reveal his name; the same person had provided him with the poisonous material and taught him how to use it. The governor survived for only twenty-four hours, during which time he gave convincing signs of repentance, while still maintaining the truth of his first declaration.'[31]

Given the fate of Antoine Hainques, Pierre Brindeau, Jean Huê and Philippe Nhan, and the earlier attempted poisoning of the Vicar Apostolic in Ayutthaya, this account seems likely to be true. In any case, Pierre Lambert was greatly weakened by this new ordeal. He even thought he was dying and asked Vachet to administer the last rites while he was still lucid. Vachet was deeply impressed by the serenity of his bishop. 'If his inner dispositions could be judged by

---

31. Launay, *Histoire Cochinchine*, 93–94. According to Professors Pierre Delaveau and Jules Vidal, it could be a case of poisoning by gelsemium elegans, a toxic liana used in Chinese and Indo-Chinese pharmacopoeia under the name gou wen.

outward appearances, it would have been difficult to find a dying man better prepared to breathe his last; I would have loved to be able to penetrate the depths of his heart to see all its movements, but to mortify my desire, I thought that it belonged to God alone to see clearly into his inner sanctum, and that it should suffice for me to see from time to time on his tongue and in his eyes a few sparks of the fire that was consuming him within.'

> Sad and weary as I was, I could not help but feel great consolation when I saw him so faithful and so peaceful, suffering intensely, yet full of confidence in God, burning with the desire to see him soon in heaven, and yet equally resigned to his orders for life or death. He tried to pronounce often enough these consoling words of David: *Misericordias Domini in aeternum cantabo* (I will sing forever of the mercies of my dear Lord). From these words it was easy to see that this divine attribute occupied him unceasingly, and that the goodness of God was the heavenly magnet which attracted his whole soul with inconceivable sweetness.[32]

Finally, it was Claude Guiart, recently arrived from Faifo in the guise of a doctor and called to the rescue by his colleague, himself a sick man, who took over the task of caring for his bishop.

Clandestine administration

On All Saints' Day, after having baptized 18 adults and confirmed 200 people despite his weakness, Pierre Lambert left on a litter. To try to pass unnoticed, he took advantage of the arrival of French merchants of Faifo, who were none other than M Maurillon and his companions. However, moving through the province of Quamghia, the Vicar Apostolic was besieged by enthusiastic Christians whose number had doubled in six years to reach a figure between 250,000 and 300,000. He was able to see the veneration that the faithful had for Antoine Hainques and Pierre Brindeau. Pierre Lambert celebrated Christmas in Binhson, where the tomb of Hainques was located. Seeing that some people prayed to him and honoured him as a saint, the Vicar Apostolic had to use his authority to put an end to this premature cult.

---

32. Launay, *Histoire Cochinchine*, 88.

All this commotion around him began to rouse public attention and he soon received a visit from a man sent by the queen's two Christian sisters to inquire about his intentions and give him advice. If he had gifts for the king, he could present himself openly at the court, but if he did not have any gifts he should keep his coming as secret as possible. Judging that the circumstances were not propitious for an official visit, the Vicar Apostolic decided to withdraw from the city to the home of a widow named Luce. There, while Claude Guiart was preparing for the first synod of Cochinchina in Faifo, he gathered together a group of women who wished to dedicate themselves to religious life. As in Tonkin, Pierre Lambert responded to this demand by proposing to them the rule of the Lovers of the Cross. Although persecution made the execution of this project particularly delicate, Mme Luce agreed to take under her protection, in her house, the little community of which she became the first superior. Two groups of five postulants soon settled in her house, and their numbers quickly multiplied.

On 15 January 1672, the Vicar Apostolic arrived in Faifo where Claude Guiart had built him an inconspicuous shelter on an island away from the city. Declining the invitations of the Christians who flocked from the neighbouring villages for him to visit them, Pierre Lambert summoned his missionaries, the two Cochinchinese priests and the principal catechists for the synod. Father d'Acosta, who was also invited, did not respond. The primary purpose of this assembly was to have the authority of the Vicar Apostolic and his delegates recognized by producing all their bulls of appointment and confirmation, and by asking for their promulgation in all the churches. This official event, however, convinced only those Christians who were already committed to the cause of the envoys of Propaganda and did not impress the supporters of the Jesuits who prolonged the schism for many years. Nevertheless, the bishop also took advantage of this meeting to settle a few disciplinary points concerning the functioning of the Christian communities and the rules of marriage, and to appoint seventeen catechists accredited by letters of mission.

After a month's stay, he left again for the province of Quinhon where the Christians, deprived of his visits by his illness, wanted to see him again in good health. Escaping the vigilance of the customs officers, he made several brief visits, during which he baptized, confirmed and even heard confessions, because he now knew the language well enough to speak directly to his faithful. When he departed, leaving the region in the care of Joseph Trang, he took with him a dozen young boys destined for the seminary of Ayutthaya. Bad weather prevented him from responding to the request of Guillaume Mahot, who, in the south, had expressed the desire to see him one last time. On March 29, Claude Guiart, appointed vicar general, was responsible for making a general visit of all the countries as soon as possible. He bade farewell to his bishop in the episcopal boat moored off the coast of Nharou, while on land the authorities, alerted by rumours, multiplied their inspections in order to find the foreigners. After three days of stormy weather, the journey was accomplished peacefully and after four weeks Pierre Lambert returned to his Siamese sanctuary where other problems awaited him.

Chapter 7
Diplomatic exercises

Pallu, Rome and the directors

François Pallu arrived in Ayutthaya on 27 May 1673, after eight long years of absence, during which he experienced many vicissitudes of a different kind, but hardly less trying than those suffered by his colleague. It is not possible to understand the sequence of events without first summarizing the impressive succession of reports, negotiations, meetings, reversals and pressures of all kinds that the peaceable Vicar Apostolic from Tours experienced. Many historians have reproached him, not without reason, for a certain inconsistency, sometimes going as far as to accuse him of doublespeak. But this judgment cannot be made without recognizing important mitigating circumstances. Placed in the position of buffer between Pierre Lambert and the directors of the Paris Foreign Missions, between Propaganda and the Jesuits, between the pope and Louis XIV, this man of good will, moderate and naturally inclined to conciliation, could not but be manipulated, from time to time, by protagonists as relentless as each other to make their contradictory causes triumph.

Fearing more than anything the unfavourable reaction of the Parisian directors, he had chosen to pass first of all through Rome where he received a warm welcome. On his arrival, the pope who had commissioned him, Alexander VII, was close to death and all business was suspended. The new pontiff, Clement IX, supported by France, was elected on 30 June 1667. In October, he granted an audience to the Vicar Apostolic, assured him of his support and went so far as to give him, for the attention of Louis XIV, a laudatory brief in favour of the Vicars Apostolic and the seminary of Foreign Missions in order to facilitate his reception in Paris where he arrived on 21 January 1668.

François Pallu's contact with the political authorities was efxcellent. The king received him personally, promised him his protection and transformed the two temporary pensions granted to the Vicars Apostolic into life pensions. Colbert, for his part, was very attentive to all the information that the bishop could provide, having in mind a better organization of the East Indies Company. Relations were much more difficult with the directors of the Paris Foreign Missions who did not want to hear of any questioning of the Jesuits and even less of the project of an apostolic congregation, 'so badly processed, so badly founded, which sins against the principles of theology and common sense'.[1]

Pallu left for Rome on 10 November 1668, followed closely by his compatriot Michel Gazil, the fiercest opponent of the congregation project. Animated by a sincere desire to be loyal to Pierre Lambert, the Vicar Apostolic did his best to defend his point of view, but his arguments were not enough to convince the cardinals, who rejected the project. The consultors, however, gave a qualified judgment on the vows of the Lovers of the Cross. Without condemning 'each one of them taken separately and in their relations with particular persons,' the Sacred Congregation judged that 'considered as a whole and with regard to those destined for the missions' they should 'be disapproved of and declared null'.[2] It was a wise decision, which gave the foreign missions a broader and more universal profile than that of the Lovers of the Cross, although the latter congregation was particularly well adapted to the context in which it was conceived, that of Siam, and therefore of Theravada Buddhism.

Apart from the rejection of the project of an apostolic congregation, the Roman authorities responded favourably to all of François Pallu's other requests. From June to September 1669, the briefs followed one another, granting the Vicars Apostolic jurisdiction over Siam and placing the religious under their jurisdiction, renewing the prohibition of trade by ecclesiastical personnel, regulating a few specific cases. The *Instructions* of 1664 were published in July, at the expense of Propaganda. Finally, on September 17, the Bishop of Heliopolis was able to leave the Eternal City, taking with him gifts and

---

1. Letter from the directors to Pierre Lambert, 28 July 1667. AMEP, volume 4, 197.
2. Henri Sy, La Société des Missions étrangères, 104. Latin text volume 253, 271 and volume 169, 31.

a letter addressed to Phra Narai in which the pope thanked the King of Siam for the favourable reception he had given his envoys.

This unconditional support for the Vicars Apostolic surprised even a man as well-informed as William Lesley, who had feared for a time that the re-establishment of diplomatic relations between Rome and Lisbon, following the Spanish-Portuguese peace concluded in January 1668, might have strengthened the position of the Padroado and the Jesuits. He even advised the directors, after much hesitation, to ask Louis XIV to intervene with his ally, the King of Portugal, in favour of the French missionaries and to propose to him a kind of colonial alliance to fight against the rising power of the Dutch in Asia. But the directors, and especially Gazil, had good reason to be afraid of arousing a desire for French patronage in their sovereign whose appetite for power they knew. For his part, Louis XIV, in the midst of a war with Spain, did not want to upset his Portuguese ally too much, while the imminent departure for Asia of a French military fleet, the Persian Squadron, exacerbated international tensions in that part of the world where Madrid was trying to defend its patronal rights over Formosa[3] and the Philippines. In any case, a royal intervention would have been useless, because the credit of the Vicars Apostolic was then so great in Rome that no manoeuvre against them could succeed.

In making preparations for his departure, François Pallu had good reason to feel relieved. Far from discrediting the cause of the Vicars Apostolic, as might have been feared, his return to Europe had, on the contrary, strengthened their position. When he celebrated Mass in December 1669 at the Jesuit novitiate in Paris on the feast of Saint Francis Xavier, he might well have hoped that in France, too, misunderstandings had disappeared, and peace had returned. Besides his authorisation to leave, the king gave him a gift of 2,000 ecus,[4] three passports for the Vicars Apostolic as well as gifts and a letter to the King of Siam. In addition, six new missionaries and four laymen (a surgeon, an apothecary-baker, a tailor and a valet) were ready to leave with him.

However, the directors of the seminary were not finished yet. The day before his departure, on 2 February 1670, the directors Gazil,

---

3. Formosa was the name of the island now commonly referred to as 'Taiwan'.
4. The écu was the name of silver and gold coins used in France from the thirteenth century until the time of the French Revolution in 1789.

Besard, Poitevin and Fermanel forced him to sign, in the presence of the Bishop of Rodez, the Carmelite César du Saint-Sacrement and M Duplessis-Monbar, a written declaration against the vows. In this declaration he promised 'before God never to observe them again, and also to prevent any of our missionaries from observing or professing them in the future, not even as the object of a simple proposal or of a solemn resolution.'[5] With regard to Pierre Lambert, the Bishop of Heliopolis also undertook to do everything possible to oblige him 'to share the same sentiments, which means to reject them entirely. It must be conveyed to him that his conduct has been generally disapproved of by all his friends, and he must be persuaded not to rely any longer on ideas that may come to him in prayer. It is our conviction that they are suspect and dangerous, and that it is safer to follow the ordinary way of doing things, even though it may appear to be less perfect than his own particular understanding, which may seem to be on a higher plane.'

This statement, made by men raised in the Ignatian school and keen to protect their good relations with the Jesuits, was a sign of a lack of understanding and a total rejection of the very principles of interior discernment dictated by Saint Ignatius. It was a refusal of that mysticism of action of which Pierre Lambert was, apart from a few human errors, such a remarkable practitioner. It was also a further symptom of the rationalist and utilitarian degradation that had been affecting the spirit of the Society of Jesus for almost a century and a harbinger of the great anti-mystical offensive that was developing in the Church, and more particularly in France at the end of the century.

Taken aback by this unexpected blackmail, François Pallu gave in, sacrificing his dignity as a bishop and his loyalty to Pierre Lambert for the survival of the mission. But the weight of cowardice and betrayal that this imposed act entailed weighed more and more heavily on his conscience during the journey that brought him back to his confrere. In Surat, the reading of Pierre Lambert's latest letters informing him of the situation in Tonkin and of his recent quarrels with the chapter of Goa, and then the arrival of Louis Chevreuil, rendered unrecognizable by eight years of harassment and captivity, brought the Vicar Apostolic with brutal force out of the irenic dream woven

---

5. Declaration of the Bishop of Heliopolis, 2 February 1670, in Henri Sy, *La Société des Missions étrangères*, 127–128.

in front of his eyes by the directors and brought him face to face with the sordid reality of the situation.

The amazing and almost unbelievable account that the unfortunate Chevreuil gave him of his tribulations lasted all night and seemed to be so serious that he immediately decided to send one of his missionaries back to Europe to inform the Holy See and ask for new protective measures. He chose Charles Sevin, a former musketeer of the king, to whom he entrusted strict instructions and a letter to the French ambassador in Lisbon. He asked the latter to demand that the king of Portugal should stop the abuses perpetrated by his subjects against the French. It was a way of reminding the sovereign of the just observance of his patronage rights and of his diplomatic commitments.

François Pallu left Surat on 17 February 1672 for Bantan where he arrived on March 30. Anxious to have a chaplain serious enough to watch over the good conduct of the Catholic French nationals, and wise enough to serve as procurator for the missionaries, he left Claude Gayme, the son of a Savoyard merchant, at this trading post of the French East India Company.

While Pierre Lambert was already waiting for him in Ayutthaya, the Bishop of Heliopolis had great difficulty in finding a boat and was forced to break up his group. Claude de Chandebois, who was ill, remained in Surat under the care of the Capuchins; the surgeon, Le Tellier, unable to adapt to missionary life, returned to Europe; Jean de Courtaulin managed to negotiate a place on a Portuguese ship and left in May. Finally, in June, an English ship leaving for Madras accepted on board the Bishop of Heliopolis and Louis Chevreuil, whom he did not want to part with, because he was his candidate to succeed Bishop Cotolendi. However, René Forget and the other three laymen had to stay ashore with most of the luggage and Louis XIV's gifts to the King of Siam, which were soon confiscated by the Dutch.

However, the ship carrying the Vicar Apostolic was blown off course by a storm to the coast of Bengal, and he had to stay in Balassor for six months. He took advantage of this time to draw up a vast plan for the establishment of the French East India Company in perfect cooperation with the French missionaries. He was even considering the foundation of a bishopric in Meliapur which would have made possible the foundation of a true French patronage in this part of India. These speculations, as ambitious as they were risky, were interrupted by the arrival of a ship that took him on board and transported him to Mergui in three weeks. On 27 May 1673, he finally arrived in Ayutthaya where new clashes had just occurred between the French and Portuguese missionaries.

New confrontations

In October 1673, seeing that the last decrees from Rome were disregarded by the religious of the Portuguese camp, whose behaviour continued to be the centre of attention, Pierre Lambert, ignoring the wait-and-see recommendations of François Pallu, took the decision to notify them about the bull *Speculatores* of 13 September 1669, stipulating that religious could not exercise the powers received from their superiors without the authorization of the Vicar Apostolic. On October 22, he sent two missionaries, Pierre Langlois and the newcomer, Jean de Courtaulin, to ask the Jesuits (Fathers Tissanier, Maldonnat, Suarez and Magalloens) and the Dominicans (Louis Fragoso and Louis du Rosaire) to present their letters patent within three days.[6] This was a symbolic gesture which renewed, while reversing, the procedure initiated by Fragoso in 1666 and officially manifested the change of jurisdiction over Siam. By mutual agreement, the religious refused to comply. On All Saints' Day, the bishop pronounced an interdict against them and had his decision posted on the door of his church. The following Sunday, the superior of the Jesuits, Joseph Tissanier, declared from the pulpit 'that he could not comply because he had a written order from his general not to recognise the Vicars Apostolic and that this bull had not been approved at the chancery of Portugal'.[7] This refusal did not prevent Pierre Lambert from scoring points, since in the following days he received a visit from the 'first Christian mandarin' (that is, a Portuguese nobleman appointed chief of the outpost of his nation by the King of Siam) who asked him 'if he could address his complaints to the pope against the religious missionaries of Siam, who were causing such great scandals relating to religion, and if he and the Christians could hope for some remedy from Rome. Having answered him that

---

6. 'Letters patent' refer to an official declaration from an authority granting rights to a person or other legal entity.
7. Letter from Pierre Lambert to the directors, 12 November 1672. AMEP, volume 858, 255.

he should not expect anything less, the bishop tells us, he took the liberty of writing to His Holiness the letter which is in this package, of which I keep the duplicate signed by him.'[8]

At the same time, the bishop wrote to the pope asking for radical measures: to recall either the Vicars Apostolic or the Jesuits. If the choice was not possible, he asked for very precise legal decisions to protect the French missionaries: prohibition of Portuguese ordinaries and religious from exercising any jurisdiction in the territories entrusted to the apostolic vicars; prohibition to form or ordain local priests from these territories; exemption for all the personnel placed under the authority of the Vicar Apostolic (missionaries, catechists and servants) from the power of the Inquisition of Goa. In support of his request, he informed the sovereign pontiff of the change in climate that had emerged from incident to incident in the missions: on the one hand, the Jesuits did not have or no longer had, in these regions, as much authority as was said. On the other hand, the Christians were beginning to tire of their servitude to them and only asked to be freed from it and to be placed under the authority of the Vicars Apostolic if they could be persuaded that the latter were supported by the Holy See. While waiting for an answer, the cold war continued in Ayutthaya until April 1673 when the return of Gabriel Bouchard, whom Pierre Lambert had sent to Manila the previous year to propose a pact of union to the Spanish religious, brought an additional element to the dispute.

It is again to Bénigne Vachet that we owe the account of this new rocky episode. 'The Franciscans, Dominicans and Augustinians received this project as if an angel had brought it to them from God. The Jesuits were not only the ones who did not want to hear about it, but also the ones who used all their influence to prevent its execution. M. Bouchard was the victim. These Fathers told the governor and the magistrates that this French clergyman was a spy disguised as a priest, that he had come to Manila only to observe the ports and to turn the best subjects against the Spanish king. It was for these reasons that M Bouchard was arrested. All the instruments had already been prepared and they would have put him to the test if the local archbishop, with a zeal worthy of this great man, had not promptly rushed in accompanied by the Inquisitor General. The

---

8. Letter, 12 November 1672, 255.

admonitions they made and the threats they used were so effective that M. Bouchard was released immediately and handed over to the archbishop, who promised to give a faithful account of the manner in which this clergyman behaved.

> M. Bouchard was lodged with the Vicar General of this prelate, who did his best to cheer him up after the bad treatment he had been given and which still threatened him. From that day on he never went out alone; either the Vicar General accompanied him on his visits, or someone else took his place. These are the circumstances of his departure: he left Manila on a Siamese ship which was about to set sail on its return journey. His embarkation caused a great deal of anger in those who were jealous of him, on seeing that the Vicar General, many of the clergy, and the superiors of religious houses, accompanied by a good number of their religious and several of the leading citizens of the city accompanied him with tears in their eyes and they did not leave the shore until they had lost sight of the ship.[9]

The reunion: Pallu rebels.

Things were at that point when François Pallu arrived in his turn, in May 1673. Already quite shaken by the account of Chevreuil, who had remained with him since his arrival in Surat and in whom he could perceive the deterioration caused by the relentless attacks of which he had been a victim, the Bishop of Heliopolis adhered unreservedly, this time, to the aggressive strategy of his confrere.

On September 3, he wrote a long letter to the directors in Paris, a veritable settling of scores, with a violence that was quite unexpected in such an affable and level-headed man. 'You forced me to sign a document that is extremely insulting to our persons and our characters', he reproached them, citing the commitment they had imposed on him. 'It was only the respect I had for the people that you had assembled for the occasion that extorted it from me, as well as the avoidance of the extreme suffering with which I was threatened, which I could not otherwise prevent at the time. Whenever I have thought about it since, I have been so indignant that I have come to believe that in order to erase all memory of it, I ought to put the document in

---

9. Memorandum of Bénigne Vachet. AMEP, volume 110b, 143.

the fire. Moreover, I consider that you also should do the same with the copy which has remained in your hands, if you have any regard for your own honour as well as ours.'[10] The list of particular faults of which he accused the directors was overwhelming: insulting and threatening words against the Bishop of Beirut; suppression of letters intended for the pope and the Sacred Congregation; falsification of the bull giving power to consecrate a new Vicar Apostolic; withholding of printed copies of the *Instructions* drawn up by the Vicars Apostolic and approved by Rome; creating mistrust of Bishop of Beirut in the missionaries sent to him.

Then he brought a full-scale indictment against the Jesuits, without any moderation of his language. Never had he been so frank.

> Believe me, gentlemen, the Jesuit fathers of these districts do not want us here. They do not know how to tolerate people who are their equal, and they are even less able to tolerate those who are superior to them. They do not want any witnesses to their conduct, which is reckless in many respects. In good faith all possible ways have been tried in order to establish a mutual working agreement with them, here, in Cochinchina, in Tonkin and in Cambodia, without any success. If they have sometimes seemed willing to enter into some kind of arrangement, it has only been a matter of pretence and dishonesty in order to achieve their own ends more successfully. It is time, gentlemen, to disabuse ourselves of this false persuasion that nothing can be done in the missions without the involvement of the Jesuit fathers. It was prudent to do so in the past when they had influence everywhere. But you know well enough that they have now lost the great credit they once had in Rome, in France and in all of Europe.[11]

François Pallu finally came to terms with reality and accepted, a little late, the advice of Propaganda, which as early as 1659, through the intermediary, William Lesley, warned him that the greatest obstacles to his mission would come not only from the Portuguese, but also from the Jesuits. He finally understood that the wind of history had

---

10. Letter of François Pallu to the directors. AMEP, volume 102, 507, quoted in Henri Sy, *La Société*, 129 to 136.
11. Letter Pallu directors in Sy. *La Société*.

definitively changed, that the Church had decided to change its missionary policy and that the French Vicars Apostolic were precisely the instruments used by Rome to bring about this missiological revolution.

He tried to open the eyes of the directors in Paris who were still blinded by a Jesuit propaganda that was basking in the glory of the authentic sanctity of Francis Xavier and was supported by personalities of great stature such as Valignano,[12] Ricci[13] or Alexander de Rhodes. Such promotion was effective at the time of the splendour of the Portuguese Empire and of the Padroado, but now it rested only on lies and disinformation. The Jesuits, supported by the economic and political power of Portugal, had been able to establish Christian communities, but they had compromised them by their political interference, and they did not know how to maintain them.

The problem was that they considered themselves to be the exclusive owners and did not want to recognize the authority of those who were mandated to establish the ordinary functioning of the universal Church. While their ambition to conquer from above clashed with the resistance of Asian societies and the coherence of their politico-religious organizations, they sought to keep Christians in their favourite system, that of reduction. This arrangement consisted in creating a closed society under their control, without any communication with the outside world, with all the risks of drifting into totalitarianism or discredit that this entailed when the missionary framework, losing its original rigour, sank into mediocrity, slackness, abuses and scandal. 'I am not looking for the causes,' continued François Pallu.

> I am only saying that the bad conduct they have been guilty of in Japan, in Ethiopia, in the land of St. Thomas,[14] in Macassar, in Cochinchina and in Tonkin, not to mention now in China, has made them the objects of suspicion and odious in all

---

12. Alessandro Valignano (1539–1606) was an Italian Jesuit who played a leading role in introducing the Catholic faith to Asia, especially to China and Japan, and in establishing the Jesuit missions in these countries.
13. Matteo Ricci (1552–1610), an Italian Jesuit, a mathematician and scientist, who spoke Chinese fluently, was one of the founders of the missions in China. He immersed himself in the Chinese culture in order to graft the faith into the Chinese culture.
14. For Christians, the apostle Thomas is the patron saint of India.

> these kingdoms. After having been ignominiously chased away, people are not even willing to hear their name, which means that they now have much less power there than any other missionaries, if any of them find a way to get in; this is what we are experiencing now in Cochinchina and Tonkin. Everyone knows that it was not the Jesuits who introduced us there. The Jesuits were so resentful at seeing us in their place that I doubt very much that the local people were sorry to see their expulsion. They have used so many tricks and so much cunning to force us to leave, either willingly or by violent means, that there is reason to believe that it would be a great consolation to them in their exile to see us exiled with them. You know from the reports that have been sent to you that all the opposition they used against us has only served to make their passions better known, and to discredit them more, and at the same time to win for us more esteem among the Christians and to increase our acceptance by them.[15]

Finally, the Bishop of Heliopolis, strengthened by the dignity conferred on him by his episcopal character, reminded the directors of the limits of their power and reaffirmed the authority of the Vicars Apostolic who alone were mandated to decide on the conduct of the missions.

> The zeal you have for our missions causes you to overstep the mark. You give the impression that you want to govern them even though you are very far away, and you have no experience of either the places or the people. The actual direction is in the hands of the Vicars Apostolic who have the title and grace for this purpose. They are appointed by God himself who has called them to this work, and the Church has provided them with all the necessary faculties and powers. As regards our relationship with the Jesuit Fathers in these districts, bearing in mind the advice you have given us and all that I have set out in this discourse, we beg you not to concern yourselves about it any further and to be at peace. We assure you that in this as in everything else we will do nothing without having carefully thought it through with the utmost rigour, in all the circumstances in which we find ourselves. We shall base our decisions on whatever we believe will be most pleasing to

---

15. Letter of Pallu to the directors in Sy, *La Société*.

God, whom alone we wish to please, and whatever is most advantageous to the good of our missions, which we seek above all else.[16]

A contested election: Louis Laneau as Vicar Apostolic

Having agreed about the attitude to adopt towards the directors in Paris, the two bishops still had an important and delicate problem to settle, that of the election of a third Vicar Apostolic who would have jurisdiction over Siam and North China. The Roman texts stipulated that this person should be chosen from among the first men to leave for the missions. The candidate favoured by all, whether in Paris, Rome or Ayutthaya, was Jacques de Bourges, but he was now assigned to Tonkin with Deydier. Hainques and Brindeau were dead. Of the three pioneer teams, only Louis Laneau and Louis Chevreuil remained. The former had the support of Pierre Lambert. He had a very good knowledge of the Siamese world and great popularity with the locals, both at court and among the Talapoins,[17] with whom he frequently conversed, and among the ordinary people.

Ever since he had been entrusted with the apostolate among the Siamese in 1664, Louis Laneau had devoted himself with great zeal to this task. As early as 1665, he travelled around the villages surrounding the capital. Aware of the obstacle constituted by the political-religious system of Buddhism, and therefore of the need to adopt a long-term strategy of gradual acceptance, he chose, in an evangelical spirit, to focus on the outcasts of Siamese society: prisoners, the sick and the poor, for whom he opened a 'small hospice,' i. e. a dispensary, in the French camp, to which patients flocked, attracted by his reputation as a doctor. Devoting all his free time to the study of the language, he translated into Siamese the principal prayers and a summary of doctrine; he wrote in the same language a treatise on theology, and undertook the preparation of a grammar and a dictionary in Siamese and in Pali.[18]

As for Louis Chevreuil, he was the preferred candidate of François Pallu, who had been his companion since the distant days of their studies in Paris. According to Vachet, Louis Chevreuil was a member

---

16. Letter Pallu directors in Sy, *La Société*.
17. Talapoins is a name for Buddhist monks.
18. Pali is an ancient language of India, and it is the language of the Buddhist scriptures.

of the group of Good Friends who went to Rome in 1656 to support the mission of the Vicars Apostolic. He himself was even considered for the episcopate, but at the last moment Ignatius Cotolendi was preferred. Either because he still believed him to be the most capable of exercising this office, or because he wanted to compensate him for the abuse he had suffered in Cambodia, Macau and Goa, François Pallu seemed very much attached to the candidacy of Chevreuil.

The disagreement was all the more embarrassing because each Vicar Apostolic was convinced that he had priority over the other. In fact, Pierre Lambert had received in Ayutthaya the original of the writ *E sublimi* of 28 February 1665, which authorized the two bishops to elect a third and stipulated that in the event that they could not agree, the power was granted to Lambert alone, Pallu being able to exercise it only if his confrere was dead. But in France, Pallu was given a copy of the same brief, authenticated by the Archbishop of Paris, which did not include the restrictive clause in favour of Lambert and implied that the Bishop of Heliopolis alone had the right to choose. Was it a deliberate falsification of the document or a simple error of the copyist? François Pallu particularly, revolted by all the pressure that he had submitted to from the directors of the seminary at the time of his sojourn in Paris, opted for the first assumption and reproached them openly for this abuse whereas Pierre Lambert, great man that he was, pretended to believe an error had occurred. Bénigne Vachet described the scene that took place between the two men: 'The Bishop of Beirut, laughing, said to him: "Don't you see, Sir, that it is a copyist's mistake to put your name in place of my name?" And without wishing to prolong the matter, he added: This error should not stop us from acting. Since we are both here together, let us disregard what has happened and let us see if together we can come to a decision about these two missionaries.'[19] Pierre Lambert then proposed to his confrere that they should imitate the apostles and draw lots, thereby leaving the choice to the Holy Spirit.

> Two slips of paper were obtained, one with Louis Laneau written on it and the other with Louis Chevreuil. The prelates then prayed the prayer of the apostles which is found in the Acts of the Apostles (1:24–26) for a similar case. Mgr de Beirut put them in his square cap and having mixed them

---

19. Memoir by Bénigne Vachet. AMEP, volume 110b, 233.

together, presented it to Mgr d'Heliopolis who drew the first one that his hand came upon. Having opened it, he seemed surprised to read Louis Laneau on it. Mgr de Beirut, who noticed his astonishment, said to him: 'Mgr, fold this slip as it was before and draw a paper a second time.' Without praying, Mgr. d'Heliopolis put his hand in the cap and brought forth the same slip. Confused by his own temerity, he threw himself at the knees of Mgr de Beirut and asked his forgiveness, agreeing that M. Louis Laneau should be elected Bishop of Métellopolis, Vicar Apostolic of Siam.[20]

It was soon evident that Louis laneau was the better man for the task, for François Pallu himself soon had to admit that Louis Chevreuil, irreparably traumatized by his ordeals, would have been incapable of exercising the office that he wanted to entrust to him. Bénigne Vachet tells us, in fact, that after Laneau's election 'they examined M. Chevreuil's report, and gave him all the time he wanted in order to explain the ideas that troubled his imagination. At that time, Mgr de Beirut, who knew more than anyone else about such matters, convinced Mgr d'Heliopolis that all that he had reported and written was pure illusion and fantasy, which God had allowed in order to test the fidelity of his servant.'[21]

---

20. Memoir, Bénigne Vachet, 233.
21. On 30 July 1675, Pierre Lambert clarified this point in a letter to Cardinal Bona. AMEP, volume 858: 309. 'Two or three years ago, an account was sent to your Eminence in which one of us, named Louis Chevreuil, exposes different types of misdeeds which, he says, take place in different parts of the region. As they are not all very well known, we have not yet been able to evaluate them properly. But what seemed to be the most serious of all is his claim that he had very often been presented with hosts made of rice flour and that many priests used such bread in the sacrifice of the Mass. But after a long investigation we finally discovered that these hosts were made in accordance with the Christian law, and it was very clear that he had been misled by haphazard assumptions. We felt it our duty to inform Your Eminence of this.' The bishop is referring here to the report that Chevreuil had written on Pallu's orders at their meeting in Surat. He had enough to reproach the Portuguese religious and he could not allow erroneous accusations to be made which would undermine the credibility of the French missionaries and play into the hands of their adversaries. Louis Chevreuil never regained his mental health and was sometimes a heavy burden for his confreres. After having exercised the office of procurator of the mission of Siam until 1677, as far as his condition allowed, he ended his life in Camp Saint-Joseph, doing what he could in the seminary. Because of his condition, he was allowed to go free during the revolution of 1688–1689. He died in Ayutthaya on 10 November 1691, aged sixty-six.

Suspicions, rumours and whispers

However, even though it was the only one possible, the election of Louis Laneau did not satisfy everyone in the St Joseph camp, because, like François Pallu, some missionaries, while recognizing the human and spiritual qualities of the new Vicar Apostolic, doubted his real capacity to exercise such important power. Indeed, while Louis Laneau had shown himself to be a pastor of exemplary zeal and devotion, he had also shown a certain dislike for administrative tasks. Moreover, he had given little time to the college and administration in the capital, preferring to use his energy in the countryside. Many of his confreres considered him an idealist, and his hope of converting the Siamese a utopian dream.

Over the years, a growing uneasiness would affect the relations in Ayutthaya between the 'old' missionaries (the survivors of the first three teams who were relatively united among themselves) and the 'new' ones who, before leaving Paris, were subjected to a veritable indoctrination by the directors against Pierre Lambert and his way of life. Ever since Rome had rejected the ascetic rules of the Lovers of the Cross, the Bishop of Beirut had become more suspect than ever in the eyes of the Parisian leaders, even though he had obeyed and renounced perpetual fasting. The directors ordered the young departing missionaries to keep an eye on him and send them a report about his conduct and the behaviour of those close to him. Philippe de Chamesson wrote to them in 1672, 'We all eat meat except for Mgr Laneau, who very rarely eats it because it does not agree with him. Since Mgr de Beirut returned from Cochinchina, he has always eaten meat.'[22]

Thus Louis Laneau who, suffering from incurable dropsy and digestive problems, had to follow a very strict diet regime, was accused of disobedience and was obliged to justify himself to the directors.

> I can assure you of our submission when we received the response from Rome regarding our affairs, meaning the rules that had been put in place here. Also, I beg you not to believe that I was being disobedient or attached to what I had

---

22. Letter from Philippe de Chamesson to the directors, Siam, 2 November 1672. AMEP, volume 858, 237–238. This systematic prejudice against Lambert is also contained in the reproaches that Pallu addresses to the directors in his letter of 3 November 1673.

> become accustomed to do. While I continue to abstain from meat as usual, the great physical weakness with which I have been afflicted since my time in Persia does not allow me to do otherwise. The climate is very different from that of Paris, and does not allow the use of heavy meat nor its consumption in such large quantities as in France or Europe. This is what causes so many deaths amongst Europeans who come to the Indies and want to live there as they did in their own country. The doctors who have spoken about these matters in the Indies have provided enough tangible reasons as to leave no doubt about this necessity. Besides, a missionary who is accustomed to good food will have great difficulty in carrying out missionary work in villages where there is almost nothing. I had this experience whenever I left this house, and M. Perez has the same experience on the island of Juncelam. To kill animals in front of friendly people would give them the same aversion for us as they would have for a very great sinner.[23]

On several occasions in the following years, Louis Laneau took up this idea and tried to convince the directors and his confreres of the need to adopt a vegetarian diet in a Buddhist environment. Indeed, his arguments in favour of adapting to local religious customs, which often caused him to be compared to Roberto de Nobili SJ, seem to be fully legitimate today. However, they were never considered seriously and the question of food became a sort of fixed idea which poisoned relations between the Vicars Apostolic and the directors. Thus, while it is reasonable to hold that the rules of the Lovers of the Cross were too restrictive to be adapted to all contexts and to all missionary temperaments, it is also true that the stubbornness of the directors in their determination to standardize the ways of life and to 'normalize' them, that is to say, to want to align them completely with the Western model, seems to be abusive and inadequate today.

Of course, when they criticized Louis Laneau, it was Pierre Lambert who remained the main target of the directors, and it was on him that they sought to put pressure through his closest companion. And even though he did everything possible to avoid any cause for complaint, for example by forcing himself to eat meat, the bishop of Beirut was deeply hurt by their perpetual mistrust and surveillance.

---

23. Letter from Louis Laneau to the directors of the seminary, Ayutthaya. 20 October 1670. AMEP, volume 858, 229–230.

For in spite of his rigour and detachment, he was a generous man, full of solicitude, who loved his fellow missionaries deeply and never neglected to help them materially, morally or spiritually. His apparent indifference in times of hardship and annoyance, his demands on himself and others, were not so much the mark of a natural insensitivity as the fruit of a relentless inner self-discipline.

The rejection of the Congregation project deeply affected him because, given his spirituality and the precise circumstances in which he lived, it seemed to him to be truly born of divine inspiration and indispensable both for convincing the Siamese and for avoiding the medium-term slackness of his own missionaries. Since this refusal, he allowed himself to be overcome by a feeling of abandonment and misunderstanding which, aggravated by his more and more frequent illnesses and the permanent tension of his struggle against the religious of Padroado, caused him to adopt an attitude of withdrawal and isolation. Little by little, he was afflicted with an emotional distress which he hid under an affectation of coldness.

It was in this tense atmosphere that the three Vicars Apostolic, overcoming their disagreements, drew up the *Recommendations* for the government of the seminary of Siam. Inspired by the *Instructions* of 1665, it gave rules of conduct for the missionaries, the seminarians and the servants, and defined the principles of management of all the ecclesial facilities of Camp Saint-Joseph. After Laneau's consecration, this plan of action was completed on 14 April 1674 by the signing of a concordat between the three Vicars Apostolic, which established the superiority of the Vicar Apostolic residing in Siam and advocated the pooling of all personal income as well as the equal sharing of material and human resources between the seminary and the three vicariates.

However, Pierre Lambert also had another idea in mind, for he no longer had any confidence in the directors whom he considered incapable of understanding the situation of the missionaries in the field. He knew that the conflict with the Jesuits was insoluble in the short term, and that consequently the disagreement with their French supporters and protectors was likely to last a long time and even to worsen. The result would be significant damage to missionary recruitment which was already noticeably insufficient.

For some time, he had been looking for an alternative solution and, in September 1673, he succeeded in convincing his two confreres to send a circular letter to M. de Bretonvilliers, Superior General of

Saint-Sulpice,[24] inviting all the ecclesiastics of France to come and work in the missions.

> We beg you to do this in the name of so many thousands of souls who perish every day for lack of missionaries; we beg you to do this in the interests of the universal Church, to whose service you have dedicated yourselves and which can, by your means, extend its boundaries to the very ends of the world; we beg you to do this for the honour of the clergy of France, to whom our missions belong for many reasons. Casting the eyes of our solicitude in all directions, we have focused them particularly on your seminaries which all bear the characteristics of their first founder of very holy and happy memory, who burned with zeal for the salvation of infidels. The late Father Olier poured out his heart to the Bishop of Heliopolis shortly before his death, assuring him that he would be most happy to spend the rest of his days in the service of the church in Tonkin.[25]

In the end, this proposal of union with Saint Sulpice, renewed in 1676, was not accepted. The directors kept control of recruitment but gradually distanced themselves from the Jesuits, and the Paris Society of Foreign Missions consolidated its status as an independent association of priests committed for life to the ministry *ad exteros*, without undergoing any major institutional upheavals in the course of its history. But this attempt showed that the spirit which animated the discussions of the first three Vicars Apostolic in the autumn of 1673 in Ayutthaya was very much ahead of its time and already foreshadowed the spirit that inspired the sending of *fidei donum* priests[26] much later.

---

24. The Saint Sulpice Seminary was established in 1641 in Vaugirard, a village close to Paris, by Jean-Jacques Olier, who founded the Society of the Priests of Saint Sulpice.
25. Circular letter to all the ecclesiastics of France inviting them to come and work in the missions, addressed to M. de Bretonvilliers, Superior General of Saint Sulpice. AMEP, volume 876, 860–861.
26. *Fidei donum* priests are diocesan priests sent by their bishops to help evangelize mission territories away from their home dioceses.

The receptions of Phra Narai

While the three apostolic vicars were preoccupied with all these problems of general administration, a solemn event was being prepared at the court of Phra Narai, the official reception of the messages of Louis XIV and Clement IX brought by François Pallu. However, the protocol arrangements encountered difficulties because Pierre Lambert wanted to take advantage of this occasion to enter into direct contact with the sovereign, which was contrary to Siamese etiquette. The negotiations lasted more than four months, but the tenacious Vicar Apostolic was finally successful. 'It was difficult to find out how these letters could be delivered, because this prince never gave a private audience to any foreigner, and besides, the bishops considered it extremely important to present them to him themselves,' said the Mission Journal. After His Majesty had been sufficiently informed of the quality and importance of the two sovereigns who had written to him, he made it known to our prelates that, to mark the esteem in which he held them, he wished to receive them with extraordinary pomp in a public audience.

'This resolution gave rise to a new problem regarding the manner in which the two bishops should appear in his presence, because no one can be seated, or standing, or shod, or otherwise than prostrate on the ground; this is such an inviolable custom among them that even ambassadors are not exempt from it. The bishops made their representations during three or four months without any agreement being reached. There were several things in the ceremonies that they were asked to do which they found unacceptable. They were quite definite in refusing to do anything that would harm the respect due to religion, the dignity of their persons and the glory of France, whose great monarch had recently won such brilliant victories that the publicity about them reverberated throughout the world. The king was willing to modify protocol on certain points. He agreed that they could wear their shoes, could be seated on a special richly embroidered carpet, and that they could make their civilities in the European manner.'[27]

Perhaps to persuade Phra Narai, he was reminded that France was then at war with his own enemies, the Dutch, who had confiscated in Bantan the gifts that were to accompany the letters of the pope

---

27. Relation des missions et des voyages, 107, Siam, Documents historiques, t. 1: 43.

and the king. So it was that the embassy visit took place with all the pomp and circumstance expected on 18 October 1673. In front of an audience of dignitaries prostrate at the foot of the throne, the three bishops sat down and bowed 'three times to the king;' then a mandarin read the two messages that had been translated by Laneau. The king then asked the French some questions, through a minister. Favourably impressed by the dignity of his visitors, he announced to them a few days later his intention to send an ambassador to Europe to carry his answers to the pope and to the King of France. Moreover, he invited them to another meeting with less protocol at his hunting residence in Louvo.

On November 19, the bishops, accompanied by their missionaries, embarked on the twenty-six-oar boat that the king had sent them. In Louvo, they were lodged in a house close to the palace and on November 22 they went to the reception, mounted on two elephants of the royal herd. 'The two bishops climbed onto one, where there was a seat with a railing of half a foot all around. They were seated together in surplice and hood, and Mgr de Metellopolis was mounted on the other in cassock and long cloak. The king, magnificently adorned with the golden crown on his cap studded all over with diamonds, was on a black elephant.'

'He had several officers of his court at his feet showing the utmost respect; the minister and a mandarin on two elephants, but without a seat, bowed low. As soon as the bishops were in sight, the minister came to meet them to introduce them to the king, to whom they bowed three times. This prince received them very kindly, and had them approach so close to him that the tusks of their elephants were able to touch each other. This surprised the whole court, and caused the court mandarins who are powerful there to murmur about such a special honour, which had never been bestowed on anyone of their nation.'[28]

François Pallu himself was astonished to note the good will which his confrere Lambert enjoyed with a monarch as inaccessible as the King of Siam, and he did not fail to point this out to the French authorities. 'It is through the care taken by Mgr de Beirut that this affair had such a favourable outcome. There were no small difficulties to overcome, mainly due to the secret opposition of some powerful

---

28. Mission diary. AMEP, volume 854, 856–857.

people and even of whole nations', he wrote to Colbert. 'I hope by the grace of God, from which this worthy prelate is accustomed to draw his enlightenment and strength, that he will derive many advantages from this event in laying solid foundations for our holy faith in this kingdom. He has already achieved this in the kingdoms of Tonkin and Cochinchina, of which he has made himself the master, so to speak, in very difficult times, notwithstanding the formal opposition of the rulers, and the hardships and threats of our own ministers of the Gospel.'[29]

An ambiguous position

Indeed, at first, the king seemed quite willing to grant new favours to the missionaries. On his return to the capital, he called Louis Laneau to the court to announce that he wished to enlarge Camp Saint-Joseph and to see a large brick house built there 'which we intend to make into a church,' as Pierre Lambert explained to one of his correspondents. No doubt the simultaneous presentation of the letters from the pope and the French king contributed to increase in Phra Narai's mind the confusion between political and religious power and led him to consider the future building as a French embassy suited to the dignity of his nation, whereas for the missionaries it was above all a place of worship, similar to a cathedral, destined to give the Christian presence in Siam an official status and to receive a growing crowd of converts.

A form of cooperation in trompe-l'œil was thus established between the king and the Vicars Apostolic, in which each one followed his own idea without raising questions about the real intentions of the partner. The fact remains that the sovereign followed the project very closely. He had the plans drawn up by the French for their church-residence sent to him and, one day when he was walking in his ceremonial galley on the Menam River, he chose the location himself, on the camp of the Cochinchinese who were forced to move elsewhere to the great embarrassment of the missionaries.

In the midst of these great projects, in December 1673, when a storm had just brought back to Ayutthaya one of the fiercest adversaries

---

29. Letter from François Pallu to Colbert, Siam, 8 November 1673. AMEP, volume 857, 281.

of the French, the Jesuit Philippe Marini, Pierre Lambert once again fell seriously ill. 'I am much weaker and more indisposed than usual, and this makes me believe, with some justification, that the good God is tired of my poor service and that in his mercy, he does not wish to withdraw me from this unfortunate exile lest I be more unfaithful to him. If this were not so, I would find it difficult to refuse this king's wish that I should accompany his ambassadors whom he has resolved to send to His Holiness and to His Most Christian Majesty next year,' he wrote on December 3.[30]

Indeed, Phra Narai, who was anxious to make use of such a fine intermediary, sent two of his physicians to him. One of them was a Chinese from Canton whom the missionaries immediately undertook to catechize. They were hoping for a conversion that would have a great impact on the court where Laneau used his numerous connections to advance his work in favour of Christianity. In the end, the doctor was not converted, but he cured his patient who, on 2 February 1674, wrote a letter of thanks to the sovereign. It is astonishing to note how Pierre Lambert, who until then had been so cautious and reserved in his relations with the authorities, now allowed himself to be drawn into the political game, with the consummate ease and skill of a former civil dignitary. It was because this mystic was also a pragmatist that he followed external developments very closely. Now, in the immediate future two considerations urged him to take action. On the one hand, he still feared Muslim competition and sought to exploit the temporary advantage enjoyed by the missionaries because of the king's diplomatic projects. On the other hand, in Cochinchina, unforeseen circumstances forced him to adjust to a completely new situation.

The official appeal from Cochinchina

Indeed, two years earlier, an incident that could have had serious consequences finally allowed the Bishop of Beirut to make contact with the Cochinchese government. While returning from his first clandestine stay in his vicariate, in April 1672, on the Menam River, at the entrance to Ayutthava, his boat encountered the craft of the

---

30. Letter from Pierre Lambert to Philippe de Chamesson, Siam, 3 December 1673. AMEP, volume 858, 270.

Cochinchinese ambassador who was leaving for home. It was at the time of a war between the two Vietnamese states when the bishop had with him a dozen young Cochinchinese whom he intended to send to the seminary of Ayutthaya where they would be educated with Tonkinese nationals. To cut short the suspicions of the ambassador, who wanted to investigate and seize these young people who had departed illegally from their country, Pierre Lambert decided to lay his cards on the table, or almost.

Without actually admitting where he came from, the Vicar Apostolic asked the ambassador to take a letter to his sovereign in which he explained the reasons for his presence in Asia and requested permission to carry out his mission. It was a skilful and well-considered plea, written in Chinese characters and Asian style in terms similar to the one that had won over Phra Narai a few years earlier. 'We were born in the West, in the part of the world called Europe, more than ten thousand leagues from here. Many years ago, while still in our homeland, through reports of your fame, we learned that Your Majesty, whose heart is full of goodness and clemency, had allowed the message of truth to be preached in your kingdom. We heard that a multitude of foreign nations came from all directions to give Your Majesty signs of their gratitude and offer you their most humble services. From that time on, we planned to come and assure you of our profound respect for you as missionaries, that is to say, as messengers sent to bring to you and your people words of truth and justice. We arrived in the kingdom of Siam with this hope, but on arrival we were informed that Your Majesty had forbidden the preaching of the message by your edicts to all the subjects who owed you obedience; since that time we have not dared to leave here to go and pay you our respects, for fear of incurring your displeasure. However, as we believe now that you think more favourably of us, we beg you to approve of a personal visit by us to assure you of our esteem for you and our fidelity, and to speak a few words of the most solid virtue, so that you may be persuaded that the message we announce is the true one.'[31]

This bluff succeeded. The offer was accepted and in March 1673, Bénigne Vachet, accompanied by a new Cochinchinese priest,

---

31. Letter from Pierre Lambert to the King of Cochinchina, in *Relations et voyages, 1672–75*, quoted in Launay. Histoire *Cochinchine*, 125–126.

Manuel Bon, set sail for Faifo with a letter and gifts destined for Chua Hien-Vuong: a branch of coral, a Venetian mirror set in an agate stone, a silver alarm clock and another of copper. In November, after many ups and downs and the death of Claude Guiart, who died under suspicious circumstances on June 3,[32] Guillaume Mahot was able to go to court in place of Vachet, who was bedridden by illness. The king received the request of the Vicar Apostolic and replied that he granted freedom of worship to the Christians and invited him to Cochinchina where he could reside in complete peace. The reasons for this reversal are complex. According to the little story reported by the irrepressible Vachet, always on the lookout for court gossip, 'at that time, relations between the king and queen were rather strained and he sought to restore their friendship. It was in the apartment of this princess that the minister had an audience. When the queen saw the branch of coral, she praised it so highly that the king presented it to her, saying that he was delighted to have found a curiosity that pleased her.'[33]

Why not? The heart can have its reasons that the reasons of state do not know... But one can also advance more political explanations: while the military situation stabilized in the north of the kingdom thanks to the victorious resistance of the Cochinchinese troops to a new Tonkinese assault, it became tense in the south where Chua Hien-Vuong was planning an expedition to Cambodia, which would not fail to provoke a reaction from his Siamese neighbour. No doubt the Chua, alerted by his intelligence services to what was happening in Ayutthaya, wished to profit from the diplomatic advantages offered by such an influential figure as the Bishop of Beirut and at the same

---

32. 'Although his best friends had warned him several times that he was not careful enough about the people he allowed into his house, his natural goodness could not suspect anyone of the evil that some were guilty of. He had never enjoyed more perfect health than when he was attacked violently by a burning pain that caused him to say that he was poisoned, for in less than twenty-four hours he changed this mortal life into a happier one. The Christians suspected a newcomer to whom he gave too much credit. After his death, the marks of the poison appeared unexpectedly on the 1st and 3rd of June 1674. The infamous poisoner was pursued, but he was not caught. This unfortunate man, a few days later, died as if enraged, not wanting to receive either sacraments or consolation, confessing his crime which he considered unworthy of forgiveness.' Memoir of Bénigne Vachet. AMEP, volume 110b, 137.
33. Launay, Histoire*Cochinchine*, 128.

time to distance him from Phra Narai. Thus, during the following years, the Vicar Apostolic, by playing both sides, finally became a hostage of the rivalry between the two sovereigns.

In February 1674, a Cochinchinese ship brought an invitation from Hien-Vuong to Ayutthaya. Phra Narai, informed in his turn, worried about the intentions of the bishop. The bishop replied, as a good Norman,[34] that he could not 'exempt himself from going to thank the prince for the honour he has done him in allowing him to remain in his kingdom, and for allowing the freedom of the Catholic religion. Moreover, if the King of Siam wishes him to remain here under the same conditions, the obligation he has, combined with his inclination, would encourage him to end his days here for the service of God and that of His Majesty'.[35]

In March, Louis Laneau returned to Camp Saint-Joseph after a three-month stay at court. In an attempt to create the nucleus of a Siamese Christian community more substantial than the few scattered conversions recorded until then, he asked the king for about fifty families for the service of the missionaries, 'who are the most suitable for embracing the Christian religion, i. e. who have neither talapoins nor pagodas'.[36] The French understood very well by this time that without the agreement of the king, the conversion of the true Siamese, i.e. the Buddhists, would remain impossible or at least very marginal. And as Phra Narai was absolutely committed to his embassy project, they decided to subject him to a kind of diplomatic blackmail. If he 'persists in wanting the Bishop of Beirut to remain in his country, he will do so on condition that His Majesty grants letters patent, by which he allows his subjects to embrace the Catholic religion and missionaries to preach it everywhere'.[37]

While waiting for a new opportunity to present itself, Pierre Lambert, assisted by François Pallu and Louis Chevreuil, conferred episcopal ordination on Louis Laneau on Easter Sunday, March 25.

In April a second Cochinese emissary arrived. Hien-Vuong insisted, he was still waiting for 'his' Vicar Apostolic, or at least one of his missionaries. Pierre Lambert thought it was time to act and to put Phra Narai's back against the wall. He notified the court of his

---

34. A Norman was a native of Normandy, a province of north-west France.
35. Mission Journal, AMEP, volume 876: 898. In Launay, Siam, volume 1, 53–54.
36. Mission Journal, Launay, 53–54.
37. Mission Journal, Launay, 53–54.

arrival and left for Louvo with Laneau on May 6, while Pallu prepared his departure for Tonkin. While officially the reason for his visit was to 'take leave of His Majesty, thank him for all his kindness and ask him for a passport to go to Cochinchina',[38] Pierre Lambert tried to convince a mandarin among his friends to propose his deal to the king. But the mandarin excused himself, explaining to the bishop 'that he was asking too much, that he should be happy with all the favours the king had bestowed on him contrary to all the customs of the kingdom; that, in his opinion, it was enough that the king allowed Christians of all nations to be made his subjects without saying anything about it, even though he was very much aware of it. Moreover, by having a church built at his own expense, there could be no doubt that he approved of the Catholic religion'.[39] Thus, the affair ended abruptly and the king even refused the passport because he 'wants to send some ambassadors to Europe this year', and because he wished 'that one of the bishops should accompany them, but he very much wishes that the Bishop of Beirut should remain in his kingdom because of the friendship which he has for him and because he believes him qualified to preserve his alliance with his Supreme Christian Majesty'.[40] Pierre Lambert had to submit, although the embassy project was delayed until the end of the Franco-Dutch war, which made the sea routes even less safe than usual. All he could do for his mission was to send two men immediately, in June, to provide support: Gabriel Bouchard, destined for Champa, and Jean de Courtaulin, named pro-vicar alongside Guillaume Mahot.

While the bishops were busy with their negotiations, Father Philippe Marini SJ, for his part, did everything he could to harm them. On the feast of Saint Ignatius, he preached against them, declaring that 'if there were only Italians living where there were Portuguese, no one would welcome the bulls supposedly granted to the Vicars Apostolic, who breathe falsehood and secrecy, so that all the religious of our society must oppose them with all their power'.[41]

It was in this poisonous atmosphere that François Pallu prepared to leave for Tonkin on board a sailing ship chartered by a Norman merchant, M. de Hautmesnil, to whom he had rendered a service

---

38. Mission Journal, Launay, 53–54.
39. Mission Journal, Launay, 53–54.
40. Mission Journal, Launay, 53–54.
41. Mission Journal, Launay, 53–54.

during his stopover at Fort-Dauphin and who had since linked his interests to those of the Vicar Apostolic. The ship, named La Conception, carried 13,000 pounds of merchandise, 10,000 of which were owned by the mission, which the merchant intended to resell in Tonkin. This venture was not entirely in keeping with the rigorous spirit of Pierre Lambert, who was forced to give up some of his scruples about commerce, but it fitted in quite well with the more flexible viewpoint of his colleague, who was very open to economic-missionary cooperation.

It also had the great advantage of making the King of Tonkin wait and of relieving de Bourges and Deydier, whose presence in Phô-hiên was only justified by the imminent arrival of the first ships of the East Indies Company which for four years had been desperately awaited. Moreover, it was clearly understood that Mgr Pallu would not receive any profit from the sales and that he would return quickly to Siam since it was finally agreed that he would accompany the embassy of Phra Narai. When they parted on August 20, almost seventeen years after their first meeting in Rome, François Pallu and Pierre Lambert did not know that they would not see each other again. The first left for an unintended tour of the world. When he returned to Ayutthaya in 1682, the second had ceased to suffer and to fight for three years and was resting in peace in the cemetery of Saint-Joseph.

Chapter 8
Last battles, last victories

A suspicion laden pause

The winter of 1674–1675 was a time of anxiety and expectation for Pierre Lambert. Administratively, his burden seemed less heavy, since, following the departure of François Pallu for his vicariate in Tonkin and the appointment of Louis Laneau to Siam, he was officially responsible only for Cochinchina. But his diplomatic prestige and his moral credit kept him in Ayutthaya where, for the king as well as for the missionaries, he occupied a pivotal role. Whether he liked it or not, he continued to bear the burden of all the churches, with their recurring problems: the lack of men, the lack of money, the opposition of the Jesuits and the Portuguese. The Spanish Dominicans in the Philippines promised to send six of their men, but the Jesuits persuaded the governor of Manila to prevent their departure. In addition, shortly before All Saints Day, Louis of the Mother of God, the Portuguese Franciscan who had been working at the seminary since the previous year, was excommunicated and declared an apostate by one of his confreres, Anthony of Saint Catherine.

In December 1674, a ship driven off course by a storm between Tonkin and the Philippines brought news to Ayutthaya of François Deydier and Jacques de Bourges, but none of François Pallu who had not yet arrived at his mission. Fearing that his confrere had perished in a shipwreck, aware of his own weakening condition and concerned about the future of the French enterprise, Pierre Lambert immediately wrote to Rome to ask that the three Vicars Apostolic be allowed to choose their successors, that a fourth position be created for China, and that the incumbent of Siam be designated as general administrator of all the missions. Shortly afterwards, he learned that Philippe de Chamesson, the missionaries' most trusted lay companion, had died in prison after being captured by the troops of the King of Golconda, then at war with France.

In the spring of 1675, an old acquaintance of the French, the Jesuit Thomas Valguarnera, disembarked in Ayutthaya. He was returning to his mission at the end of his mandate as visitor to the province of Japan. While there he had taken the opportunity to inform Rome of all the failings in general he had perceived in the missionaries from Paris, and of the Bishop of Beirut in particular. He was accompanied by a Portuguese priest, Jean d'Abreu de Lima, appointed by the chapter of Goa as visitor to the diocese of Malacca and as such, charged with the task of countering the power over Siam that Pierre Lambert claimed for himself, wrongfully according to Jean d'Abreu. To carry out this task, he brandished the usual weapons: Christians were ordered to obey him under pain of excommunication and priests who did not submit to his jurisdiction would be placed under an edict.

On March 25, Jean d'Abreu notified the French missionaries of his presence. Louis Laneau, who as Vicar Apostolic of Siam was now its official leader, informed him of his own election and, notwithstanding d'Abreu's claims, on Holy Saturday, April 13, ordained a priest of Filipino origin, Jean-Baptiste Bangayana, and conferred minor orders on twelve native seminarians. A few days later, on the 21st, he declared Jean d'Abreu suspended for having administered the sacraments without his episcopal authorization, before being in turn excommunicated by his opponent, who renewed his orders concerning Christians. As usual, the contradictory sentences were displayed at the door of the churches of each camp. When he left Siam shortly afterwards, in the company of the Jesuit Fathers Tissanier and Marini, Jean d'Abreu transferred his powers to a Portuguese secular priest, Nicolas da Motta, who had already opposed Pierre Lambert in the past and who now had the task of maintaining the pressure. Thus, when, in the following month of August, Laneau sent to the religious the papal brief *Cœlestibus et apostolicis* which dismissed Fragoso's claims against Pierre Lambert and ordered him to leave Siam, the superior of the Dominicans, Emmanuel de la Nativité acquiesced after some reluctance, but Thomas Valguarnera SJ rejected it on the pretext that it had not passed through the chancery of Lisbon.

Although he certainly supported in private his young confrere, and perhaps even encouraged him, Pierre Lambert seemed to be curiously absent from this new quarrel. It was because, from now on, the affairs of Siam did not concern him directly, but more importantly because two much more serious problems preoccupied him. First of all, there was the fate of François Pallu, who had just been arrested in Manila, where his ship had been diverted by a storm. And while the prisoner, in the letters he sent to Europe, expressed satisfaction at the good conduct of the Jesuits towards him, he seemed to be unaware of the cause of his misadventure. For Pierre Lambert, on the contrary, matters seemed to be much clearer: 'He was driven by a violent storm to the Philippine Islands and then betrayed by a spy of some kind who handed him over to the Fathers of the Society of Jesus, who held him prisoner. Moreover, the ship was confiscated by the royal taxation authorities and the captain is being held prisoner.'[1] So the Bishop of Beirut asked the Roman authorities to intervene with the Spanish Government to obtain the release of the Vicar Apostolic and the restitution of his goods, including a large subsidy for Tonkin which amounted to several thousand silver coins. It created a very large hole in the French mission's budget which already had a serious deficit.

An emergency situation in Cochinchina

This financial loss was all the more serious because Pierre Lambert needed money to travel to Cochinchina. In May, Guillaume Mahot and Bénigne Vachet arrived in Ayutthaya on a boat lent by Hien-Vuong to bring the bishop to his vicariate. The report they gave him encouraged him to hasten his departure, for the situation of the mission had become very difficult. The schism was aggravated because the Jesuits and the French missionaries were now almost equal in number. In fact, at the same time as Fathers Courtaulin and Bouchard arrived, two new Jesuit Fathers from Macau—a Sicilian, Joseph Candone, and a French returnee, Ignace Baudet—arrived clandestinely. Guillaume Mahot, who had been reluctantly acting as pro-vicar since the death of Claude Guiart, put forward a proposal to them: 'Not to require any submission from them for a year and a

---

1. Letter from Pierre Lambert to the Propaganda, incomplete, s. d, spring–summer 1675. AMEP, volume 857, 349. When he left Manila, François Pallu understood that the Jesuits were not totally unrelated to his arrest, the official reason for which was, as for Bouchard before him, the suspicion of spying for France, which was then at war with Spain. Indeed, he told the directors in 1677 that five Jesuits from Manila had filed a complaint against him, accusing him of trading and being a Jansenist (cf Baudiment, note 1, 306).

half, on condition that they agree that, after the year and a half has expired without receiving anything from Rome, they will accept the bull of Clement IX.'[2] The Jesuits refused, and while Baudet moved to the south where he could observe and annoy Bouchard, Candone went to hide in Hué at the home of the founder, Jean de la Croix. The latter's son, Clément, took it upon himself to take to the court twenty-seven articles denouncing the French.

This request, in which the claw of the Jesuits is clearly recognizable, 'contained in its malignity some truths, but in addition so many lies, so much slander and deceit that it could not have been more appalling if the devil had dictated it', Vachet declared.[3] Fortunately, the latter, while convalescing in Faifo, found a way to make friends with several high-ranking figures, including the sister of the Minister of State for Foreigners, Ou Phu Ma, who was also the king's son-in-law. At the end of complex manoeuvres that he described with his usual prolixity, Vachet succeeded in burying this file, the consequences of which could have been catastrophic for the French, because some of the charges, although fallacious, were extremely serious. They were accused of no more and no less than conspiring with the enemy for having brought two Tonkinese spies into Cochinchina (which was completely false); they were educating Tonkinese and Cochinchinese together in Siam (which was true) and the missionaries of Tonkin were corresponding with those of Cochinchina (which was neither true nor false since all the news passed through Aytutthaya). They were also reproached for having chosen 'in the province of Quangnhiac the most beautiful daughters of the Christians to enclose them in a house whose entrance is forbidden to men, but not to the missionaries, who can enter whenever they wish' (poor Lovers of the Cross). Moreover, they were keeping with them as servants some young fellows 'who are students, whom they are educating so that they can become priests of the country'.[4]

---

2. Letter from Guillaume Mahot to Propaganda. AMEP, volume 734, 90, in Launay, *Histoire Cochinchine*, 123. Launay, does not reproduce this letter in its entirety and omits in particular this sentence, which is nevertheless so representative of the provost's profound weariness: 'In truth we are better treated by the good people, the Moors and the heretics than by the fathers of the Society of Jesus.'
3. Memoir by Bénigne Vachet, AMEP, volume 11, 32 ff, in Launay, *Histoire Cochinchine*, 134 ff.
4. Memoir, Benigne Vachet, in Launay.

These difficulties with the Jesuits, embarrassing but normal, were aggravated by internal dissensions which testified to the moral wear and tear and spiritual exhaustion from which the French missions were beginning to suffer, after fifteen years of harsh conditions. In reality, the mission of Cochinchina had not recovered from the disappearance of its two pillars, Pierre Brindeau and especially Antoine Hainques whose charisma and spiritual strength were capable of cementing the Christian community without authoritarianism but with firmness, two qualities that were not apparent in his successors. In general, many of the new missionaries did not seem to be of the quality of the earlier ones, perhaps in part because the grace of state and that mixture of enthusiasm and illusion proper to any beginning enterprise were beginning to wear thin; perhaps also because in Paris their training was less demanding and the directors less careful in their recruitment. It was not that good will and conviction were lacking in the new recruits, but enthusiasm was sometimes absent, which made them appear as more ordinary, less inspired, and more vulnerable to the bidding of their own will.

Thus, in Cochinchina, Guillaume Mahot, who had neither the charisma nor the taste for command, was quickly overwhelmed by the newcomer, Jean de Courtaulin, to whom Pierre Lambert had granted the powers of pro-vicar in case of the absence or physical incapacity of Mahot. Courtaulin, trained at the seminary of Saint-Sulpice in Paris, combined great intellectual abilities with an equivalent physical strength and an over-confident and arrogant spirit that quickly provoked exasperated reactions from Vachet. After convincing Mahot to relinquish his title, the new pro-vicar embarked on an ambitious strategy that soon threatened the precarious balance of relationships that his colleagues had managed to establish with the authorities.

He overstepped all normal bounds and showed a great lack of prudence by proposing to the minister who received him in Hué a great program of hydraulic development, and by building in Faifo a church that was too conspicuous, thereby annoying the leaders and almost provoking a persecution. He imprudently ventured into the strategic zone of the north near the Tonkinese border, and launched a problematic and premature 'mission of the savages' among the Laotians which resulted in the death of one of the three local priests, Manuel Bon, who was poisoned by polluted water. During his journeys, he reformed parishes and convents everywhere, and imposed his authority on all, to the point of being able to proudly announce to his bishop a year after his arrival: 'Everywhere the subordination of all the evangelical workers to Your Grace is very well established. They recognize you there by name and by nickname. Previously it was known by hearsay that there was a bishop in Siam who had come here to assist the Christians. Now the Christians recognize you as their true pastor, and pray to God for Your Grace in this capacity; your pro-vicar is also well-known and obeyed there.'[5]

As well as Hien-Vuong's repeated invitation, this news prompted the Vicar Apostolic to travel to the field to form a personal opinion and to try to solve the problems himself. He therefore had to request a new authorization to leave from Phra Narai who only gave his agreement after having made his Cochinese crew promise to bring him back the following year.

Accompanied by Mahot and Vachet, Pierre Lambert left Ayutthaya on 23 July 1675. The day before, he made his will which stipulated that at his death, all his goods should go to the seminary of Paris to be assigned mainly to the financing of the formation of the Cochinchinese clergy.

A triumphant visit

The three Frenchmen arrived in Faifo on 6 September 1675. After meeting with the priests, catechists and the main lay leaders of the city, Pierre Lambert hired a junk belonging to Christians at his own expense and left for the capital with Vachet and Courtaulin. Because of the recent death of his son, the king refused to receive him but sent his son-in-law Ou Phu Ma, the foreign minister, to meet him. He welcomed the bishop very warmly, gave him complete freedom to visit the kingdom, and proposed that he take up his ordinary residence in Faifo, at a respectful distance from the court, where he could nevertheless stay periodically. The prelate made all his official visits openly displaying the insignia of his episcopal dignity, the rochet, the cape and the pectoral cross, while his missionaries all wore their cassocks with undisguised satisfaction. Obviously, such a welcome greatly upset the Jesuits and particularly Joseph Candone

---

5. Letter from Jean de Courtaulin to Pierre Lambert, 30 August 1674.

who claimed to be vicar general of Malacca, and therefore superior of the mission, but who was living in hiding with Jean de la Croix, disguised as a Japanese.

In order to cut short the schism which was sowing confusion and discord among the Cochinchinese Christians, the Vicar Apostolic decided to take advantage of his position of strength to impose his legitimate authority, and sent Bénigne Vachet to make known to Fathers Candone and d'Acosta the writ *Speculatores,* which placed the regulars[6] under the authority of the Vicars Apostolic in the territory of their jurisdiction, and its decrees of reception by the Inquisition of Goa. The confrontation, summed up by the directors, was quite eventful.

> First, Father Candone received the writ and the decrees with respect, putting them on his head and chest, but then he threw the writ on the ground. M. Vachet reproached him for the way he treated the Pope's orders. Father Candone answered that they meant nothing to him. After that, the aforementioned gentleman left the room and found Father d'Acosta who considered the matter to be unimportant. On leaving the house, a servant followed him and having seen him get into his boat wanted to pass to him all the papers he had left behind but, accidentally or otherwise, they fell into the water. M. Vachet picked them up and gave them to Father Candone who, having taken them, threw them in the mud. Vachet gave him a sharp reprimand and then withdrew.[7]

At the end of the legal period of reception, Pierre Lambert suspended and excommunicated the refractory pair. Father Candone, invoking his alleged position of vicar general of the bishopric of Malacca, replied by treating Pierre Lambert with contempt and excommunicated him in turn, as well as all those who received the sacraments from the hands of the French missionaries. This trial of strength, however painful and ridiculous it may seem today, achieved the desired result. Most of the catechists and Christians soon rallied

---

6. 'Regulars' are religious in the Catholic Church who make vows, follow a rule of life and usually live in community. Jesuits, Franciscans and Dominicans are 'regulars.'
7. Extracts from the letters of Mgr de Beirut of Siam, 10 November 1676. AMEP, volume 858, 345 sq.

to the Vicar Apostolic, the Jesuits having been unable to provide arguments that were sufficiently convincing to justify their position, which was, indeed, legally indefensible. And the pastoral tour that the bishop soon undertook in the provinces confirmed his prestige and his authority over the church of Cochinchina.

Pierre Lambert had indeed received permission from the Chua to administer to Christians in complete freedom, provided that large gatherings were avoided. The tolerance of the government had its limits, which related to public order and social cohesion, which did not shock the Vicar Apostolic, since discretion was one of the strongest recommendations advocated by the Roman *Instructions* and that he had already been practising successfully for several years in Siam. The beginnings of his administration were reserved for the Christians of the capital who gave him an enthusiastic but exhausting welcome. They 'flocked to him in droves', said Vachet, 'both to enjoy the presence of their pastor and to receive his blessing and the sacraments. We stayed there some fifteen days so busily occupied that often I saw this prelate throw himself on his bed, soaked with so much sweat that he looked like someone who had come out of a river. He did not allow his cassock to be pulled off, since no sooner was he on the bed than he had to return promptly to the church.'[8] In two weeks, the bishop administered 4,500 confirmations, 300 baptisms, and many marriages.

Such a conspicuous success could become dangerous, so Pierre Lambert decided to leave quickly for the southern provinces, which were clamouring for his arrival; he went first to Faifo, where he spent the Christmas holidays. Everywhere the enthusiasm of the faithful was the same and the work was just as overwhelming. 'In order to satisfy everyone, we had to walk all day long, and when evening arrived or at any other time, we had to go first to the confessional and spend the whole night administering the sacraments and giving instructions. Scarcely had we finished in the morning than disputes broke out on all sides about who could take us more quickly to a place where there was a similar or greater work to be done, all believing that it would be to their advantage to have the pastor go to their own churches.'[9]

---

8. Letter from Bénigne Vachet to the directors of the Seminary, Siam, 20 October 1677. AMEP, volume 734, 251, in Launay, *Histoire Cochinchine*, 180.
9. Letter, Vachet, 20 October 1677.

Several marvellous events took place during this triumphal visit. One such happening in particular deserves to be recorded, because the story has been told and re-told from generation to generation among the local Christians. The event took place in the region of Hué, where two young married people came to the missionaries one day carrying their infant child in their arms. It was Vachet who received them and described the event.

> I examined the child closely; to me he seemed to be dead, for he had no pulse and no heartbeat. His face was livid, and I could perceive no sign of life in him. I said to them, 'What do you want to do? The child is dead, and we must not trouble our prelate, who is busy.' Then these poor people threw themselves at my feet, urging me to give them the consolation they asked for. I told them to wait and returned to the prelate, to whom I confided what the problem was without concealing anything. "'But', he replied, 'do you believe that this child is dead?' I answered that I was not the only one to think so, and that all those who were present when I examined him were of the same opinion as I, that I had wanted to send away these grieving parents, but that they did not want to depart until he had given them his blessing, and especially to the child. Immediately M. de Beirut got up and the whole company followed him into the chapel. He then said to me in a distinctive tone of voice that I had never noticed in him before: 'Take this child and give him to me.' I took him from his mother's arms and presented him to the bishop, who received him in his own arms. He carried him to the altar where he laid him, then knelt with his head bent over the little body. I was very close to him, and for half an hour I heard only a few sighs and saw tears flowing from his eyes. He spoke only these words: 'I thank you, my God.' At the same time he took the child, gave him to me and said, 'Give this child back to his mother.' I marvelled to see this little being looking at me with his eyes sparkling, his mouth laughing and his face coloured in an unusual way for this country. I had no sooner given him to his mother than he searched for her breast to take his daily nourishment. My lord bishop returned at once with his attendants, and told me to send away the people while telling them not to cause a stir; but our host opposed it and wanted to give them something to eat. It was in vain that we tried to hide this marvel. They were all eager to have the father and mother and the child come to their home.

'The bishop stayed more than three weeks at the court without being able to return home. Five years after this event, Mgr de Beirut having already died, I brought to Cochinchina the Bishop of Metellopolis to whom I had told the story in all its circumstances; when he arrived at the court, I had forewarned the father and mother to bring to us the child who was in perfect health. The prelate confirmed him and I was the godfather. We changed his name, so that he would be called Pierre from then on, as it was the name of his second father who had given him life. Not only did the healing of this child bring peace to his family, but it could also be said that it was the cause of the conversion of his grandfather, his grandmother, his uncle, and also the conversion of more than fifty other people, relatives or friends.'[10]

Resolute opponents

Other incidents, less favourable, spoiled the tour of the Vicar Apostolic, whose popularity aroused much jealousy, both among mandarins hostile to Christianity and among dissident Christians. The day after Christmas, following a denunciation, a real attack was

---

10. Memoir of Bénigne Vachet, AMEP, volume 111, 6 and 11, in Launay, *Histoire Cochinchine*, 181–182. In March 2000, while visiting Hué, I met the parish priest. The first thing he told me about was this cure that everyone there considered to be a miracle. Moreover, during his lifetime, Pierre Lambert already had a reputation as a miracle worker among his missionaries, as François Deydier seemed to testify when he said about Pallu: 'The most holy prelate I know, even though I know some of them, who, or rather, through whom God has worked and is still working miracles.' (Letter from François Deydier to clerics, Tonkin, 6 December 1677. AMEP, volume 651, 66). It is likely that he is referring to Lambert. Following this event, Vachet again relates the deliverance of a possessed woman who demanded the presence of the Vicar Apostolic. The latter's reaction shows how cautiously, confidently and humbly Pierre Lambert dealt with this type of case, which was classic in the 17th century, both in Vietnam and in France: 'My said Lord of Bérythe did not want to go, nor even allow the woman to be brought into his presence, alleging to me with his usual gentleness that it was up to us to impose laws on the devil and that it was not reasonable for him to come and brave our door, that I should remain there in his presence, that the woman had been delivered, which happened at the moment he spoke to me. The devil came out and boasted that he would return three days later, but he was not able to do so. I could talk to you for a long time about similar matters. (Letter from Bénigne Vachet to the directors of the seminary, Siam, 20 October 1677. AMEP, volume 734, 251, Launay, *Histoire Cochinchine*, 180. Another shorter version of this fact is given by Courtaulin. AMEP, volume 734, 235.

organized against the faithful gathered in the church of Faifo. Several dozen Christians, mostly poor people from the hospital, were arrested and mistreated in front of the bishop and his powerless missionaries.

A few days later, about the time of the Epiphany, the Vicar Apostolic returned to Hué to request a passport in order to be able to return to Siam, as he had promised, at the next sailing season which began in February. He was welcomed there 'by the Christians with great joy, by kind people with extreme veneration and respect'.[11] He was lodged with a friend of the crown prince, Ou Tho Mat, a former Jesuit catechist. There he received Christians of the three northern provinces who came to make their submission and receive Confirmation.

In the home of Jean de la Croix, there was consternation. The founder and his son tried to obtain an audience with the Vicar Apostolic to assert their rights and those of Portugal, but Pierre Lambert replied that he refused to speak to people who did not obey the apostolic writs of the Holy See, and who were not willing to submit to a bishop recognized by the inquisitors of the Holy Office of Goa.

In order to take revenge, Jean de la Croix decided to have the Vicar Apostolic kidnapped by the Macau ship which docked at Faifo in mid-February. The Jesuit Jean Cardoso, who was in charge of the execution of these evil plans, disembarked with rich presents, with the intention of obtaining from the king permission to kidnap the French missionaries. To achieve his ends, the religious chose denunciation and insinuation. With Jean de la Croix as his intermediary to the king, 'he had Mgr de Beirut accused without being named, but simply referred to as a French bishop who went to Tonkin and from there to Cochinchina in secret, from where he had kidnapped subjects whom he took to Siam. These accusations were crimes that merited the death penalty in Cochinchina. It was believed that the fathers did not intend this extreme punishment, but they hoped at least that they would be given permission to take Mgr de Beirut and the other missionaries to Macau in their ship.'[12]

'This process did not worry the Vicar Apostolic who was well aware of the intentions of his adversaries but understood perfectly well the advantage that he held over the Jesuits at the court. He therefore chose

---

11. Report from Cochinchine 1675–1676 by M de Courtaulin. AMEP, volume 734, 219, in Launay, *Histoire Cochinchine*, 178.
12. Extracts from the letters of Mgr de Bérythe of Siam, 10 November 1676. AMEP, volume 858, 345 sq.

clemency in preference to revenge. 'The only difficulty this news gave us', he wrote later to M de Brisacier, 'was whether I ought to have had this provincial father arrested, being in a position to do so, and it would only have cost me a word to the minister who is the king's son-in-law and to the governor of the province who were looking for opportunities to oblige me. But after I had knelt at the foot of the crucifix, I had no other wish than to follow the evangelical counsels and to leave this matter in the hands of God.'[13]

This excessively evangelical behaviour, which accorded very well with the nobility of spirit of Pierre Lambert, did not lack panache compared to the baseness of the attack, but it was not appreciated by all.

On his return to Ayutthaya, the bishop was reproached for having missed such a splendid opportunity to get rid of his adversaries for good. 'I am accused of having been too moderate towards them in these quarters and of not having made sufficient use of our power to have them imprisoned and punished,' he confided to Monseigneur de Laval. 'But if it is a fault, we were willing to commit it in order to practise the councils of our Divine Master.'[14]

Without regretting this gesture of leniency, which was also a silent lesson in dignity for his adversaries, Pierre Lambert was not so naive as to believe that it would be enough to 'convert' the Jesuits, and he knew perfectly well that the use of political weapons would have been much more effective in neutralising them. That is why he asked François Pallu to request of Propaganda the authority for the apostolic vicars to have recourse to the local secular arm in case of necessity, in order to counterbalance the abusive support given by the Padroado to its own missionaries. 'They will obey only when forced to do so. It is very important to make this known to Rome, and that it is necessary that we have enough power in the places where we are established to oblige the Jesuits to recognize the Apostolic Constitutions. It is important that the authorities in Rome continue to support us, that they allow us to have recourse to secular tribunals, and that they punish those who have fomented and continue to foment this schism.'[15]

---

13. Letter from Pierre Lambert to M de Brisacier, Siam, 16 November 1676. AMEP, volume 858, 361.
14. Letter from Pierre Lambert to M de Québec, Siam, 14 November 1676. AMEP, volume 858, 353.
15. Letter from Pierre Lambert and Louis Laneau to François Pallu, Siam, 16 November 1676. AMEP, volume 419, 298–301.

Before leaving his mission, Pierre Lambert went to the province of Quangnghia where he ordained a new Cochinchinese priest, Louis Doan, the only seminarian who had persevered in his studies and received the vows of the first Lovers of the Cross. At Fumoy, he confirmed Jean de Courtaulin as pro-vicar since Mahot, too tired, returned with him to Siam. This choice proved to be unfortunate. Unappreciated by his French and Cochinchinese colleagues, the pro-vicar multiplied abuses of power and imprudence. A few months before his death, the Vicar Apostolic was obliged to limit his authority by appointing Gabriel Bouchard to restrain him.

The last stand

In June 1676, the Vicar Apostolic returned to Siam, where a new contingent of missionaries soon arrived: Pierre Geffrard de Lespinay, Guillaume Le Clergues, Charles Thomas, Pierre Le Noir and Charles Sevin, Pallu's emissary. The latter brought back from Rome the brief *Decet Romanum* which exempted the Vicars Apostolic from the jurisdiction of the Inquisition of Goa and confirmed all the measures taken previously in their favour. Also, he brought a letter from the Jesuit general, Paul Oliva, enjoining his men to submit to the authority of the Vicars Apostolic.

Although greatly fatigued physically by his journeys in Cochinchina and in a state of health which worsened day by day, Pierre Lambert used the last of his strength to put pressure on the missionaries of Padroado in their entrenchments. He had the last Roman decisions served on the religious of Ayutthaya, who took refuge, as usual, behind the authority of the King of Portugal to justify their refusal.

This was the last trial of strength between the strong-willed Vicar Apostolic and his opponents in Ayutthaya. The following year, in fact, a letter from the new Archbishop of Goa, the Cistercian Antoine Brandao, informed the Vicars Apostolic that the rights of Jean d'Abreu, governor of the church of Malacca, extended only over the domains of the King of Portugal and that they could not be exercised in any way in the territories entrusted to their jurisdiction. After this legal clarification, the deaths of the two greatest adversaries of the French in Siam, Father Fragoso and Father Valguarnera, also contributed to conciliation. Thus, fifteen years after his arrival in Asia, Pierre

Lambert could legitimately consider that his combative strategy had borne fruit. The Vicars Apostolic and their men were well and truly established in their missions in Indochina, and the supremacy of the Padroado, whatever its claims, was irremediably shaken.

Exhausted by hardship, work and illness, Pierre Lambert had only a few months to live, but, more than ever, this tireless fighter deserved the praise that François Pallu gave him in 1673.

> Any other than Bishop de Beirut would have succumbed under the weight of the task; but he knew how to treat people so well and to moderate all things by his gentleness, patience and forbearance, by the example of a very holy life, always reliable, without ever being upset in any way, but especially by his earnest prayers to Our Lord, that finally he brought back all the spirits that had been pushed aside; he made himself the master of them and disposed of them in any way he pleased. All those who know Bishop de Beirut knew that it would be difficult to find a person more suitable than him for the commission he exercises. It is to him, after God, that we owe the establishments of Siam, Cochinchina and Tonkin. In their construction, many difficulties had to be overcome and turbulent storms withstood. He has protected the last two missions so well against the schism that confronted them, that they have remained unwavering in their loyalty, and in fact they have become much stronger and have increased in numbers, notwithstanding the envy and the continuous efforts of our rivals.

'God has given him a fearless spirit that does not know what it is to surrender, nor even to relent, as long as he can see a reason for his stance. Nevertheless, he knows how to yield when it is necessary, and how to concede in order to attain the main objective. He is admirable especially where prudence is required. Finally, he has not undertaken anything of consequence here that he has not eventually succeeded in doing. His adversaries have been the Portuguese, the Dutch, the English, Moors, Chinese, and Siamese, and several formidable people over whom he prevailed. He obliged them to give way without ever offending them and he did this while hardly ever leaving his room and never appearing agitated, so to speak.'[16]

---

16. Letter from François Pallu to the directors of the Seminary, Siam, 3 September 1673. AMEP, volume 102, 108, in Launay, *Histoire Cochinchine*, 238.

Another missionary, Jean de Courtaulin, expressed a very similar judgment, and one that was just as eulogistic: 'The Bishop of Beirut is an eagle that flies above the clouds; his prayer and his solitude are constant; and notwithstanding that, he is so admirably vigilant that he does not allow the slightest opportunity to pass by without doing his best to procure what is best for his missionaries and for their advancement. He had very unfortunate and difficult encounters with the Portuguese, the Moors and the Chinese, all of whom eventually left him in peace and did not interrupt the management of his missions. He achieved this without making an enemy.'[17]

While a certain calm seemed to settle over the region, at least in Ayutthaya, Pierre Lambert did not stop fighting with the European ecclesiastical authorities. During his trip to Cochinchina, he himself validated a certain number of concessions made to the faithful and sought to harmonize the Church's discipline and devotional practices as far as possible with local traditions, for example, by requesting that Christians be able to celebrate the memorial of their martyrs at the time of the Chinese New Year in order to be able to take part in the collective rejoicings without any difficulty. But he saw in the Jesuits' pastoral work certain accommodations that he found inadmissible. Upon his return to Ayutthaya, he sent to Rome for examination by the cardinals a Portuguese set of principles translated into Italian by Father Marini and printed in Lyons in 1665 during his visit to Europe. More determined than ever to impose Roman control in the region, he wrote to one of the cardinals:

> I beg V. E. not to believe that we are weary of enduring such a great quarrel, but I beg her to be of assistance by noting its cause for the sake of the propagation of the faith, which is certainly greatly impeded by the inconsistencies of the Jesuits. We cannot agree with them about superstitions which we find disgusting, and exemptions from the observance of the positive law for the Christians of our missions, nor about the errors which they make in the administration of the sacraments. One of the remedies I propose for these great evils is the removal of two or three Jesuits who are in Tonkin and Cochinchina, as a punishment for their faults. Also, all those who are sent to these missions by their superiors in future

---

17. Quoted in Launay, *Histoire Cochinchine*, Siam, 36.

> should be obliged by a decree of His Holiness to recognize the Vicars Apostolic and to follow the decrees of the sovereign pontiffs in doctrinal matters and in the administration of the sacraments under pain of heavy penalties.[18]

Finally, since 1662, the discourse of the Vicar Apostolic had not changed much. He still put forward the same arguments with as much firmness, even if there could be detected in them a little less passion, a little more assurance, and that serenity which the feeling of accomplished duty confers. So it was, that having reached the end of his race, with his physical strength decreasing day by day, he knew that his fight had not been in vain, for although he had not always been listened to in Paris, authorities in Rome had paid close attention to his words. Also, as he was always a great gentleman, he made a gesture of reconciliation to the directors to whom he wrote on 16 November 1676:

> Finally, we must point out that respect for and recognition of the Jesuits is not as great as might be imagined. If we had wanted to make use of the power we have, some of these religious would have received well-deserved punishment. We think it is useful to inform you of this so that you will know that they are not to be feared as much as you think, and that we will emerge from these disputes with our reputation enhanced, please God. Assuming this to be correct, it seems that the matters of concern which gave rise to our misunderstandings must be abandoned and that it is important for us from now on to act in concert in the conduct of our missions, and this is what we beg of you with all our heart.[19]

Anxious to preserve a unity of action for the general good of the nascent Paris Foreign Mission Society and perhaps to attenuate the effects of some of its rather too virulent reactions, Pierre Lambert, nevertheless, no longer entertained any illusions about a deep rapprochement with the Parisian leaders. Because, even if the emotional wounds and the loss of self-esteem caused or suffered on both sides were disregarded, he knew that spiritual communion

---

18. Letter from Pierre Lambert to a cardinal, Siam, 4 September 1676. AMEP, volume 876, 829.
19. Letter from Pierre Lambert to directors of the seminary, Siam, 16 November 1676. AMEP, volume 419, 303–305.

was no longer possible between men once united by the same ideal, but now separated by living conditions that were too dissimilar. For him, the directors, who were far from the actual mission field and unaware of the renunciations and radical efforts required, had lost their original idealism. They had succumbed to a life of ease and had become incapable of understanding the daily life of the men on the ground, perhaps even of providing sound management of the Paris Foreign Mission Society.

The state of affairs

In spite of the difficulties and disagreements, the results of the work carried out by the Vicars Apostolic and their missionaries were largely positive. Barely fifteen years after their arrival in Asia, they had made considerable progress, if we take into account all the opposition they had to endure and their inadequate means. But the situation of the various French missions was paradoxical. While the missions in Vietnam recorded spectacular baptism statistics despite persecution, the Jesuit schism and lack of personnel in Siam, where the king's tolerance allowed the official installation of basic institutions—chapel, seminary, hospital—conversions were rare in proportion to the number of missionaries.

In 1676, two more priests arrived in Ayutthaya, Etienne Paumard and François Leroux, accompanied by a layman, René Charbonneau. In the following year, René Forget and Claude Gayme joined their confreres after a stay of several years in Bantan. Counting the pioneers and the two bishops, the Siamese team was composed of twelve men, some of whom were preparing to leave for other missions. If we can believe the opinion of one of the newcomers, Pierre Le Noir, the internal divisions did not affect the authority or the prestige of Pierre Lambert, whose charisma as a leader was able to transcend the opposition of individuals. 'I received untold pleasure and consolation from the sight and the conversation of the bishops, but principally from Monseigneur de Beirut, whom I consider to be the first and principal cause of all of our missions. It is a pleasure to fight for our beloved Saviour under his gentle and wise guidance, from which flows the strong attachment to our missions of all of our very dear gentlemen.'[20]

---

20. Letter from Pierre Le Noir to a director, Siam, 24 January 1677. AMEP, volume 861, 33.

The Siam mission had five residences: Tenasserim in the southwest, Phitsanulok in the northeast, Ayutthava, Bangkok, and another undetermined residence in the centre, these last three all located at intervals along the course of the Menam River. The missionaries were stationed according to the needs of the mission or their ability to adapt. Pierre Langlois, tired of the seminary, was sent in 1677 to Phitsanulok where the Portuguese governor, Amador Coelho de Mello, a great friend of the French, had requested a missionary. Claude de Chandebois took charge of the parish of the Immaculate Conception in Bangkok. On account of the austerity of his life and his great charity, he was held in high esteem amongst the poor and the sick, although, like his confrere Etienne Paumard, he showed little inclination to learn oriental languages. Claude Gayme was appointed procurator in 1677 in place of Louis Chevreuil who was granted permission by Pierre Lambert to return to Cochinchina in the company of Pierre Le Noir and Charles Thomas. Bénigne Vachet, who was ill, returned to Siam for treatment, and Leroux succumbed to scurvy which he contracted during his trip.

As for Louis Laneau, he seemed to abandon his administrative responsibilities in some measure in order to devote himself almost entirely to the tasks of evangelization. Pierre Lambert, who was in charge of the general direction of the missions, still had the same admiration for the pastoral qualities of his confrere. To his friend Dominique George he wrote, 'This bishop is a miracle. He has an excellent command of the language. He preaches and instructs by himself, and has composed several books to give this people a knowledge of our holy mysteries.'[21] He therefore showed himself to be in perfect solidarity with the inculturation initiatives that Laneau persisted in wanting to introduce into the mission of Siam in spite of the determined opposition of the directors and some of his confreres. Although he did not relax his efforts, Laneau, the Vicar Apostolic of Siam, suffered from the fact that the mission to which he had devoted himself body and soul for fifteen years and for which he had officially been put in charge, remained the least loved of the French missions. Even today the question can be asked whether Laneau was just a likeable dreamer lost in his illusions, or a genuinely spiritual

---

21. Letter from Pierre Lambert to Dominique George, Siam, 19 November 1676. In *Semaine religieuse de Bayeux*, May 1918.

man gifted with a long-term missiological vision which failed due to historical circumstances; even at the present time historians remain divided on this question.

One of the major concerns of the Siam mission remained the operation of the seminary, which was essentially used for the Vietnam missions since the majority of the Latin students were Cochinchinese or Tonkinese, but which no one wanted to take care of over the long term. After promising beginnings and great projects, including that of setting up a printing press in Ayutthaya, Pierre Langlois became discouraged and asked to be changed in 1677. He was briefly replaced by Gayme, then Vachet and finally by Geffrard. This instability of the teaching staff did not help to maintain discipline among the seminarians whose conduct often left something to be desired. After a number of defections, the twelve remaining seminarians were transferred to Bangkok to the residence of Claude de Chandebois whose ascetic life was intended to serve as an example to them. As for the schoolchildren's section, which included younger children of more varied nationalities, it remained in Ayutthaya where it enjoyed a certain stability thanks to the disinterested care of the Portuguese Franciscan Louis de la Mère de Dieu, helped on occasion by a Frenchman passing through.

Fortunately, there was another establishment that gave less reason for concern and more satisfaction to the two Vicars Apostolic: the hospital, a project dear to Pierre Lambert but essentially inaugurated and developed by Louis Laneau. With a capacity of twenty-five beds for the most serious cases, it also received seventy or eighty outpatients. While Louis Laneau was in a way the chief medical officer, most of the care was provided by René Charbonneau. Although it was materially expensive for the mission, the hospital was of great spiritual benefit to those therapists of the soul, Louis Laneau and Pierre Lambert. 'God works many extraordinary cures by means of oil and holy water, as well as in the other places where we preach the Gospel', enthused the Bishop of Beirut. 'We are viewers of the wonders that God performed in the past at the birth of the Church. They provide a reason for us to rejoice and they serve as a source of encouragement for the labours of a missionary, which certainly are not small, but which are also often accompanied by an interior joy that cannot be explained.'[22] In contact with the poorest and most afflicted, he found a joy that was

---

22. Letter from Pierre Lambert to M. de Québec, Siam, 14 November 1676. AMEP, volume 858, 353.

evangelical in nature the greatest consolation for his worries and sorrows. To some extent this moral compensation helped the Vicar Apostolic to bear the weight of a burden that became more and more overwhelming as his own strength declined.

From 1676 on, serious financial difficulties were added to the usual problems. Besides the difficulties of communication, war, and shipwrecks, the help from France arrived only in dribs and drabs whereas the missions, growing strongly, required significantly greater support. In France, Cardinal de Bouillon refused to pay Pierre Lambert the annuity due to him from the revenues of the Abbey of Saint-Ouen. In the Philippines, the Jesuits, contrary to their promises, withheld the property they had confiscated from François Pallu. Upon his return from Cochinchina, Pierre Lambert was obliged to borrow 2,500 écus from the King of Siam, a sum which was insufficient to satisfy the budgetary demands of each mission. This lack of financial aid aggravated the dissensions and jealousies between the missions.

On 29 November 1677, Pierre Lambert co-signed with Louis Laneau the last letter he addressed to François Pallu, a document that could be considered, in some measure, to be the expression of his last wishes. Feeling that he would no longer have the strength to leave Siam, whether to return to Cochinchina or to accompany the Siamese embassy to France as Phra Narai wished, he asked his colleague to take whatever steps he judged necessary for the perpetuation of their common work. Three main problems preoccupied the Bishop of Beirut: the financial situation of the missions, recruitment, and the consolidation of the diplomatic position that the Vicars Apostolic had acquired, unintentionally on their part, in certain countries of Southeast Asia.

For finance, he relied less on the generosity of private individuals, which was too uncertain, than on the regularity of the ecclesiastical revenues due to the bishops. The payment of these famous pensions had to be requested from the providers, King Louis XIV and the Cardinal de Bouillon among others who, undoubtedly secretly influenced by the Jesuits, were inclined to drag their feet. As far as recruitment was concerned, Pierre Lambert no longer expected much from the directors of the seminary in terms of either the number or the quality of missionaries. He therefore persevered without qualms in his project of union with Saint-Sulpice or another congregation. He had even fewer scruples of conscience towards the directors because he believed that they, in wanting to avoid annoying the Jesuits for political reasons, had made no attempt to emphasize to the king the diplomatic importance of the Vicars Apostolic.

However, keenly aware of the seriousness of international issues, Pierre Lambert ended up entering, more or less in spite of himself, into a political role which sometimes led him to cross the line of non-intervention that he had initially set for himself. A cornerstone of the diplomatic relations between Siam and France, he was also sought as a negotiator by the King of Golconda. In November 1677, in an astonishing move on his part, he asked the director of the French East India Company, François Baron, to send two cannons to the King of Cochinchina, no doubt to thank him for his favours and to encourage him to continue his policy of tolerance toward the French missionaries. Even if he acted through the intermediary of the French East India Company and did not involve himself in these negotiations, which were very foreign to the evangelical spirit, he came dangerously close through this initiative to the behaviour for which he reproached the Jesuits. It is regrettable that at the end of his life the Vicar Apostolic, so vigilant at the beginning, allowed himself to be involved in the world of politics. But one may also wonder whether, given the context, it was really possible for him to do otherwise.

Under the sign of the cross

On 16 August 1678, after abandoning his desire to return to Cochinchina because of his state of health and excessive suffering, Pierre Lambert was obliged to go to bed from which he never rose again. For almost a year, he endured terrible sufferings that no care succeeded in relieving. As much as the missionaries, Phra Narai was alarmed by this disease which compromised his cherished embassy plans. 'The king sent his doctors,' wrote Claude Gayme, one of the bishop's nurses, 'and as we know from reliable sources, he assembled all his best doctors in front of him and wanted to be present at their consultation. Being himself subject to some similar infirmity, he sent some of his most precious medicines, which in the beginning brought the bishop some relief, but they were unable to eliminate the continual pain he felt. The king made it clear to his doctors that he did not want the bishop to die.'[23]

---

23. Letter from Claude Gayme to François Pallu, Siam, 31 August 1678. AMEP, volume 877, 617–618.

To show his sympathy for the French, the king offered them a large gilded pulpit, which revived Laneau's hopes of a possible conversion. 'There was no opposition from the mandarins or from the king, who repeated a few days ago that he did not prevent anyone from becoming a Christian, and he talked for a long time about our way of life, and about the obligations of Christians once they had embraced the religion', he wrote to François Pallu.

'He no longer goes to his pagoda as he used to do every year, and at the end of last year he forbade entry to the pagodas, but it is not clear why he did so.[24] It is certain that he no longer devotes himself to his idols as he used to, and the people usually say that he follows the religion of the foreigners. May God enlighten him completely. The house he wished us to build is finished; all that remains to be done is to apply some whitewash to it. It is one of the most beautiful buildings in the kingdom.'[25]

But these hopes were of small comfort when compared to the burden that was oppressing the Vicars Apostolic. In the midst of his suffering, Pierre Lambert still had to help Louis Laneau face the new difficulties that burdened the mission. In China, it was the defection of the Dominican, Grégoire Lo, who had been approached by the French to be the first native bishop. In Siam, there were still problems of money and personnel with the voluntary return to Europe of one of the most ardent missionaries, Charles Sevin, who complained of being underemployed, and the defection of René Charbonneau who found celibacy unbearable. 'Brother René is a blessing for those with whom he works, but the devil cannot tolerate him, and he is asking to be withdrawn and occupied elsewhere,' lamented Louis Laneau. 'His trial is his attraction to women and he imagines that this will cause him to be damned. We cannot yet be sure that this fantasy will pass, but if not, it would be a great loss for the mission. That is why, if in the future a few lay surgeons are sent, it would be appropriate to employ them in France in a hospital among women to find out whether they are suitable. This should nevertheless be done with all necessary discretion so as not to put them in danger of offending God. But if they are not capable of passing this test in France, they will not be

---

24. A pagoda is a building in East Asia used for religious purposes by Buddhists and Hindus.
25. Letter from Louis Laneau to François Pallu, Siam, 4 September 1678. AMEP, volume 877, 629–630.

of much use in this country.'²⁶ This crisis, which highlighted the real difficulty, on the human level, of having different states of life live together under a common rule, discouraged the Vicars Apostolic from associating themselves with lay collaborators and contributed to the clericalization of the French missionary enterprise. 'It seems that eventually he will want to get married', concluded Laneau, 'and that is why I think that it is not a good idea to have laypeople in these places unless they are of proven virtue. It is better to have clergy practising medicine or other similar things rather than to take on laypeople, and although the necessity of medicine is more and more obvious, the little that is known of it by clergy may suffice.'²⁷

The year 1679 was a difficult one for all the missionaries of Camp Saint-Joseph, constantly aware of the interminable agony of the Bishop of Beirut who went through 'a purgatory of pain for ten whole months, enduring unimaginable suffering,' wrote Laneau.²⁸ The last months of his life were indeed a long physical and moral ordeal which horrified and shocked his companions. Such suffering moved even the most bitter opponents of the Bishop of Beirut to take pity on him and, on the threshold of death, Christian charity finally appeared. Passing through Ayutthaya, Fathers Jean d'Abreu and Nicolas da Motta came to visit him, while a Portuguese from Macau brought him a new remedy. But the illness was fatal. Pierre Lambert died at four o'clock in the morning on 15 June 1679 at the age of figfty-five.

In a confidential letter to the directors, Louis Laneau gave a striking description of the bishop's cruel end. A doctor of bodies and a doctor of souls, a man familiar with human suffering, Pierre Lambert's most intimate disciple concealed nothing in a cold clinical report. He delivered in parallel a poignant 'spiritual autopsy report' of his master and confidant. '

> He died in severe pain, as our Lord made him feel the excessive weight of his cross with which he had been so enamoured during his life. We have not dared to include all the particulars

---

26. Letter from Louis Laneau to the directors, Siam, 4 October 1678. AMEP, volume 858, 422.
27. Letter from Louis Laneau to the directors, Siam, 25 October 1678. AMEP, volume 858, 427.
28. Letter from Louis Laneau to the directors, Siam, 25 October 1679. AMEP, volume 858, 425.

of his sufferings in the report, lest they seem unbelievable to those who do not know how God treats his most intimate favourites, but since we must not keep anything hidden from one another, it is fitting that I tell you something about it. For many years he had been experiencing great difficulty in urinating; but this did not prevent him from fulfilling his ordinary duties, although he did not dare to go to Cochinchina last year. On the day of the Assumption, an abscess, which was at first thought to be haemorrhoids, degenerated into a fistula. This caused him even greater pain, and he could hardly bear to have the necessary remedies applied.

'The king of Siam sent his physicians to him, who gave him many remedies but all to no avail; instead, they made matters worse. Afterwards came a first fever, followed by typhus, then a burning thirst. Further, although a loss of bladder control suggested that he did not have gallstones, after his death, three large stones were found stuck to each other. Previously nothing was known of this problem, since he had never consented to the use of a probe, no doubt considering it indecent. Along with these stones, his bladder was found to be decaying and ulcerated; also, one of his kidneys, as big as a fist, had an ulcer, which caused his urine to give off a disgusting smell. During the first stages of this illness he used to rise from his bed, but eventually he was obliged to remain in bed, which caused bedsores to develop in several places on his body. In the end he was only skin and bone and he could not attend to his own needs.

'It was heart-breaking to hear his cries when his pains resumed, something that occurred almost every quarter of an hour or half an hour. However, he often said that all this was as nothing compared to the dryness and sadness with which his soul was filled, for Our Lord took away all interior consolations from him, and there remained only a small spark from some unknown light which prevented him from giving in to despair. He experienced such unfamiliar anxiety and darkness that caused an agonizing confusion. He was carried from one place to another, and in his room he kept changing beds. However, as he could see that people found such behaviour strange, he begged them not to be scandalized, for it was necessary in order to cope with the excruciating pain. Although his senses were in a state of confusion and misery, nevertheless he enjoyed a deep peace in the depths of his soul; although his human nature experienced extreme pain, a certain serenity existed in the deepest recesses of his soul.'

He made his complaints to Our Lord, just as Job did at the height of his suffering. His recurring prayer consisted of these words: 'Auge dolorem, auge patientiam' ('Increase my pain, increase my patience.') saying that although he sometimes uttered words of impatience, he did not consent to them, and that he wanted only what God wanted. It was suggested to him that he should make a vow in order to obtain the restoration of his health from God. After telling me about this suggestion, he concluded that he did not dare ask God for health, as he did not know if this was expedient, given his age and infirmities, given the fact that he could no longer kneel down or do penance, and that he might give bad example to the missionaries.'

'He was comforted by our visits to him, but because we were busy about many things, it was often difficult to assist him. He himself would send us away, saying that we should go and do God's work and leave him to suffer. His judgment never wavered; he always responded to everything that was suggested to him as if he were in good health. He often received communion, and his eagerness to receive the last sacraments of the Church was edifying.'

Finally, he gave up his spirit to God as a true man of sorrows, having always lived in the midst of crosses and sufferings, which were internal in nature rather than external. God made him pass through these trials in order to annihilate entirely any remaining egotism and to render him incapable, so to speak, of having any complacency about what God was doing through him.'[29] At the end of a life filled with honour and struggles, Pierre Lambert died in a state of physical wretchedness and spiritual abandonment, far worse than the penances he had voluntarily embraced a quarter of a century earlier during his pilgrimage to Rennes. But here, for what conversion, for what atonement, for what redemption, for what forgiveness? It is perhaps the ultimate secret of this elite soul that we are unable to penetrate.

One last act, however, throws a revealing light on a career so exceptional, so fruitful and so painful. In 1675, before leaving for Cochinchina and at a time when he already knew he was seriously

---

29. Letter from Louis Laneau to the directors of the seminary, Siam, 2 November 1679, AMEP, volume 860, 25, in Launay, *Histoire Cochinchine*, 73.

ill, Pierre Lambert had written in his will: 'I leave to the church of the Jesuit priests of Macau, as a token of my friendship for them, the crucifix that my late brother left me a few days before his death.'[30] This symbolic gesture alone summed up the unexpected radicalism of this eminent mystic of the Cross. By bequeathing to his fiercest adversaries this object with its twofold emotional and spiritual value, the only article perhaps for which he would have had any attachment, an image moreover of his unique love, he erased at his death all traces of human resentment and put the Jesuits back in their rightful place as brothers in Jesus Christ. With great panache and a touch of evangelical provocation, he unilaterally signed the end of the relentless battle he had waged against them, in total conformity with the ideal of his Ignatian formation: only for the greater glory of God and in perfect obedience to the pope.

Posthumous tributes

Although it had been foreseen for a long time, the death of Pierre Lambert plunged his associates into a state of anxiety. 'The king felt very strongly about his death', wrote Claude Gayme a month after his death, 'and the late Mgr de Beirut is to be praised for winning the esteem of princes and kings everywhere by his remarkable composure which inspired respect for his person. The Portuguese, who feared him like fire, think that now they will have no more difficulties in their pursuits, but the good Lord will provide. It is very true that in our missions there is no leader like him, but the work that has been started will continue as long as there is peace among the evangelical workers and they seek God alone.'[31] For Louis Laneau, who until then had always remained in the shadow of the great man, his death came as an enormous shock and left him totally distraught. 'You can imagine the state we are in after losing him and not knowing when the Bishop of Heliopolis will return,'[32] he wrote to the directors.

---

30. Last will and testament of Pierre Lambert. AMEP, volume 8, 151, quoted in Chappoulie, *Une controverse entre missionnaires à Siam au XVIIe siècle*, t. l, 378.
31. Letter from Claude Gayme to the directors, Siam, 15 July 1679. AMEP, volume 877, 672–673
32. Letter from Louis Laneau to the directors, Siam, 25 October 1679. AMEP, volume 858, 425.

After the death of the Bishop of Beirut, who was a real lightning rod for the French missions, difficulties bore down on them from all sides. Whereas in Ayutthaya the king demanded the money he had lent to the Vicar Apostolic, in Cochinchina the adversaries of the missionaries raised their voices and resumed their harassment of them. 'While the great reputation that the Bishop of Beirut had acquired in his travels in Cochinchina had been sufficient for the missionaries to carry out their duties peacefully enough', wrote Vachet,

> the news of his death on 15 June 1679, in the seminary of Siam, was no sooner known there, than at once the most malicious rumours were spread about the mission. It was the common opinion, even in the houses of the greatest lords, that the missionaries, having lost this outstanding figure, would be forced to abandon their work. It was spread abroad everywhere that it was not true that there was a newly consecrated bishop in Siam; as for the Bishop of Heliopolis, the Spaniards had disposed of him so well that there was more fear for his safety than hope of seeing him again. These false impressions would have had very unfortunate consequences if the missionaries had not gained the support of a number of Christians who were resilient enough not to succumb to the prevailing rumours.[33]

The authority of the Bishop of Beirut, his dignity, his sense of responsibility, his determination and his intelligence had impressed all those who approached him. This was true of his adversaries as well as his allies, kings as well as common people, confreres and missionaries, even when they did not agree with him. In Rome, where the news was not yet known, Innocent XI, determined to support him in his struggle, wrote him a very encouraging letter in praise of his work on 4 October 1679, nearly four months after his death.

> In addition to being aware of the respect you have for us, not because of our personal merits, but because Divine Providence has placed us in this See for the government of the Church, we have experienced great joy in learning of the abundant

---

33. Bénigne Vachet. Report of the Journey of Mgr Laneau to Cochinchina. AMEP, volume 734, 685, in Launay, *Histoire Cochinchine*, 239.

harvest with which the Lord's field is now being enriched in these far-off regions. Assured as we are that you are working ardently for this admirable work, and that you are burning with zeal for the propagation of the Catholic faith, with the most intimate feeling of our paternal charity, we embrace you in the Lord, and assure you that our help will always assist the pious efforts that you constantly make in order to reach your noble goal and to acquire the reward that is prepared for you in heaven. Nor are you unaware of the decisions taken by the cardinals in charge of the Congregation of Propaganda, which were made known to our venerable brother, the Bishop of Heliopolis. In the implementation of these decisions we pray God to shower upon you the gifts of his grace, and we affectionately impart to you the apostolic blessing.[34]

The following year, having taken severe measures against the Jesuits by imposing on them the oath of obedience to the Vicars Apostolic and by finally obtaining from General Oliva SJ[35] the effective recall of the most disruptive elements, the Holy See confirmed the authority of the French bishops over all the missions of Asia. With the brief *Onerosa pastoralis officii* of 1 April 1680, he appointed Pierre Lambert general administrator of all the missions of Indochina (Siam, Cochinchina, Tonkin and 'other adjacent missions', that is Pegu, Ava, Cambodia, Laos) while François Pallu received the same title for the missions in China. At the death of the latter in 1684, Louis Laneau, Pierre Lambert's favourite disciple, inherited the joint responsibilities of his two predecessors and was named administrator general of the missions in Asia. This was the highest office ever held by a member of the Society of Foreign Missions of Paris, but it was also an office that was beyond him and it disappeared with his death. Thus, even after his disappearance, Pierre Lambert's influence continued to affect Roman decisions for some time, as if the tremendous energy he had deployed in the service of his mission had not been extinguished with his last earthly breath.

---

34. Brief of praise from the Pope to Pierre Lambert, 4 October 1679. AMEP, volume 269, 167, in Launay, *Histoire générale*, t. 1, 254.
35. Fr Giovanni Paolo Oliva was the eleventh Superior General of the Jesuits. He held this position from 1664 until 1681.

Chapter 9
A Missiology in Search of Balance

A consistent record

By consecrating François Pallu in its internal historiography as the 'principal founder of the Foreign Missions,' the Paris Foreign Missions Society (MEP) largely obscured the founding role of Pierre Lambert de la Motte to whom it owed much more than it seemed to realize, forgetting in the first place that without his decisive intervention in Rome in 1658 it might never have existed. The Bishop of Beirut also played an important part, both administratively and financially, in the creation of the seminary of Paris, and it is also to him that the Society owed the opening of its first Asian seminary in Ayutthaya and the installation of its first missionary base which gave birth to the mission of Siam, today Thailand. Finally, it was he who sent the first French missionaries to Vietnam and Cambodia. By his authority, his firmness and his solicitude, he helped them to maintain their positions and to resist the violent reactions of rejection from the Jesuits. It is in him that all the MEP missionary groups implanted in Southeast Asia were more or less rooted. The Vicar Apostolic also had a permanent concern for China, whose maritime provinces were under his jurisdiction, but he did not have the means to maintain a missionary presence there after the expulsion of Pierre Brindeau.

On the moral level, the contribution of Pierre Lambert, although more hidden, was no less important, for the nascent Society owed its survival in large part to the credit which the Bishop of Beirut enjoyed with Propaganda throughout his career. The Roman refusal to institutionalize the project of the Lovers of the Cross as a missionary congregation should not obscure the unconditional support given by successive cardinals and popes to his actions and his struggles. In the same way, the few political concessions he made in favour of his country should not conceal the remarkable loyalty he showed to the Holy See, although one can reproach him, as we have already pointed out, for his unfortunate intervention in the opening of Franco-Siamese diplomatic relations, the consequences of which were so disastrous for the mission. With this regrettable exception, his exemplary submission to the orders from Rome must be underlined. His submission proved to be costly, on account of various physical attacks as well as defamation campaigns of which he was the target during his lifetime, and of which his memory is still a victim today. Yet, despite the risks he faced and the accumulation of obstacles, Pierre Lambert tried to fulfil faithfully the episcopal mandate that had been entrusted to him.

It is obvious that his greatest problem was not differences of method (which were only in matters of detail), nor doctrinal disagreements, but rather a jurisdictional problem that provoked the most dramatic confrontations with the missionaries of Padroado, and above all with the Jesuits, whose special vow of obedience[1] had been transferred from the Pope to the King of Portugal in a strange and an extremely unfortunate move. By imperturbably playing the card of a Padroado in decline, the Jesuits in Asia made Pierre Lambert an unshakeable adversary, and they signed their long-term doom. Had they been willing to enter the ecclesial game with a little more goodwill, they would have found in the Bishop of Beirut an ally and a brother. But their choice was deliberate because it allowed them to maintain their autonomy from the Holy See, for, as Roland Jacques remarked in his analysis: 'It was this freedom of action that appeared to be a particularly important goal for them to attain and then to preserve at all costs. The Portuguese royal authority acted as the guarantor of the mission without interfering directly in spiritual matters. This allowed the Society of Jesus to organize the mission and the emerging churches in accordance with its own ideas and methods. The intention of Propaganda Fide, on the contrary, was to bring all religious into line without exception, to give a major position to bishops who did not come from religious orders, and to control more strictly from Rome all initiatives and ways of acting in missionary matters.'[2]

---

1. The Jesuits took a fourth vow to carry out any work the pope wished them to undertake.
2. Roland Jacques. *Naissance et développement du Padroado portugais d'Orient des origines à 1659* (Lisbon: Calouste Gulbenkian Foundation, 1999), 169.

Pierre Lambert had no personal desire for power, but he obviously possessed a charism as a leader. Assured of the legitimacy of his authority, he exercised it with confidence, with the consummate skill of the senior civil servant and the rigorous integrity of the Norman jurist that he had been in his youth. He was thus able to stand up to the Padroado as long as he felt the support of Rome, and this support was never lacking. At the same time an unswerving faithfulness to the principles of his spirituality preserved him from the temptation to abuse his power, no matter what his detractors might say. Whereas he was able to resist claims of the directors of the seminary which he considered excessive and inappropriate, he knew how to listen to the advice of his companions and always submitted to the decisions of Rome, even when they contradicted his most intimate and firm convictions, as in the case of fasting. The directors of the Paris Foreign Missions were unable to understand the eminent dignity and crucifying fidelity with which the Bishop of Beirut assumed his mandate. Their incomprehension was on a level with that of the Jesuits, who, by their constitutions were strangers to the episcopal ministry, if not actively opposed to it.[3] This lack of understanding of Pierre Lambert has persisted to the present day.

The Church of Vietnam, for its part, owes to Pierre Lambert the ordination of its first native priests, the foundations of its organization established by the first two synods of 1670 and 1672, and the foundation of the Lovers of the Cross. Without the energetic and courageous interventions of the Vicar Apostolic of Cochinchina, without the three perilous expeditions carried out at the risk of his life in his mission land, the first Christian communities, deprived of pastors and persecuted, would have had great difficulty in surviving at a time when the Jesuits were no longer in a position to ensure an ongoing and effective presence.

While the remarkable work accomplished by the first Jesuit evangelizers around the central figure of Alexander de Rhodes cannot be denied, the constancy and courage of the first French priests led by their bishop must also be acknowledged. To be deplored is the criminal obstinacy that the missionaries of the Society of Jesus sometimes showed in opposing their presence.

---

3. Ignatius of Loyola (c 1491–1556), the founder and first superior general of the Jesuits, was strongly opposed to members of the Society being appointed to the ecclesiastical offices of bishops and cardinals, judging such positions being opposed to the spirit of religious life.

In any appraisal of the work of Pierre Lambert in Siam, it must be noted that it was he who gave the people and their leaders a dignified and authentic Christian image of the Catholic religion. He also knew how to show attention and respect, if not for their doctrine, at least for the religious behaviour of the Buddhists, in particular his 'colleagues', the bonzes (monks).

Through his concern for the poorest, the prisoners and the sick for whom he founded the first hospital, he showed the Siamese the true face of evangelical charity. Without personally taking care of the apostolate in this country, which was not his responsibility, and in spite of the opposition of many of his companions, he unconditionally supported the inculturation initiatives attempted by Louis Laneau.

Finally, it should be remembered that by choosing Ayutthaya as the support base of his missions, Pierre Lambert was the founder of the Apostolic Vicariate of Siam and that he inaugurated the uninterrupted presence of the Foreign Missions in Thailand which exists there to this day. Until the beginning of the 20th century, the Paris Foreign Missions Society carried out almost alone what was essential for the evangelization there, supplying the country's bishops for more than two hundred and fifty years and training many generations of Thai priests and nuns.

Unfortunately, during all this time, the founding intuitions of the Bishop of Beirut and his confrere of Metellopolis were forgotten by their successors, and they have only very gradually reappeared in the last few years, thanks to new missiological data which should incite scholars to reconsider not only the contribution of Louis Laneau in the field of inculturation, but also, and perhaps above all, that of Pierre Lambert in terms of missiology and of missionary spirituality. During the first years of the French mission in Asia, in fact, the responsibility for defining the detailed rules for the implementation of the Roman *Instructions* fell essentially on the latter, the only Vicar Apostolic present in the field. Even if he did so in collaboration with his companions, and in particular with François Pallu with whom he initiated the synod of Ayutthaya, his strong personality was very influential in formulating the decisions adopted.

The right use of human resources

Directly inspired by the Roman *Instructions*, the *Monita ad Missionarios* of 1665 repeated and even amplified the disapproval of the use of human means. Deeply shocked by the behaviour of the

Padroado religious, especially in India where they had witnessed the excesses caused by the wrongful exercise of trade and other secular activities, Pierre Lambert and his companions had been able to see the uselessness and even the harmful effects of such actions, not only on the person of the missionaries, but also on the results of their work. For in addition to being scandalous when they openly opposed the moral teaching of the Church or simple human justice—as in the case of interest-bearing loans or the pursuit of excessive profits—these practices, even when they were humanly harmless, only distracted the missionaries from their true purpose, the proclamation of the Gospel.[4]

In this respect, therefore, their condemnation was very firm.

> If we are to believe experience, purely human supports do more harm than good towards the propagation of the faith; their use has never led to the adoption of true religion, but rather to a shadow or a phantom of religion. They weaken the faith of the workers of the Gospel themselves, they diminish their hope, they suspend and hold back the surge of love that should continually raise them to God.
>
> Indeed, depressed by transitory things, they forget to turn towards the true sun of faith. Deprived of that ardour which animated the Apostles and made their work fruitful, they cannot bring into being a truly viable Church. In such a perilous situation, they wither away themselves as a plant languishes and dies when the sun's rays no longer bring it joy. And so, in provinces and kingdoms almost everywhere, religion is abandoned when the human means that had been used to lead people to accept the faith could not be exercised. Or else, as soon as a storm of persecution arises, religion is overthrown without any difficulty and without leaving any trace of the faith that had not been able to put down deep roots.[5]

---

4. Regarding interest-bearing loans, much has been written about the teaching of Christian and non-Christian religions on this topic. The practice has generally been condemned. In the 1917 Code of Canon Law the Catholic Church changed its position and allowed church money to be used to accrue interest. Nonetheless, it regarded the charging of interest as sinful when, in doing so, it took advantage of a person in need as well as when it meant investing in corporations involved in the harming of God's creatures.
5. *Monita ad Missionarios*, Instructions to the missionaries of the S. Congregation of Propaganda (Paris: AMEP, 2000), 40.

'Thus astronomy and other mathematical sciences, painting, mechanical arts and the like, all these are a burden and a hindrance to the missionary rather than a real help. All the time he spends on them is taken from prayer and other apostolic functions; moreover, they attract to the missionary esteem and fame which fill him with the smoke of vainglory, amuse the curiosity of the audience and, by fixing their attention on such things, distract them from matters of salvation. It even happens sometimes that missionaries, wanting to appear expert and knowledgeable in these arts, in order to gain credit and authority for their religious preaching, achieve precisely the opposite effect; they are believed to be too clever, they are distrusted, and they are denied all credibility.'[6] These condemnations were not dictated by simple considerations of principle, for the French missionaries could point to the situation of the Jesuits who were losing ground wherever they had tried to get involved by these human means, as if the example of Japan had not been enough to convince them of the fragility of the results of a method based on seduction and compromise.[7]

In Peking (Beijing), they were still tolerated for their scientific skills, but Christianity was banned. In Vietnam, their involvement in the arms trade and their status as mandarins provoked jealousy and persecution. In Siam, the superior of the Jesuits, Thomas Valguarnera, had become an engineer to supervise the construction of the walls of Ayutthaya, but this did not advance the progress of the mission nor did it favour the position of the Christians, since the king welcomed with equal benevolence and employed indiscriminately all foreigners who could be of use to his kingdom.

To emphasise his difference, and to be able to exist alongside the other Europeans who, Catholic or not, made commerce their main activity, Pierre Lambert chose to give a privileged place to the only two human actions compatible with the state of religious life: teaching and charitable work. For this, once again, he benefited from all the experience he had acquired in France. Teaching was recommended by the Roman *Instructions* and aimed essentially at establishing seedbeds from which the future native clergy would emerge. The

---

6. *Monita ad Missionarios*, 48.
7. Francis Xavier was the first Jesuit to set foot in Japan in 1549. The missionary work expanded peacefully until 1614 when Christianity was banned and in the mid-seventeenth century all missionaries were expelled and converts were executed.

college in Ayutthaya, even though it welcomed non-Christians (in particular some young Siamese sent by Phra Narai) and provided a general elementary and secondary education for its youngest students, was above all conceived as a seminary. But the concern for a popular education for the sole purpose of improving the condition of the underprivileged classes was not absent from the preoccupations of the Bishop of Beirut, since he made the instruction of women, 'both Christian and pagan', a priority for the Lovers of the Cross. As regards works of charity, the Vicar Apostolic had a particular concern for prisoners who, in Siam, lived in deplorable conditions. But above all, hedeveloped ways of caring for the sick, and in particular for the poorest who had no means of help. For them, he conceived the idea of opening a small dispensary in Camp Saint-Joseph, where he himself began to treat them as he had learned to do in the hospitals of Caen and Rouen. But absorbed by his many administrative tasks, he soon entrusted the care of this initiative to Louis Laneau who worked there with admirable devotion and thus acquired, through practice, an advanced medical knowledge for the time.

For even if the most commonly used remedies were prayer and holy water, the French did not neglect more professional procedures, and for serious cases they called upon native doctors, most often Chinese. Soon an introduction to the practice of medicine became part of the training of missionaries. Laymen, also, with specialized skills were called upon, such as the highly skilled 'nurse-surgeon', René Charbonneau, who assisted Louis Laneau for many years. As for women, Pierre Lambert entrusted the task of caring for them to the Lovers of the Cross 'in order to use this path to deal with them in matters of salvation and conversion.'[8]

For the Vicar Apostolic, the care of the sick was not simply a humanitarian concern as it might be conceived today. From his perspective, the salvation of the body was nothing if it did not allow for the salvation of the soul. By healing the sick, the missionaries were doing more than a charitable work as it might be understood in France. Rather, they were imitating Christ and the Apostles for whom physical healings were an introduction to the proclamation of the Kingdom of God. This is why we find in the writings of the missionaries several accounts of spontaneous cures that can be

---

8. Launay. *Histoire Tonkin*, 104.

considered 'miraculous', although the historical distance from them does not allow the necessary verifications. On the other hand, the French also encountered failures, the most resounding of which was the attempted cure of the brother of the King of Siam in 1666. This unfortunate episode marked the limits of this method, at least when it was guided by human interest motives.

The subtleties and contradictions of adaptation to local customs

Contrary to the image of a rigorist and reactionary prelate that some historiography has painted, Pierre Lambert was a fervent supporter of methods of adaptation. He could hardly do otherwise, since these methods were recommended by the Roman *Instructions*. But on the other hand, since he left a great deal of personal latitude to his missionaries, he never gave general directions, preferring to respond to problems case by case when his advice was sought. Some missionaries, like Jacques de Bourges in Tonkin, were sufficiently confident and intelligent to decide for themselves what concessions were useful or necessary. That is why there was little controversy in this mission. The situation was more complex in Cochinchina, either because of the abusive authoritarianism and narrow-mindedness of certain missionaries, or because of their scrupulous and more indecisive temperament which caused them to defer to the decision of their bishop. Pierre Lambert's main concern was to avoid arousing the distrust of local institutions towards Christians so as not to provoke persecution.

But he was just as concerned not to authorize practices whose explicitly religious character was in clear conflict with the profession of Christian faith. One can therefore speak of a moderate tolerance or an enlightened rigor that can be seen in the answers he gave in 1667 to several cases submitted by his envoy to Cochinchina, Antoine Hainques.

> The first case concerned the 'thien ku'. the altar erected in the house of the Cochinchinese Christians. He definitely would not allow its presence, because '*est signum intrinsece malum et protestativum falsae sectae, quod nequit separi a ratione cultus*'. (It is an intrinsically evil sign and expressive of a false sect, inseparable from worship.) In the second case, the question

is whether the 'neu' or superstition which they carry out at the beginning of the year can be tolerated. A bamboo pole and a basket are set up at the entrance of the house and in the basket food is placed in order to propitiate the demon during the course of the year. It was decided that Christians could be allowed to set up this bamboo and this basket without putting food in it, because then the evil of this superstition or this bad custom would be removed from Christians, who would then understand that this sign does nothing more than mark the beginning of the year.

As for the marks of reverence and genuflections they make to their dead relatives, I think they can be tolerated, and the relatives honoured after their death, as was the custom during their lifetime. With regard to the feast honouring the dead, it seems that, strictly speaking, it can be argued that Christians can offer food and drink to their dead relatives in order to honour them, but only at a political service, and in order to avoid problems that would ensue if they did not do so. This custom of serving food and drink to the dead is observed in many places after the death of great people, as we see after the death of our kings, and it has been practised for some years now, after the death of the late archbishop of Paris.[9]

In spite of his prudence and rigor, Pierre Lambert often encountered resistance from Propaganda, whose practice was often much more restrictive than was intended by the formulations in the *Instructions*. Anxious not to disobey the Holy See in order to preserve the credit he had acquired in his fight against the regulars, a credit which depended on his perfect loyalty, the Bishop of Beirut, without being discouraged, tried to have decisions accepted which seemed justified to him, but he was not always successful. One of the most characteristic cases was that of the Chinese New Year, for which he requested a dispensation as soon as he became aware of the customary festivities that marked this celebration. On 4 September 1663, he wrote to Propaganda: 'In these kingdoms, it is customary to celebrate the first three days of

---

9. Launay. *Histoire Cochinchine*, 53–54. At funerals, Buddhists complement their chanting and singing with food, which shows respect for the dead and encourages people to be generous. It also shows the dead that they are still loved as they were in life.

the Lunar New Year with great solemnity. As it often happens that these days fall on Friday and Saturday, or during Lent, we ask for a dispensation which would allow meat to be eaten without scruples, and we also ask for an indulgence to be granted to those who will visit the church, give alms or do some other pious work.'[10] But the cardinals were not convinced by his argument and replied curtly: 'Since this solemnity has nothing to do with the Church and does not represent any mystery of the Christian faith, there is no reason to grant anything.'[11]

However, in 1667, when Antoine Hainques asked him again about abstinence during the New Year's holidays, Pierre Lambert gave an answer that was sufficiently evasive and general to allow Christians to break the fast without openly disobeying the Roman decisions. 'As for eating meat on forbidden days, this can be done when it would cause great harm to Catholics if they did not do so.'[12] A former student of the Jesuits, the Vicar Apostolic of Cochinchina knew how to practise freedom of conscience when circumstances required it. But he was not a man to indulge in vagueness, and his legal training had given him the art of formulating arguments. He therefore found a new reason to submit the case by proposing to Christianize these feasts in order to make them acceptable to the Roman censors. In 1676, on his return from his second trip to Cochinchina, he asked that Christians be granted permission to honour their martyrs at the Lunar New Year so that they could participate in the traditional collective festivities without any problem.

Pierre Lambert did not have the same scruples in agreeing to Louis Laneau's request for Siam in 1677. The latter thought that the apostolate in the Buddhist milieu would be easier if the French missionaries could wear the habit of the bonzes, who were highly respected by the population, rather than the Western cassock which associated them with the European religious from whom they sought to distance themselves. After careful consideration, the Bishop of Beirut gave his approval and the missionaries were able to wear the habit of the Buddhist monks for their apostolic journeys, which put them, at least in appearance, in line with the innovative Jesuits such

---

10. Jean Guennou. *Missions étrangères de Paris* (Paris: Fayard, 1986), 190.
11. Guennou. MEP, 190.
12. Launay. *Histoire Cochinchine*, 54.

as Roberto de Nobili and Matteo Ricci.[13] But the Jesuits in Ayutthaya did not agree and, after the death of Pierre Lambert, they complained to François Pallu who saw fit to submit the matter to Rome. The Bishop of Heliopolis wrote to Propaganda to request permission for the missionaries to wear either the costume of the bonzes, or at least a cassock of the same colour, yellow or orange. But this suggestion was definitely not appreciated by the men of Propaganda, who answered categorically: 'Negative, etiam quoad colorem.'[14] ('Negative, even as regards the colour.')

The father of the Vietnamese clergy

The Roman *Instructions* of 1659 stipulated firmly that the primary objective of the Vicars Apostolic was the formation of a native clergy placed under their authority, pending conditions favourable to the constitution of a local hierarchy, which they were considering with caution. Indeed, contrary to what was happening in Europe and in the colonies where they were dependent on political power, Propaganda wanted to control episcopal appointments in the new churches that were being formed. As soon as the French missionaries had decided to set up their base in Ayutthaya, Pierre Lambert set about creating a seminary there, bringing together young schoolchildren, native seminarians and French missionaries in charge of teaching or others who were simply passing through Siam.

The first native candidates for the priesthood, mostly Vietnamese, were recruited from among former catechists according to strict selection criteria defined in the *Monita*. The instructions concerning the formation of Asian clergy owed much, through Pierre Lambert, to the priestly ideal of the French School of Spirituality. They recommended great rigor in the celebration of worship and the administration of the sacraments, which implied a priori a perfect understanding of their meaning. In order to be worthy celebrants of their sacred functions, native priests should not only have had a theoretical or formal knowledge of them, but also an internalized

---

13. Roberto di Nobili SJ (1577–1656) adopted local customs in India to gain acceptance by the Hindus and so be able to win converts to Christianity. Matteo Ricci SJ (1552–1610) also sought to win converts in China by adopting the language and culture of the people.
14. Guennou. MEP, 192.

appreciation of them through the regular practice of prayer, in order to achieve that spirit of oblation and adherence to Christ advocated by all the great French formators in the wake of Cardinal de Bérulle. Opened in 1665 for candidates for ordination from Macau, the theology class of the seminary of Ayutthaya directed by Louis Laneau, welcomed seminarians who were mostly catechists sent by the missionaries of Cochinchina and Tonkin. On March 31, 1668, the Bishop of Beirut ordained the first Vietnamese priest, a Cochinchinese named Joseph Trang, as well as the one who was to become his successor at the head of the Church of Cochinchina, the Eurasian François Perez. A few weeks later came the turn of the first two Tonkinese, Jean Huê and Benoît Hiên, followed the next year by another Cochinchinese, Luc Ben. In 1670, upon his arrival in Tonkin, the Vicar Apostolic conferred the priesthood on seven new candidates from among the senior catechists, all selected by François Deydier.

The synod which was held immediately after these ordinations entrusted each of the nine Tonkinese priests with the direction of a district. Thanks to this system of direct administration, many Christians who had been abandoned for years were able to receive the sacraments again. 'The Tonkinese priests render us a great service,' wrote Jacques de Bourges in one of his reports,

> some through the Sacrament of Penance and by their preaching in parishes that have not been visited for many years, others by going to visit the sick who, without them, would not have received the Sacrament of Penance and Extreme Unction before dying. We cannot bless Providence enough for so many benefits. Thanks be to God, this year these poor souls received the help they needed; for the nine priests ordained by Bishop de Beirut went through the villages, administered the sacraments, and baptized more than 6,463 people, heard the confessions of more than 15,000, many of whom had never been to Confession before, and others who had not received this sacrament for twenty or thirty years, which came at the right time for a number of old men on the edge of their grave.[15]

---

15. An account of what happened in Tonkin. AMEP, volume 677, 244.

Although the French missionaries, considered to be the direct representatives of the Vicar Apostolic, retained the responsibility for directing the mission in his name, Pierre Lambert insisted that the greatest equality should reign among the members of the clerical community, without distinction of rank or nationality, in accordance with the regulations he had already instituted for the seminary of Ayutthaya. Pierre Lambert wrote to William Lesley: 'During my stay of more than six months in Tonkin, I tried to persuade those who were destined for the service of the Church to have everything in common among themselves. You will certainly be pleased to hear that amongst our two missionaries, the nine priests of the country, the forty-eight clerics whom I ordained, and the seminarians who make up the community, there is no meum ni tuum (mine or yours), that they live in the way decided upon by the synod whose decisions I sent to Rome.'[16]

Recruitment was more difficult in Cochinchina where the Christian community was less numerous and less well organized. In 1672, Pierre Lambert brought back from his first visit ten young men destined for the seminary of Ayutthaya, of whom only six were still persevering in 1675. Highly appreciated by the French missionaries and living very harmoniously with them, the first Vietnamese priests were, on the other hand, the target of violent criticism from the Jesuits, who considered their formation insufficient. In 1670, Father Tissanier, appointed superior of the Jesuits in Ayutthaya to replace Father Valguarnera, wrote, 'M. de Beirut ordained seven Tonkinese priests who had been our catechists or servants, but who were not sufficiently well trained for this high ministry. Two French priests dressed as merchants entered Cochinchina with two other extremely ignorant Cochinchese priests, one of whom could not pronounce the formula of absolution without having the words written on a piece of paper.'[17]

One of the main problems facing both the seminarians and their teachers was indeed the learning of Latin, since the *Instructions* of 1659 had not renewed the authorization granted in 1615 by Paul V to the Jesuits in China to celebrate the liturgy in the national language.

---

16. Launay. *Histoire Tonkin*, 111.
17. Letter from Joseph Tissanier to Father Ignace Meveilo, 30 May 1675. AMEP, volume 858, 243.

On several occasions, Peter Lambert asked that this authorization be renewed in favour of the Vicars Apostolic in the territory of their missions. But Rome, fearing a schism, refused and only allowed subjects too old to learn Latin to recite the liturgical formulas by heart, without understanding them. This explains the linguistic approximations denounced by the Jesuits, an approach that was understandable since the Vietnamese priests of the first generation, trained on the job by the missionaries in precarious conditions, were generally not admitted to the priesthood before the age of 40. The apprenticeship was obviously easier for the younger ones who benefited from a classical education at the seminary of Ayutthaya. This allowed them to acquire quickly a certain autonomy of judgment in relation to the Europeans.

Thus, as Pierre Langlois, the superior of the seminary of Ayutthaya, reported: 'Those who now understand Latin are surprised to see with their own eyes that these fathers (the Jesuits) practise the opposite of what is taught in their books, and so they understand why they did not want to teach them Latin even though they had asked them to do so. They say that it is because these fathers feared that one day they would be contradicted by their own pupils and disciples. These reasons help to explain why Christians are drawn more readily to submission to the orders of the Holy See and to the Vicars Apostolic; they see their fellow clerics and priests, who are knowledgeable, leave the Jesuits and adhere entirely to the Holy See and to the Vicars Apostolic without any of them wavering.'[18]

In spite of the criticism of the Portuguese religious, which, as these remarks show, was not entirely disinterested, Pierre Lambert favoured the quickest possible promotion of an indigenous clergy. If he took the risk of ordaining men who did not always have the required level of intellectual training, he remained very demanding regarding the moral and spiritual qualities of the candidates, and overall the priests ordained by him did excellent pastoral work. Towards the end of his life, however, discipline at the Ayutthaya seminary became somewhat lax, partly because of the instability of the teaching staff. So in 1680, Louis Laneau decided to move the seminary to Mahapram, away from the city and thus from the hustle and bustle and temptations of the world.

---

18. Letter from Pierre Langlois to Michel Gazil, Siam, 24 December 1674, AMEP, volume 858, 285.

The auxiliary personnel

As a former lay activist who received Holy Orders rather late, Pierre Lambert never showed any clerical exclusivism. As early as 1662, his project for a Congregation of the Lovers of the Cross was open to lay people 'not in wedlock,' without specifying their sex. A few years later, in 1668, the Vicar Apostolic specified that no one should be excluded, of whatever sex or condition, and that the congregation should be represented everywhere, 'in the towns and villages, by a number of faithful.' Here we find the influence of the mystical and missionary flowering of the 17th century in France, which involved men as well as women, laity as well as clerics and nuns.

In his youth, Pierre Lambert had worked with people from different backgrounds who, like Jean de Bernières, Jean Eudes, Vincent de Paul and many others less well known, were not only very spiritual men leading a rigorous ascetic life, but also people very involved in social and missionary activity. The Company of the Blessed Sacrament, to which he belonged, was made up of men only, and included both clerics and lay people without distinction. But he had also often collaborated with women, apostolic religious like the Daughters of the Cross or lay benefactors like the Duchess of Aiguillon.[19] The Bishop of Beirut could not, therefore, conceive of the organization of the missionary apostolate apart from this militant mix which had borne so much fruit in the Church of France.

The teams of missionaries who accompanied the first Vicars Apostolic included lay people, most of whom died or gave up along the way. Only the former naval officer, Philippe de Chamesson, persevered to the end and rendered great service to the missionaries as a guide and negotiator. A few others followed, such as the surgeon René Charbonneau, but experience showed that generally, lay people had difficulty coping with the constraints and difficulties of missionary life, so that the experiment was quickly abandoned. In order to better stand the test of time, perhaps these lay people should

---

19. The Duchess of Aiguillon (1604–1675) was the niece of Cardinal Richelieu, the prime minister of King Louis XIII. She used her considerable wealth to aid charitable works as well as to found and promote Catholic ministries in France and mission countries in Asia and French North America. She played an important part in the foundation of the Société des Missions Étrangères de Paris and its affiliated seminary (known for short as the MEP seminary).

have been more closely linked to the missionary priests by a true spiritual community. In fact, this is precisely what the project of the Lovers of the Cross intended. This project was inspired by the organization of the Order of Minims which included three branches, one for male religious, one for female religious and a third order for the laity, of which Pierre Lambert was a member.

In the spirit of the Vicar Apostolic, the Congregation of the Lovers of the Cross was also to have a tripartite structure in which all the members would be linked by a common spirituality but assigned to different tasks. Since the men's branch was rejected by Rome and the lay branch, approved as a confraternity, quickly collapsed, only the women's branch of the Lovers of the Cross flourished with the success that we know and it perpetuated the missionary ideal of its founder.

Faced with the failure of his project, Pierre Lambert had to make do, for the recruitment of auxiliary personnel, with an institution that had largely proved itself, that of the catechists. He took over the organization given to them by the Jesuits, in particular by Alexandre de Rhodes. Charged with the task of assisting the priests in their apostolate but also with filling in for them in case of absence at a time when the missionaries were often expelled or imprisoned, the catechists had to possess solid moral virtues: zeal, good character, and exemplary conduct. They had to observe the same rules of life as the missionaries, who chose them from among their pupils.

But there were also spontaneous applications that could be accepted if they met the required criteria. The catechists were mostly celibate since some of them were destined for the priesthood, but this was not an absolute obligation and married men of good character could perform the functions defined in the *Monita*.

> Their task is to instruct others; that is to say, they must be fully capable of teaching true doctrine faithfully, and the initiation they give to catechumens must conform in every way with the principles of piety and holiness. With regard to the infidels in whose midst they live, they should attach great importance to combating their errors by going back to their source; it is even desirable that they be able to read their books: it would be a means of better understanding the thousand dreams, fables and countless superstitions of which they are full; it would be a blessing to meet and to indicate one or other point on which they are in agreement with us. This will teach them the easy

way to refute their errors by taking up with them their own arguments; and by relevant material drawn from their own books, they will be able to affirm and prove the truth of the Christian religion more easily."[20]

Like the Lovers of the Cross, the catechists had specific responsibilities that required of them, if not a scholarly training, at least an enlightened faith and genuine spiritual qualities. Far from confining them to a subordinate role, Pierre Lambert sought to promote them to the priesthood.

While he had only a handful of European missionaries to assist him, the first Vicar Apostolic of Cochinchina knew how to make the potential wealth of the young Vietnamese Christian community bear fruit by providing them with their own indigenous leaders, priests, catechists and nuns who worked together according to well defined and complementary functions. In seventeen years of uninterrupted presence in the missionary field, Pierre Lambert, who had already demonstrated his exceptional organizational abilities in Rouen, was the true pillar of the French mission. In spite of the constant harassment of the Padroado religious who were united against him, he succeeded in setting up the ecclesiastical structures of the churches of Siam and Vietnam, while at the same time winning the respect and good will of the sovereigns of these nations.

In Europe, the greatest difficulties came from those who should have been his closest allies, the directors of the Paris Foreign Missions. However, as a faithful agent of the Roman reform, Pierre Lambert exercised his office in perfect conformity with the spirit of his country of origin, that of the French School of Spirituality which was shared by the greatest ecclesiastical figures of his time and which left an indelible mark on the Church of France. Thus, it can be affirmed that if today certain points of convergence still exist between the Church of France and the Church of Vietnam, it is not so much in the colonial period of the nineteenth and twentieth centuries that we should look for their origins as in a previous age, in the heroic and troubled times when Pierre Lambert de la Motte laid the foundations of the one on the heritage of the other.

---

20. *Monita ad Missionarios*, 136.

Chapter 10
A spiritual heritage to be rediscovered

Pierre Lambert was a man of the seventeenth century, shaped by the cultural and religious criteria of his time. Hence his language, his sensitivity, his way of thinking, his conception of the world, may seem old-fashioned to us today. Religiously, as bishop, he was closely dependent on the highly regulated centralism of the post-Tridentine Church.[1] Dogmas, beliefs, and practices of piety, as well as public and private behaviour, were rigorously codified at that time. Catholics were placed under the close supervision of clerics who, themselves, had to set an example.

The first Vicar Apostolic of Cochinchina was also marked by the rigorism that characterized the French spirituality of his time. This French spirit, described as 'classical' in contrast to the 'baroque' character of Italian or Iberian piety,[2] was manifested by austerity, renunciation, asceticism, contempt for the body, the struggle against passions and especially against self-love. Contrary to widespread opinion, rigorism was not the prerogative of Jansenism, but affected all the great souls of that time, from Vincent de Paul to Armand-Jean de Rancé, from the spiritual Jesuits in the mould of Louis Lallemant to the disciples of Cardinal de Bérulle. And while the most political and worldly members of the Society of Jesus adhered to Molina's lax theses, the most austere orders—Carmelites, Capuchins and

---

1. The Catholic Church held an ecumenical Council between 1545 and 1563 in the town of Trent in northern Italy. The Council of Trent (Latin: Concilium Tridentinum) responded to the teachings of Protestant reformers and the need to eliminate abuses in Catholic Church practices. 'Post-Tridentine' refers to the time after this Council.
2. 'Iberian' refers to what is Spanish and Portuguese.

Minims—nevertheless exerted a great influence on the pillars of the Catholic Church. Located through his eclectic training at the crossroads of these various currents, Pierre Lambert, in this severe context, developed an authentic spiritual freedom, the inner freedom of true mystics.

An initial conflict

From an early age, Pierre Lambert aspired to a radical contemplative life. Initially, his thoughts about the Lovers of the Cross, conceived at the age of nine were, in fact, a passionate aspiration for the 'perfect life'—that is, according to the terminology of his time, to a life of union with God—that none of the religious institutes he knew at that time seemed likely to satisfy. On the contrary, shortly after this intuition, he received from the Jesuits, a formation entirely oriented towards engagement with the world.

Even if his teachers at the time were men on an incomparably higher spiritual plane than most of the largely secularized Jesuits he met on mission, even if he had no point of comparison that would allow him to measure what he lacked, even if his intelligence, piety, charitable devotion, apostolic zeal and sense of discipline made him an exemplary student worthy of recruitment into the circles of the elite formed by Marian congregations, he was not completely at ease in this milieu. For him, the Ignatian model was excessively focused on externals, too much confined to the constant concern for action that was the basis of its social effectiveness. This formal perfection, this systematic and normative asceticism which was intended to serve as a public standard, did not fulfil his own desire for a 'perfect life', the desire of his childhood, the passionate and heart-felt desire of every mystic, that of life 'in God.'

Driven by the collective dynamics of the college, family obligations and social constraints, Pierre Lambert allowed many years to pass before clearly perceiving his restlessness and deciding to change his way of life. His second conversion occurred in 1654 when, disappointed by the evolution of the political events in which he was involved, he decided to leave the world. This withdrawal, however, while radical in its demands, was neither absolute nor definitive in its form. By choosing the Hermitage of Jean de Bernières, a place highly regarded for its charitable and missionary commitment, in preference, for example to a retreat in La Trappe or among the Carthusians, the future Vicar Apostolic of Cochinchina showed that, consciously or not, he was now, or perhaps always was, imbued with a desire for commitment in the world. It was in this environment, with the various people he met there, that he learned to unify the active life and the contemplative life. Throughout his life he drew from the Bérullian notion of 'adherence to Christ' the balance needed between the 'Jesuit activity' required by his missionary vocation and the 'Carmelite passion for God' inherent in his temperament. Soon after, John Eudes transmitted to him the priestly spirituality of annihilation that made him feel, on the day of his diaconal ordination, his interior vocation to the 'martyrdom of love.'

It is curious to note that two hundred years later, another Norman mystic, Thérèse of the Infant Jesus, in her Carmel of Lisieux,[3] made the same discovery that led her to holiness and earned her the title of universal patroness of missions alongside the most famous Jesuit missionary, Saint Francis Xavier. This concurrence was not simply the result of chance, because, between Pierre Lambert and Thérèse Martin, there was more than a simple geographical concordance focused on Lisieux, where the former was born and where the latter died. There was, transcending all that differentiated their lives and their similar mentalities, an obvious correspondence.

Both were ardent and eminently contemplative souls, challenged from an early age by the mystery of the incarnation through the fervent reading of *The Imitation of Christ*.[4] From this encounter, both of them chose to follow Christ and imitate him, especially in the two extreme poles of his earthly life: his birth through abasement, humility, abandonment, spirit of childhood, and his death through love, suffering, sacrifice and desire to 'save souls.' Both, after a life of

---

3. St Therese of the Child Jesus (1873–1897) entered the Carmelite convent in Lisieux in April 1888 and died at the age of twenty-four. She was canonised in 1928 and declared a doctor of the Church in 1997. She had a special love of the missions and is their patron along with St Francis Xavier. 'There was a request for more sisters to help the small community in Saigon and St Therese was one of the first to volunteer.' (See https://aleteia.org/2019/10/22/how-st-therese-of-lisieux-was-nearly-sent-to-vietnam/) Her writings were published after her death as *The Story of a Soul*.
4. *The Imitation of Christ* is a devotional book written by an Augustinian monk named Thomas à Kempis between 1420 and 1427. It has inspired Christians through the centuries to live a life dedicated to Jesus Christ.

prayer and dedication, perfected their martyrdom of love in the last months of their lives, plunged into the dark night of the soul and their bodies crucified by frightful suffering.

Thus, little Thérèse, with her intuitions so simple and so brilliant at the same time, could be considered as an 'autumn rose,' a late and unexpected flower of the long underground process of spiritual germination rooted in the fertile soil of this Norman mystical milieu, which was the crucible of seventeenth century missionary France of which Pierre Lambert, although unrecognized, remains one of the most eminent figures.

The Pauline model

The political disappointment at the end of the Fronde, coinciding with the end of his family responsibilities thanks to the establishment of his brothers and sisters, was certainly a determining factor in Pierre Lambert's decision to leave his position in the world. But an authentic spiritual life is not built on negative feelings that have no purpose, ambition or duty. It needs its own dynamic. Now, in this case, it was a very ordinary incident, a fall from a horse without injury, which brought the young world-weary magistrate out of the somewhat depressed state in which he had been stagnating for several months. More or less consciously influenced by the iconography of his time which represented the conversion of Saint Paul by a fall from his horse through the power of his divine encounter, Pierre Lambert gave this innocuous event a supernatural meaning; he interpreted it as a sign from heaven. This reference to the Apostle to the Gentiles was not merely of passing interest; it had a profound effect on his spiritual development. Perceived as the archetype of the convert, Saint Paul, whose writings were, with those of Saint John, the favourite scriptural sources of the masters of the French School, also became for Pierre Lambert the missionary model *par excellence* and his main source of inspiration.

On 15 March 1661, Pierre Lambert wrote a letter from Baghdad to his spiritual director Simon Hallé, which showed that from the beginning of his apostolic career at the age of 37, he had already reached a very high level of spiritual maturity.

> Wishing therefore to give you some idea of our dispositions since our departure from France, I can tell you that it seems to me that the good Lord is the perfect master of our interior

movements. His manner of acting in us is absolute: we are no longer asked if we want something, but as soon as the soul sees or experiences God's good pleasure, it responds, not only without reflection, but also with ineffable joy. What I judge to be most admirable in this conformity, uniformity, or deiformity of will, is that in its composure, the soul is continually absorbed by exalted sentiments and a profound adoration of the most supreme majesty of God. As far as the soul is concerned, it increases its self-knowledge, and develops a most holy and implacable self-hatred. These effects undoubtedly come from their cause, that is, from the union that the soul has with its Maker. Ah, my Father, how difficult it is to remain calm when speaking of this wonderful life. You know more about it than I do, and yet, this does not prevent me from rejoicing with you in the happiness of being totally dedicated to God.[5]

This state is very closely related, in its essence, to the union with God as defined by the greatest mystics: by a radical detachment from creatures but also from his own powers, man reaches a state of interior availability that allows the birth of God in the soul, and of the soul in God. He no longer has to choose between a contemplative life and an active life since his own will, purified of all personal or human considerations, exists in harmony with the divine will. The depths of his soul, established in a close union with God, enjoy a happiness and a peace independent of external circumstances or reactions of a sensible nature that may affect his outward demeanour.

Whether it was the inaugural grace of a painful missionary career or the culmination of a demanding inner journey, Pierre Lambert seemed to experience in all its fullness, at this precise moment of his life, that state of 'adherence to Christ' so dear to his teachers of the French School. His interior delight, nourished by the inevitable asceticism of the conditions of travel and the abandonment they required, had not yet been disturbed by the trying conflicts within the Church that darkened the rest of his career.

From this mystical betrothal in the desert were born in the spirit of the Vicar Apostolic, some radical missiological convictions which clashed head-on not only with the imperialist tradition of the

---

5. Letter from Pierre Lambert to Father Simon Hallé, Babylon, 16 March 1661. AMEP, volume 136, 71.

Padroado and the practices of its religious, but also with the realist principles and the aims of economic-Catholic expansion of his French supporters. A return to evangelical simplicity, an acute awareness of the vanity of human resources and material goods, a trusting abandonment to Providence, a childlike spirit: these were indeed the dispositions that guaranteed, for Pierre Lambert, the missionary's fidelity to his vocation. As for his mission, it can be summed up apart from any quantitative, strategic or political consideration, as an essential goal: to offer to people who consented to it, the way to the only true good, 'the knowledge and the experiential love of our Lord Jesus Christ.'[6] Indeed, behind the seeming pessimism of a 'nihilist' (incorrectly referred to as 'Jansenist') conception of sinful man, too often levelled as a reproach at the Vicar Apostolic, is revealed the fundamental optimism of an apostolic soul totally absorbed by the Good News of salvation: man redeemed by Christ's sacrifice on the cross and purified by baptism to become a 'tabernacle of the Holy Spirit' and 'delight of God,' destined for divinisation.

But soon these ideal principles clashed with the trivial realities on the ground, with human mediocrity and with certain European interests which, although presented under the sign of the cross, sometimes had only a rather remote relationship with the Gospel precepts. Thus, when ten years later the Vicar Apostolic was confronted with the terrible difficulties of his mission, he turned to Saint Paul, and it was in his theology of the cross that he found the source of his own missionary dynamism.

From the beginning of his Asian ministry, in fact, Pierre Lambert understood that he was in a polemical situation that was not unrelated to that which Saint Paul experienced when faced with the Corinthians: division of communities, the claim to superiority of the Jesuit 'super-apostles' who did not hesitate to resort to the wisdom of the world to obtain conversions and thus eliminate the event of the cross, the possessiveness of these same Jesuits towards those whom they had baptized and whom they had forced to promise not to recognize any pastor foreign to their Society. Over time, the Vicar Apostolic also became more and more acutely aware of his vulnerability, of the paltry insufficiency of the human resources at his disposal by comparison with the power of the Padroado, of the mistrust and disavowal of his

---

6. Letter, Lambert to Hallé, 71.

friends, of abandonment and loneliness under the enormous weight of his overwhelming responsibilities. In such a context, the words of Saint Paul resonated for him in their dramatic existential depth: 'Christ did not send me to baptize but to proclaim the Gospel, and not with eloquent wisdom, so that the cross of Christ might not be emptied of its power. For the message about the cross is foolishness to those who are perishing, but to us who are being saved, it is the power of God' (1 Cor 1:17–18).

A lover of the cross from his youth, Pierre Lambert strove to experience on a daily basis the paradoxical fecundity of the message explained by Paul, that it pleased God to save believers, when human wisdom seemed foolishness to God, when the weakness of humans was opened to divine power, when death led to eternal life. In opposition to the worldly strategies of the Jesuits and the excessive human prudence of the Parisian directors, he chose the radical path of evangelical abandonment. It was therefore in prayer and contemplation that he found the source of all his decisions, a simple vessel of clay disposed to receive divine grace, so that, as the Apostle said, 'It is clear that this extraordinary power belongs to God and does not come from us' (2 Cor 4:7).

The obedience of faith

The folly of preaching about the cross, concealed from the wisdom of men, can only be accepted by faith. The problem of pure faith, of naked faith, occupied a large part of Pierre Lambert's meditations, especially during the first years of his ministry, when the secular excesses he observed among the Jesuits led him to a painful questioning of his own Ignatian formation. 'Whenever I open the New Testament, and see the means of acquiring holiness written in words, I accuse myself of having wasted time formerly by consulting men who did not speak this language, and I regret that I willingly allowed myself to be deceived. Let us therefore be wise, whatever the cost, and resolve to put into practice without question the teachings of the Son of God, who is concerned about our vocation, believing that this is undoubtedly what we must do to please the Divine Goodness. To examine whether we should follow an evangelical counsel is to lose the grace given to us to put it into practice.'[7]

---

7. Letter from Pierre Lambert to M Gazil, July 1663. AMEP, volume 121, 529.

A return to simplicity and evangelical radicalism: faced with casuistic subtleties and specious reasoning advanced by the Jesuits for their own justification, Pierre Lambert put forward the full force of Scripture in its original purity. It was, therefore, by contemplating Christ in his incarnation, by imitating his conduct and fulfilling his commandments that the missionary would find the assurance of being perfectly obedient.

However, the more he advanced in the ministry, the more the Vicar Apostolic found that this obedience of faith, apparently obvious to a mystic as advanced as he was, nevertheless presented some difficulties for ordinary mortals, even among those whose vocation it was to pass it on. For many of them, indeed, he noted, faith seemed to have become a set of conceptual assertions dictated by an institution; it seemed to have lost its original strength, personal trust and commitment to the One who was its source. For other so-called believers, even among the best, faith was limited to the practice of moral precepts and rules of conduct, to the respect for propriety that ensured their moral comfort without altering their material welfare. In the problematic situation in which he found himself, Pierre Lambert could not be satisfied with an intellectual faith or a faith solely concerned with moral convention. Compelled to act in order to avoid spiritual stagnation, he could not allow himself to be passively drawn into the dark night of contemplative mystics.

It was imperative for him to have a servant God, a saviour God, the God of the Bible who led his people into the wilderness where he guided and nourished them, the God of the Gospel who provided for the needs of those who sought the Kingdom above all, the Father God who never abandoned those who entrusted themselves to him. It was not by chance that the Vicar Apostolic frequently quoted chapters 5, 6 and 7 of the Gospel of Matthew, chapters concerned with the Beatitudes, the Our Father, the parables of the lilies of the field and the birds of the sky, the narrow gate, true disciples and true treasure, prayer and fasting in secret, in short, what biblical commentators call 'evangelical discourse'. To this God who put his faith to the test, the Vicar Apostolic addressed Job's last answer, the only correct answer that annulled any justification or useless advice: 'I know that you are almighty: what you conceive, you can achieve.' It was in this God that he grounded the missionary spirituality with which he nourished himself and which he transmitted to his companions. It was to this God that it was necessary to look for the source of his radical interpretation of the distrust of human means advocated in the Roman *Instructions*.

Pierre Lambert was indeed so scandalised by the abuses into which the Jesuits had allowed themselves to be dragged in the material management of their missions that, in his behaviour, he did the exact opposite of their anti-evangelical practice. Thus the renunciation not only of wealth, but also of any concern for material security was for him the first step, an essential step, on the way to missionary abandonment. 'An apostolic missionary must believe with regard to the temporal that he is more certain of his livelihood than is the greatest monarch in the world. The reason for this is that he trusts completely that he will never be abandoned by God, who is committed to him. His position is much better than that of the potentate who relies on human means which, however great they may be, are likely to perish. Scripture is pervaded with this truth. Certainly there is reason to be surprised that so few people believe this truth and act upon it.'[8]

'To believe in a practical way' was one of the most revealing of Pierre Lambert's attitudes, because for him, faith like love, was verified only by deeds. Faith in an incarnate God who manifested himself physically in human history, implied a reciprocal commitment and a permanent exchange between God and humans. It was not a question of the believer having to choose between faith and deeds.

Inner abandonment

Physical poverty and indifference to material goods that obliged the missionary to put all his trust in God were, however, only the first manifestations, all external, of a much more radical renunciation that should lead the missionary to the only authentic poverty, spiritual poverty. For man's greatest riches 'are not external goods but the powers of his soul which God asks him to renounce so that, having relinquished their ownership and enjoyment in favour of Jesus Christ and in relation to him, he may enter into that truly genuine poverty which is the first and the essential beatitude.'[9]

---

8. Handwritten Narrative, 82–83.
9. Handwritten Narrative, 83. This text can also be compared to Gal 2:20.

What the Vicar Apostolic was asking here—to renounce the powers of his soul—was, in more precise terms, the renunciation of his reason and his will, those two great sovereigns which, for the French thinkers of the seventeenth century, constituted the greatness of man. It was an exorbitant demand that Pierre Lambert justified by his conviction that the conversion of souls was not a human work for which the greatest capacities of the spirit would be required, but a divine work of which the missionary was only the incarnate support. It was not therefore, on his actions or competence, but on the contrary on his availability and his ability to dispossess himself that his apostolic efficacy would depend.

> Without this renunciation, he can do nothing heroic regarding the divine tasks entrusted to him. How, for example, will he behave when entering a pagan kingdom? By what means will he introduce the Gospel? How will he present the mysteries of our holy religion as credible when they are so far above reason? Will it be by skilful reasoning, by the lights of an acquired science or by natural demonstrations? Those who have no other resources than these will be well advised to have nothing to do with the foreign missions, for certainly they will not help their neighbour in any way, and they will risk getting lost themselves. In this profession, missionaries must deny themselves completely; they must protest to God that they do not wish to undertake anything on their own authority, and that the conversion of souls being in his hands alone, the means that concern these divine works must be commensurate with their end. That is why only he can inspire them.[10]

Such a statement was shocking at a time when philosophical discussion, as practised by the Jesuits with the scholars of Peking, was considered the best apostolic method in civilised countries. For since Francis Xavier had landed in Japan, the missionaries of the Society of Jesus believed that the spread of the Gospel would be much easier among the yellow people endowed with reason than among the Indians whom they compared to black people of an inferior civilization. They therefore placed their greatest hopes in the conversion of the Chinese and Japanese (and later the Vietnamese). Amongst them

---

10. Handwritten Narrative, 84.

they preferred to address members of the upper classes with whom intellectual contacts were possible and whom they hoped to convince by rational argument. It was the principle of conversion from above, in other words an appeal to the head, taking into account the double meaning that this term can have: seat of power for a nation and seat of understanding for an individual. However, this method had quickly found its refutation in Japan itself where the authorities had reacted violently against Christianity, which became in their eyes a political issue and a danger. Moreover, it was precisely on the argument of reason that the apostate Jesuit Ferreira had based his refutation of Christianity in 1636. 'There is not one of these teachings that satisfies the requirements of reason', he wrote. 'They make an invention the basis of their teaching; it is a plot to sow discord in the country, and to subvert society. There is not an ounce of substance in their way of explaining the future life. An examination of its fundamental tenets shows that this religion is not founded on reason.'[11]

Pierre Lambert, for his part, was not fundamentally opposed to the use of reasoning in exchanges with the infidels, but he was aware of its insufficiency, because he believed, from experience, that the divine word was addressed above all to the heart of man and that it was therefore this heart that the missionary had to reach through charity, prayer, example and the transparency of his own heart.

In addition, by setting aside reason Pierre Lambert gained another advantage in the particular situation in which he found himself. For while it was commonly accepted by the educated of that time that reason allowed man to dominate his passions, fulfil his duty and control his destiny, this axiom, perfectly adapted to the ordinary existence of an honest man of the metropolis, did not suit the situation of the Vicar Apostolic and his companions. In their case, reason, far from helping them, would have been a bad counsellor; it

---

11. Jacques Proust. *La Supercherie dévoilée, une réfutation du catholicisme au Japon au xvii siècle* (Paris: Chandeigne, 1998), 72. In 1633, the acting provincial of the Jesuits in Japan, Christovao Ferreira, had apostasised to the great despair of his peers who resolved to expel him from the Society. Married to a Japanese woman and enrolled in a Zen temple under the name Sawano Chûan, he wrote a refutation of Christianity in 1636, at the request of the Japanese authorities, which was used in the interrogation of Christians. This text has been published in its French translation by Jacques Proust, preceded by a well-documented introduction.

would have shown them that their position was untenable, that their task was impossible and that the only reasonable solution would be to abandon everything, return to Europe and devote themselves to more achievable tasks.

> Hunger, thirst, and weariness must be endured for the love of Jesus Christ as well as hatred, slander and disgrace. In bearing such sufferings his servants who preach his holy Gospel in his spirit, with a sense of gratitude and thanksgiving, are always to be respected. Thoughts of fear and warnings that our lives are under threat from violence or poison are to be ignored. In short, these blessed happenings and all those similar in nature are to be accepted as inherent in the missionary vocation, while support is provided by the belief that if the good Lord allows these things to happen to missionaries, it is very much to their advantage.[12]

Freed from fears about his personal safety by his total abandonment to Providence, the missionary also gradually detaches himself from concerns for his personal salvation. Not that he loses consciousness of his sinful nature; on the contrary, his intimacy with God only emphasizes his human imperfections. But this relationship absorbs him so completely that it cuts him off from all other preoccupations and renders him indifferent to any attempt to grasp intellectually the way of salvation. The mystical attitude impeded the theological debate on necessary grace or sufficient grace, and indulgences or predestination, which so disturbed the Christian and especially French consciences of the seventeenth century. The choice of the direct path of contemplation rendered this controversy pointless, because, in the end, all that mattered for the missionary on this earth was the possibility of living in union with a God who became man so that man might live in Christ. In his radical renunciation, Pierre Lambert remained faithful to the great spiritual orientations of the French School.

It was in this christocentric and trinitarian conception of adherence to Christ, out of obedience to the Father and in all docility to the Holy Spirit, that the missionary found the source of his personal happiness and apostolic fruitfulness. 'If the perfection of man in this life is to be like the Son of God and to imitate him in his life and actions, can

---

12. Handwritten narrative, 85.

anything be done that is more in conformity with him than to consent to the destruction of all self-will in order to receive only that spiritual illumination which is created in us through the movement of grace? When a person has lost himself in God, he is made a participant in his divine nature, and divine goodness is communicated to him in a way that cannot be explained because, as the creature sees nothing but his God, he can only be moved in the interest of this divine spirit. God makes him master of all nature and fills him with a treasure of grace to use according to his good pleasure, which is the same as that of God.'[13]

A harmonious and fruitful synthesis

Sent to Asia as a missionary bishop with the specific task of promoting an indigenous clergy, Pierre Lambert fulfilled his mandate in the light of the rich teachings he had drawn from the best sources of that golden age of French spirituality that was the seventeenth century. Strongly influenced initially by the Ignatian apostolate of the Jesuits of New France, themselves centred on the spirituality of the cross, he later integrated it with the most radical elements of the French School of Spirituality, so that he can be considered to be the adapter of this current in a version specifically oriented towards the mission *ad exteros*. Heir to both traditions, he elaborated, despite the personal struggles that strongly affected his sensitivity, a very fruitful original synthesis that superimposed the carnal depth of Bérullian mysticism on the Ignatian ideal of self-denial and zeal.

The thought of St Ignatius, contemporary with the greatest extension of the Iberian empires but also with the great fracture of European Christianity[14] and the immense effort of Catholic reconquest that followed,[15] was centred on the opposition between the two kingdoms of God and the world, symbolised by the Standard of Christ and the Standard of Satan. Under the first was grouped all Catholics under the spiritual authority of the pope whose main secular arm was at that time the King of Spain on whose empire 'the sun did

---

13. Letter from Pierre Lambert to M de Meur, July 1663. AMEP, volume 121, 527.
14. Divisions occurred in Christendom as a result of the Protestant Reformation that began in the sixteenth century.
15. The Council of Trent that began in 1545 was called by the Catholic Church to meet the crisis of the Protestant Reformation. One of the aims of the Society of Jesus was to combat Protestantism.

not set.' The second standard floated over the rest of the world, that is, all non-Catholics, whether Protestants, Jews, Muslims or 'pagans.' This conception was in perfect accord with the patronage system, but it presented the great risk of seeing the political merge with the spiritual wherever the power of the king was stronger than that of the pope, which was particularly the situation of those on mission where the religious depended legally and financially on the sovereign.

The reform initiated by Propaganda to remedy these abuses was based on the guidelines of the Council of Trent. It tried to reconcile the very modern notions of independence, unity and collegiality in the Church. By re-establishing control of all missionary activity, it sought to correct the friction that undermined the missionary clergy, and above all to suppress rivalries between orders and nations, to guarantee doctrinal orthodoxy, to control particular interests and thus to avoid the schisms that had broken up European Christendom. Its ambition was none other than to preserve the universality of the Church while ensuring equality between churches. For this, there was only one way forward: to get out of the patronage system and promote the emergence of indigenous clergy.

This grandiose project came up against enormous obstacles in Asia arising from the advantages acquired by Catholic monarchs and by religious, and especially by the Jesuits. From the beginning, the Jesuits completely ignored the role of the bishops and, during many years of working within the patronage system, had become accustomed to subordinate the authority of Rome to that of Lisbon. The application of the innovative ideas of Propaganda was also thwarted by the rigid centralism of the Council of Trent, which strengthened clerical power over lay people who were reduced to a passive role, though they played an essential role in the young churches of Asia. The Council also hindered the full exercise of authority by bishops in their respective churches.

But the ecclesiology of the Mystical Body inherited by Pierre Lambert from the French school made it possible to overcome these blockages and contradictions by considering the Church not primarily as an administrative structure, but as a living organism. This was the idea that underpinned the missionary model of the Lovers of the Cross, whose every member, whatever his or her state of life, participated in the common task of evangelization through prayer, asceticism, gifts or works. As bishop and missionary, Pierre Lambert embodied this spirituality and lived it through perpetual suffering, as an authentic mystic of the cross, taking up St Paul's motto: 'I complete in my flesh the sufferings of Christ for his body, which is the Church' (Col 1:24). He thus unknowingly foreshadowed the long tradition of martyrdom that the Society of Foreign Missions would face in the following centuries, providing it with its theological and spiritual foundations. Unfortunately, the unfavourable reputation of the Vicar Apostolic in Parisian circles and the anti-mystical reaction that raged in France under the reign of Louis XIV buried these intuitions.

Meanwhile, the exaltation of humanism by the philosophy of the Enlightenment, then positivism and its natural belief in human progress and finally the development of colonialism profoundly influenced French mentalities, even among Catholics. Thus missiological thinking was led in a much more human-centrist direction, oriented towards civilising or developmental actions. Thanks to the dedication of missionaries and the generosity of lay donors, the Church developed in many countries, and France became a great missionary country. However, the balance sheet was perhaps a little less brilliant on the spiritual level, as suggested by this question posed at the end of the 1998 Synod of the Churches of Asia by the French Vicar Apostolic of Cambodia, Bishop Destombes: 'Why does the Church in Asia, which is admired for its work in education and teaching as well as in the socio-charitable field, for its efficiency and organization—why does it gain so little from them and does not give the witness of a spiritual educator?'[16]

The missionary, a contemplative in action

Now, three centuries earlier, Pierre Lambert had made spiritual education one of the priorities of evangelisation on the same level as human development, because he believed that the two aspects were inseparable in leading humans to 'the experiential love of Jesus Christ'. But he also thought that missionaries themselves could only serve humans effectively after listening to God and he knew that this listening was not natural for the psychological human, that it required instruction, asceticism, and true interior conversion. For his part, eminent contemplative that he was, blessed with the most exalted mystical experiences, Pierre Lambert was willing to sacrifice them in order to fulfil the crucifying obligations of his mandate, taking as his sole support, Christ on the cross, the keystone, principle, driving force

---

16. Missions étrangères de Paris, no. 331, 213.

and justification of every missionary enterprise. 'Although it is true that the perfection of prayer consists in the present and passive union with God who is always present to the soul, yet our contemplation will never be perfect unless we go to God through Jesus Christ, because of the union of the two inseparable natures in the person of the Word. The soul that sees only Jesus Christ crucified unites itself to God in a very special way, very much in keeping with the life of a pilgrim that we lead. A person who is faithful to this holy practice will find in it all that can make him happy in this world, that is, the greatest secret of the interior and perfect life.'[17] Presented in this way, it seemed to be asking a great deal of the missionary, too much no doubt, because it corresponded to the difficulty of the task at hand, which was huge.

Nevertheless, in the general disruption of the missions of his time, undermined by divisions, violence, corruption and secularism, Pierre Lambert strove to embody and promote a new missionary model that today appears surprisingly consistent with what Pope John Paul II defined for our time in the encyclical *Redemptoris Missio*: 'The missionary must be 'a contemplative in action. He finds the answer to problems in the light of the divine word and in personal and community prayer. My contact with non-Christian spiritual traditions, especially those of Asia, confirmed for me that the future of the missions depends largely on contemplation. Unless the missionary is a contemplative, he cannot proclaim Christ in a credible way; he is a witness to the experience of God and must be able to say with the Apostles: "What we have contemplated . . ., the Word of life, we proclaim to you" (1Jn 1:2–3).'[18]

Jean Guennou, one of the few historians of the Foreign Missions who sought to promote the memory of the Bishop of Beirut, wrote in 1986: 'Because he was evangelical in the extreme, Bishop Lambert de la Motte remains one of the most up-to-date amongst the great missionaries of the modern era.'[19] Today more than ever, Pierre Lambert appears as a model to be rediscovered for a better understanding, apart from the many conflicts and scandals that dot his history, of the most fundamental, timeless, noble and the most hidden motives that have animated the Church's missionary impulse since her origins.

---

17. Handwritten Narrative, 167.
18. *The Mission of the Redeemer* (*Redemptoris missio*), Encyclical Letter of John Paul II (Paris: Cerf, 1991).
19. Guennou. MEP, 194.

Epilogue

The ruin of the mission of Siam

After the death of Pierre Lambert, King Phra Narai, who had made him the foundation stone of his diplomatic projects, was more demanding and more suspicious of the French missionaries, though without giving up his idea of an embassy. On 22 December 1680, two Siamese mandarins, accompanied by Claude Gayme, embarked for France aboard the Soleil d'Orient which disappeared at sea between Madagascar and the Cape of Good Hope at the end of 1681. Towards the end of 1680, on the initiative of François Pallu who, freed by the Spanish, was again in Paris, the East India Company set up a trading post in Ayutthaya. Pushed by the directors of the seminary, themselves under pressure from the Jesuits, the Bishop of Heliopolis sought at all costs to regain the support of Louis XIV, on whom he believed the fate of the French missions depended, and he reproached Louis Laneau for his lack of decision and political initiative.

In 1683, while passing through Ayutthaya, François Pallu took advantage of the absence of his colleague, who had gone to Cochinchina, to meet Phra Narai. He also established relations with the king's new favourite and first minister, Constance Phaulkon. This Greek adventurer, converted to Catholicism, sought to rely on the French to consolidate his position and so multiplied material benefits in support of the mission. Blinded by his political concerns, Pallu did not see the trap; Laneau may have warned him but was not strong enough to oppose him. A Siamese embassy left for France under the leadership of Bénigne Vachet and Artus de Lionne, a missionary and son of Louis XIV's Minister for Foreign Affairs.

In 1684, on Pallu's death, Laneau inherited his office as administrator-general of the Chinese missions. He hoped for an acceleration of conversions in Siam. The following year there arrived in Ayutthaya the first French embassy led by the Chevalier de Chaumont and the Abbé de Choisy, accompanied by the Siamese ambassadors now back in their own country. With them were six Jesuit mathematicians destined for China. The purpose of this embassy was secondarily commercial and primarily religious: to ask the King of Siam on behalf of Louis XIV to convert to Catholicism, according to the initial project drawn up by Pierre Lambert in 1666.

But this perspective was not that of Constance Phaulkon, who acted as an interpreter and took advantage of this situation to water down the content of the letters of the King of France during official audiences. Soon, the favourite judged that it was in his interest to dissociate himself from the missionaries and so he began to develop a new plan with the strong man of the Jesuits, Guy Tachard. The latter, skilful and full of ambition, hoped to supplant the influence of the apostolic vicars and become the superior of the missions of Asia. He succeeded in gaining a position for himself at the court of Siam and soon returned to Europe as a special envoy in charge of recruiting Jesuit mathematicians for the king's observatories.

Louis Laneau, increasingly overwhelmed by events, clung to the promise made by the Siamese government to the Chevalier de Chaumont to grant privileges in favour of Christian converts. Meanwhile, Constance Phaulkon, with the complicity of Guy Tachard, managed to ruin the apostolic vicar's credit with the king and prepared a smear campaign against him in Europe as well as a plot designed to make him responsible for the schism of Tonkin.

In September 1687, the Siamese embassy returned with two extraordinary envoys of Louis XIV, Simon de La Loubère and Claude Céberet. Their objective was essentially commercial. They were accompanied by fourteen Jesuits destined for Siam, including Guy Tachard SJ, and a French expeditionary force charged with occupying Bangkok and Mergui. Louis Laneau and his missionaries, now clearly opposed to the Phaulkon-Tachard party, avoided any intervention in public affairs as far as possible, but the consequences of the revolution which broke out in May 1688 fell on them. The quarrel over the succession of Phra Narai ended in the victory of Phra Petracha, a convinced Buddhist, and the elimination of Constance Phaulkon.

After an unfortunate intervention, the French expeditionary corps withdrew without respecting the commitments concluded with the Siamese authorities. The reprisals fell on Louis Laneau who had served as a living shield during the clashes and who was imprisoned in very harsh conditions along with his missionaries, the students of the college and some French nationals who had not fled. Many died in prison. For thirteen months, until December 1689, Louis Laneau, remained exposed in an open-air cage and condemned to several forms of punishment such as a wooden collar placed around his neck and chains attached to his neck and his feet. At the end of this time he was transferred to a residence under surveillance. It was during this imprisonment that he wrote the treatise *On the Deification of the Just* for his companions condemned to forced labour.

Meanwhile, in Rome, Tachard sought to discredit Laneau and Artus de Lionne who had left with the French troops of which he was chaplain. The Jesuit managed to win the confidence of Pope Alexander VIII, who created two great bishoprics in China, subject to Portuguese patronage. In Paris, a Jesuit-led campaign made the apostolic vicars look responsible for the 'martyrdom of Constance Phaulkon' and the French failure.

In April 1691, the French missionaries from Siam were released, whereupon they returned to St. Joseph's seminary. They benefited from the clemency of the king, but the mission was destroyed and from then on stagnated. In 1687, there were nineteen missionaries in Siam. Only two survived Laneau, who died on 16 May 1696. With him, the victim of political intrigues, there disappeared the first authentic attempt to introduce Christianity into a Buddhist environment that the mystic Pierre Lambert had, during his lifetime, always understood and supported.

Bibliography

Baudiment, Louis. *François Pallu, principal fondateur de la Société des Missions étrangères.* (Paris: Beauchesne, 1934).

Borges, Charles (SJ). *The Economies of Goa Jesuits, 1542–1759. An explanation of their rise and fall.* (New Delhi: Concept Publishing Company, 1994).

Bourges, Jacques de. (MEP) *Relation du voyage de Mgr l'Evêque de Bérythe au royaume de la Cochinchine, par la Turquie, la Perse, les Indes etc. jusqu'au royaume de Siam et autres lieux.* (Paris: Gérard Monfort, 2000).

Carmona, Michel. *La France de Richelieu.* (Paris: Fayard, 1984).

Certeau, Michel de (SJ). *La Fable mystique, 1: xvie-xviie siècle.* (Paris: Gallimard, 1990).

Challe, Robert. *Journal d'un voyage fait aux Indes orientales.* (Paris: Mercure de France, 2002).

Chappoulie, Henri Mgr. *Rome et les missions d'Indochine aux XVIIe et xviiie siècles.* (Paris: Bloud et Gay, 1943 et 1948).

Chatellier, Louis. *L'Europe des dévots.* (Paris: Flamarion, 1987).

Clévenot, Michel. *Les Chrétiens du xviie siècle, ombres et lumières du Grand Siècle.* (Paris: Retz, 1989).

Cognet, Louis (oratorien). *Le Jansénisme,* (Paris: PUF, 1961).

Costet, Robert. (MEP)*Siam-Laos. Histoire de la mission.* (Paris: Églises d'Asie, 2002).

Delumeau, Jean. *Le Catholicisme entre Luther et Voltaire.* (Paris: Presses universitaires de France, 1971).

Deslandres, Dominique. *Croire et faire croire, les missions françaises au xviie siècle, 1600–1658.* (Paris: Fayard, 2003).

Deville, Raymond (PSS). *L'École française de spiritualité.* (Paris: Desclée, 1987).

Étiemble. (présenté par) *Les Jésuites en Chine. La querelle des rites [1552–1773].* (Paris: Julliard, 1966).

Fauconnet-Buzelin, Françoise. *Le Père inconnu de la Mission moderne, Pierre Lambert de la Motte, premier vicaire apostolique de Cochinchine (1624–1679).* (Paris:Archives des Missions étrangères, 2006).

Federn C., *Mazarin.* (Paris: Payot, 1983).

Forest, Alain. *Les Missionnaires français au Tonkin et au Siam, xviie-xviiie siècles. Analyse comparée d'un relatif succès et d'un total échec.* (Paris: L'Harmattan, 1998).

Francois-Xavier(SJ). *Correspondance 1535–1552, lettres et documents.* (Paris: Desclée de Brouwer, 1987).

Guennou, Jean. (MEP) *Missions étrangères de Paris.* (Paris: Fayard, 1986).

Jacques, Roland (OMI). *Naissance et développement du padroado portugais d'Orient, des origines à 1659.* (Lisbonne: Fundaçao Calouste Gulbenkian, servicio de Educaçao, 1999).

Krumenacker, Yves. *L'Ecole française de spiritualité. Des mystiques, des fondateurs, des courants et leurs interprètes.* (Paris: Cerf, 1998).

Lacouture, Jean. *Jésuites, une multibiographie, 1.1: Les Conquérants.* (Paris: Le Seuil, 1991).

Lambert de la motte, Pierre (MEP) et Pallu, François (MEP). *Monita ad Misionarios. Instructions aux Missionnaires de la S. Congrégation de la Propagande, rédigées en 1665.* (Paris: Archives des Missions étrangères, 2000).

Laneau, Louis. (MEP) *Rencontre avec un sage bouddhiste.* (Paris: Cerf, Genève, Ad Solem, 1998).

Laneau, Louis. (MEP) *La Divinisation par Jésus-Christ.* (Paris: Missions étrangères de Paris, 1987).

Lange, Claude. (MEP) *L'Église catholique et la Société des Missions étrangères au Vietnam (vicariat apostolique de Cochinchine) aux xviie et xiiie siècles.* (Paris: L'Harmattan, 2005).

Launay, Adrien. (MEP) *Histoire de la mission du Tonkin. Documents historiques, t.I: 1658–1717.* (Paris: Les Indes savantes, 2000).

Launay, Adrien. (MEP) *Histoire de la mission du Siam (1662–1911).* (Paris: Les Indes savantes, 2000).

Launay, Adrien. (MEP) *Histoire de la mission de Cochinchine (1658–1728).* Paris: Les Indes savantes, 2000).

Lebrun, François. *Le xviie siècle.* (Paris: Armand Collin, 1967).

Mantienne, Frédéric. *Les Relations politiques et commerciales entre la France et la péninsule indochinoise (xviie siècle).* (Paris: Les Indes savantes, 2001).

Milcent, Paul (eudiste). *Saint Jean Eudes.* (Paris: Cerf, 1992).

Pitaud, Bernard (PSS). *Nicolas Roland et les Sœurs de l'Enfant—Jésus, l'Ecole française à Reims au xviie siècle.* (Paris: Cerf, 2001).

Proust, Jacques. *La Supercherie dévoilée. Une réfutation du catholicisme au Japon au xviie siècle.* (Paris: Chandeigne, 1998).

Sy, Henri. (MEP) *La Société des Missions étrangères, les débuts 1653–1663.* (Paris: Églises d'Asie, 1998).

Sy, Henri. (MEP)*La Société des Missions étrangères, la fondation du séminaire, 1663–1670.* (Paris: Églises d'Asie, 2000).

Tallon, Alain. *La Compagnie du Saint-Sacrement, spiritualité et société, 1629–1667.* (Paris: Cerf, 1990).

Taveneaux, René. *Le Catholicisme dans la France classique, 1610–1715.* (Paris: Sedes, 1994).

Triboulet, Raymond. Gaston de Renty 1611–1649. *Un homme du monde, un homme de Dieu.* (Paris: Beauchesne, 1991).

Valignano, Alexandre SJ. *Les Jésuites au Japon, relations missionnaires (1583).* (Paris: Desclée de Brouwer, 1990).

Van der Cruise, Dirk. *Le Noble Désir de courir le monde, voyager au xviie siècle.* (Paris: Fayard, 2002).

Index of Names

A

Abada (Paul de]: 127.
Abbas (Chah): 52, 53. 79.
Abreu (Jean d'): 184, 195, 205.
Acosta (Barthélémy d'): 148, 149, 150.
Acosta (Paul d']: 102, 103, 104, 117.
Acarie (Barbe): 1.
Aiguillon (duchesse d'): 25, 62.
Alberici (cardinal): 37.
Albier (Pierre d'): 82, 83.
Alexandre VII: 37, 210.
Agnès: 140.
Ambroise de Preuilly: 55, 115.
Annat (François): 70, 87, 90.
Anthony de Santo-Felice: 33.
Aquaviva (Claude): 69.

B

Bagot (Jean): 29, 36, 77.
Bangayana (Jean-Baptiste): 184.
Barberini (Cardinal Antoine): 40.
Baron (François): 203.
Baudet (Ignace): 147, 185, 186.
Ben (Luc): 111, 120, 122, 146, 148, 151.
Bernières (Jourdaine de): 20.
Bernières-Louvigny (Jean de): 13, 16, 18, 21 225, 230.
Bérulle (Pierre de, cardinal): 3, 4, 222, 229.
Bon (Manuel): 178, 187.
Bona (cardinal): 80.
Bonneau (Jacques): 42.
Borges (Charles): 67.
Borges (Onufre): 82.
Bossuet (Jacques-Bénigne): 1.
Bouchard (Gabriel): 121, 123, 130, 161, 162, 180, 185, 186, 195.
Boudon (Henri-Marie): 19, 20.
Bouillon (Cardinal de): 202.
Bourdoise (Adrien): 14.
Bourges (Jacques de): xiii, xvi, 46, 51, 71, 72, 77, 86, 87, 89, 90, 91, 102, 113, 117, 121, 122, 123, 130, 131, 140, 166, 181, 183, 218, 222.
Brandao (Antoine): 195.
Bras-nu: 8, 9.
Brindeau (Pierre): 110, 118, 131, 137, 140, 142, 144, 167, 168, 193, 194, 198, 205, 206, 223, 247, 278.
Brisacier (Jean-Charles de): 19, 22, 34, 38, 44, 45, 255.
Buzomi (François): 34.

C

Camus (Jean-Pierre): 20.
Candone (Joseph): 185, 186, 188, 189.
Cardoso (Jean): 59, 193.
Carré (Barthélémy): 67.
Carré (accounts manmger): 13.
Carvalho (Diego): 34.
Castro (Mathieu de): 33.
Céberet: 246.
Certeau (Michel de): 2.
César du Saint-Sacrement: 158.
Challe (Robert): 67.
Chamesson (Philippe de): 45, 77, 82, 91, 102, 144, 169, 176, 184, 225.
Chandebois (Claude de): 159, 200, 201.
Charbonneau (René): 199, 201, 204, 217, 225.
Charlotte of Savoy: 3.
Chaumont (chevalier de): 246.
Chieu (Jacques): 132.
Chrysostom of Saint-Lô: 18.
Chevreuil (Louis): 77, 82, 94, 98, 99, 101, 103, 122, 131, 143, 147, 158, 159, 162, 166, 167, 168, 179, 200.
Choisy (abbé de): 246
Clément IX: 108, 141, 155, 173, 186.
Clément XIV: xi.
Coelho de Mello (Amador): 200.
Colbert (Jean-Baptiste): 42, 45, 88, 156, 175.
Condé (Prince de): 13.
Condren (Charles de): 19.
Conti (prince de): 13.
Corneille (Pierre): xii, 10, 11, 47.
Cospéan (Philippe): 20.
Cotolendi (Ignace): 63, 77, 120, 123, 144, 159, 167.
Coton (Pierre): 69.
Courtaulin (Jean de): 159, 160, 180, 185, 187, 188, 192, 193, 195, 197.

D

Délia Rocca (Charles): 123.
Destombes (Émile): 243.
Deydier (François): xiii, xvi, 46, 51, 73, 74, 76, 93, 103, 104, 111, 118, 122, 123, 125, 126, 127, 129, 130, 132, 135, 145, 166, 181, 183, 192, 222.
Doan (Louis): 195.
Dufour (Charles): 46.
Dumas (Alexandre): 63.
Duplessis-Montbar (Christophe): 158.
Duval de Bonneval: 13.

E

Emmanuel de la Nativité: 184.
Ephrem de Nevers: 33, 55.

F

Fénelon (François de): 1.
Fermanel (Pierre): 9, 54
Fermanel (Lucas): 45, 70, 90.
Fieschi (Philippe): 129, 130, 132.
Forget (René): 159, 199.
Fragoso (Louis): 104-107, 160, 184, 195.
François de Sales (saint): 1.
Francis-Xavier (saint): xi, 31, 65, 105, 145, 157, 164, 216, 231.
Fronde ville (Henri de): 2.
Fuciti (Dominique): 122, 129, 131, 132, 147.

G

Gabriel Lallemant (saint): 12.
Gamma (Louis de): 97.
Gassion (colonel Jean de): 9.
Gault (Jean-Baptiste): 42.

Gautier: 42.
Gayme (Claude): 159, 199, 200, 201, 203, 208, 245.
Gazil (Michel): 39, 78, 84, 85, 86, 122, 156.
Geffrard de Lespinay (Pierre): 195.
George (Dominique): 14, 200
Gilles de Bourges: 55.
Gondi (Jean-François de): 12.
Grieu d'Estimauville de Pape- rottes (Jacques de): 14.
Guennou (Jean): 143, 220, 221, 244.
Guiart (Claude): 121, 122, 123, 140, 142, 143, 146, 151, 152, 154, 178, 185.

H

Hainques (Antoine): 77, 93, 98, 99, 101, 103, 110, 111, 114, 118, 120, 122, 142, 143, 146, 147, 151, 152, 166, 187, 218, 220.
Hallé (Simon): 29, 52, 232, 233, 234.
Harcourt (comte d'): 13.
Harlay de Champvallon (François II): 26, 45, 46.
Hautmesnil de: 180.
Hayneuve (Julien): 11.
Henri IV (de Navarre): 4.
Henriette: 4.
Heudey de Pommainville (Catherine): 4.
Heudey de Pommainville (Nicolas de): 4.
Hien (Benoît): 118, 128, 135.
Hien-Vuong: 178, 179, 185, 188.
Huê (Jean): 118, 128, 135, 143, 151, 222.

I

Ignatius of Loyola (Saint): 11.
Ingoli (François): 31, 33.

Innocent X: 35, 37.
Innocent XI: 209.
Isaac Jogues (saint): 11, 12.

J

Jacques (Roland): 212.
Jans (Henri): 45.
Jean de Brébeuf (saint): 11, 12.
Jean Eudes (saint): 1, 16, 19, 20, 138, 225.
Jean de la Croix (saint): 99, 122. 193.
Jean de Saint-Samson: 6.
John Paul II (Pope): x, 244.
Jeanne de Chantal (saint): 1.
John Baptist de la Salle (saint): 28.
Joseph de Paris: 6.
Junet (capitaine): 123, 125, 130.

K

Kien (Simon): 132.

L

La Croix (Jean de): 99, 122, 142, 150, 186, 189, 193.
Lallemant (Louis): 11, 69, 229.
La Loubère (Simon): 246.
Lambert (William I) (ancestor of Pierre): 23.
Lambert (Guillaume II) (great-grandfatherof Pierre): 23.
Lambert (Marie) (younger sister of Pierre): 25.
Lambert (Nicolas) (brother of Pierre): 25, 49, 111, 140.
Lambert (Pierre I) (father of Pierre): 24, 28.
Laneau (Louis): xiii, xvi, 77, 93, 103, 104, 107, 109, 110, 111, 115, 116, 117, 118, 120, 123, 140, 141, 166, 167, 169, 170, 171, 174, 176, 179,

183, 184, 194, 200, 201, 202, 204, 205, 208, 209, 210, 214, 217, 222, 224, 245, 247.
Langlois [Pierre]: 144, 160, 200, 201, 224.
Laval (François de Montmorency-): xiii, 20, 36, 194.
Lebouthiller: 45.
Le Clergues (Guillaume): 195.
Le Cornu de Bimorel (François): 27.
Le Cornu de Bimorel (Laurent): 27.
Le Faure (Jacques]: 7, 115.
Legras (Nicolas): 45.
Le Noir (Pierre): 199, 200.
Leroux (François): 262, 263.
Lesley (William): 38, 40, 46, 157, 163, 223.
Le Tellier: 159.
Lionne (Artus de): 245, 247.
Lo (Grégoire): 204.
Longueville (Duke de): 13, 14, 26.
Longueville (Duchess de): 26.
Louis XI: 3.
Louis XIII: 4, 27.
Louis XIV: 4, 21, 44, 45, 47, 70, 89, 102, 112, 155, 157, 159, 173, 202.
Louis de la Mère de Dieu: 201.
Louis du Rosaire: 160.
Luce: 153.
Lucie: 94.

M

Magalloens (Gabriel): 160.
Mahot (Guillaume): 121, 122, 123, 140, 146, 147, 148, 154, 178, 180, 185, 186, 187, 188, 195.
Maldonnat (Jean-Baptiste): 160.
Mantienne (Frédéric): 88.
Marie de l'incarnation: 20.
Marie de Médicis: 4.
Marini (Philippe): 87, 113, 114, 115, 118, 122, 123, 176, 180, 184, 197.

Marquez (Pierre): 147, 148.
Martin (François): 67.
Martin (Ignace): 129.
Matignon (Duke): 8.
Mauduit (Marie): 4, 5, 9.
Maurillon: 146, 151, 152.
Mazarin (Cardinal): 4, 12, 13, 16, 42, 47.
Mechtilde du Saint-Sacrement: 20.
Mersenne (Marin): 7.
Molière: xii, 17, 47.
Molina (Luis): 229.
Montpensier (Mlle de): 53.
Motta (Nicolas da): 142, 184, 205.

N

Nhan (Philippe]: 132, 143, 151.
Nicolas Barré: 28.
Nobili (Roberto de): 170, 221.
Nyel (Adrien): 27, 28.

O

Olier (Jean-Jacques): 1, 172.
Oliva (Paul): 105, 210.
Ou Phu Ma: 186, 188.

P

Pallu (Anne) (aunt of François): 62.
Pallu (Étienne) (grandfather of François): 62.
Pallu (Étienne) (father of François): 62.
Pallu (François) (titular bishop of Heliopolis): 9, 13, 56, 57, 58, 59, 60, 61, 62, 63, 64, 75, 79, 83, 96, 97, 98, 100, 101, 102, 103, 105, 108, 109, 110, 111, 113, 118, 120, 121, 122, 126, 127, 128, 130, 132, 133, 135, 137, 140, 147, 164, 165, 175, 176, 177, 178, 179, 189, 182,

183, 184, 186, 187, 188, 189, 193, 194, 200, 201, 203, 205, 212, 214, 215, 216, 222, 223, 224, 230, 231, 234, 241, 265, 266.
Pascal (Blaise): 15, 47, 80.
Pascal (Étienne) (father of Blaise): 10, 11.
Pascal (Gilberte) (sister of Blaise): 10.
Pascal (Jacqueline) (sister of Blaise): 10.
Paul (Saint): 15, 17, 60, 145, 232, 234, 235.
Paul V: 141.
Paul VI: x.
Paumard (Étienne): 199, 200.
Perez (François): 97, 117, 140, 170, 222.
Phaulkon (Constance): 245, 246, 247.
Philip II: 3.
Phra Naraï: 95, 96, 111, 113, 118, 157, 173, 175, 177, 179, 181, 188, 202, 203, 217, 245, 246.
Phra Petracha: 246.
Piques (Bernard): 36.
Poitevin (Armand): 158.
Poutet (Yves): 28, 29.
Pressard: 45.

Q

Quillet (Chantal): 16.
Quintanaduenas (Antoine): 104, 106.

R

Racine (Jean): xii, 47.
Rancé (Armand de): 229.
Renty (Gaston de): 17, 36, 40, 41.
Retz (cardinal de), see Gondi (Jean-François de).

Rhodes (Alexandre de): 30, 34, 35, 36, 37, 53, 126, 134, 135, 164, 213, 226.
Rhodes (Raphaël de): 98, 127, 128, 133.
Ricci (Matteo): 164, 221.
Richelieu (Cardinal): 4, 8, 225.
Rigordi (François): 53.
Rocha (Balthasar da): 128, 130, 132.
Rodrigues (Manuel): 97, 98, 103.
Roland (Nicolas): 28.

S

Sassi: 122.
Savary (François): 121.
Sawano Chuân, 239.
Séguier (chancelier): 9.
Servien (Abel): 23.
Sevin (Charles): 159, 214, 256, 269.
Sirisuthammarajà: 134.
Suarez (R. P.): 160.
Surin (Joseph): 69.

T

Tachard (Guy): 70. 246, 247.
Thérèse of the Infant Jesus (saint): 232.
Thomas (Charles): 195, 200.
Trinh-Trang: 126.
Tissanier (Joseph): 82, 83, 160, 184, 223.
Trang (Joseph): 118, 120, 143, 146, 148, 154, 222.
Tri (Vite): 132.
Tru (Léon): 132.

U

Urban VIII: 114.
Ursule de la Conception: 20.

V

Vachet (Bénigne): 63, 75, 142, 144, 145, 146, 147, 148, 150, 151, 161, 162, 166, 167, 168, 177, 185, 186, 187, 188, 189, 190, 191, 192, 200, 201, 209, 245.
Valente (Diego): 33.
Valguarnera (Thomas): 95, 115, 184, 195, 216, 223.
Valignano (Alexandre): 87, 164, 251.
Vallées (Marie des): 20.
Vaz (Louis): 105.
Vericelli (Ange-Marie): 104.
Ventadour (duke of): 2.
Ventadour (duchess of): 2.
Villeneuve (Mme de): 27.
Vincent de Paul (saint): 1, 14, 22, 26, 136, 225, 229.
Vitelleschi (Mutius): 69.

Z

Zacharie de Lisieux: 4.